MW01249064

Government
by
Political Spin

by Dr. David Turell

Huntington House Publishers

Huntington House Publishers
P.O. Box 53788
Lafayette, Louisiana 70505

PRINTED IN THE UNITED STATES OF AMERICA

Library of Congress Card Catalog Number 99-67674
ISBN 1-56384-172-X

Dedication

To Grandpa Mike,
who came to this country from Russia
at age seven as an orphan, to join his older sister.
He became fully Americanized,
an avid Brooklyn Dodger fan, a deep-sea fisherman,
and was addicted to driving powerful sedans.
With only a grammar school education,
married by age seventeen,
he raised a family and developed a business,
which when sold, made him a millionaire.
He lived the immigrant's dream,
possible only in this country.

Contents

Preface

The idea for this book has been kicking around in my head for nearly twelve years. It stems from conversations I had with my internal medical patients. We talked about their health problems, of course, but often the conversation meandered to other subjects. Being a family internist involves knowing the family, its background, its outlook, its aspirations, its troubles. Knowing these intimate details helped me to further understand my patients and the pressures that might be affecting their conditions and illnesses. The politics of the country affect people, their intentions, and their views of life. Through what they told me in the privacy of my office, I feel I have heard their true feelings, not sentiments edited for outside consumption. Most doctors assume that the patients' discussion of themselves is clearly the truth about themselves, and I think, having tested patients intellectually in conversation and seeing them maintain their viewpoints, that I have heard how people truly feel about life in this country. Those conversations changed my viewpoint. I gradually realized that I would not be satisfied with myself, unless I expressed what I had discovered in this book.

I started out life as a New York liberal. In my childhood mind, seeing the ravages of the Great Depression, FDR had saved the country. By the age of twenty, I was all heart—the standard definition of a liberal. Washington could solve all of our problems: send the money there and let them do it. The beginning of success for the civil rights movement with the government's help in the 1960s served at first to console me. When, in my forties, I began to recognize the monolithic bureaucratic controls and waste that had developed in Washington, I felt the first conservative stirrings in my brain. Following the famous definition, as life's experience and logical thought patterns took control of me, by fifty I was conservative. And now approaching seventy, having read Charles Murray's book, *What It Means to Be a Libertarian* (1997), I find that is what I have become. I follow the concepts of J.S. Mill (1859) that society should restrict individual liberty only for society's own protection, and should not legislate control over individual moral judgments or physical behaviors. Restrictions should be applied only when those individual moral or physical behaviors have an adverse or potential effect upon other individuals that they cannot control (Wolfson, *Wall Street Journal* [*WSJ*], 13 August 1998). In reality, individuals are only as strong as the society they create and maintain allegiance to.

Retiring young from the practice of medicine (in order to do all the things I ever wanted to do in life but didn't have time for), has given me time to think and ponder, to read widely, and become angrier and angrier about the tone and direction of this country. This book represents what I heard from my patients, and six plus retirement years of reflection. I feel driven to write it.

This book is presented as a group of interlocking essays. As a result, some of the same ideas may pop up from different perspectives. They are not meant to be repetitive, but as counterpoints in music, with variations on the same theme, all to make you think of how you can help to continue the success of this country.

A note about my use of the English language: I intend to employ masculine gender for pronouns when discussing subjects as to how a person, male or female, might react, and gender is not an issue. This is meant as no disrespect to women. I abhor the use of he/she or of alternating the use of he and she, hoping to come out 50/50.

One other observation about my methods of pulling this book together: Obviously, I started with certain intellectual principles and ideas, expanding the concepts based on books of opinion and history. But to flush out my thought that the opinions of a democratic citizenry depend on the news material presented, as well as the methods of presentation, I have collected, over a nine-year period, local and national newspaper articles and opinion columns, magazine articles, and even letters to the editor. I have used this material to present examples of the points I have made, making the book somewhat event-driven. The true intent is to solidify the principle that only a well-informed voting public can make the proper decisions, and that all sides of a question need to be properly presented and interpreted. I strongly insist that proper presentation and interpretation is severely lacking at this time, not only in the printed media, but especially on television. I wish I could reproduce examples of the woefully inadequate soundbites I have seen, but I will attempt to demonstrate how worthless television news has become.

Introduction

The title of this book, *Government by Political Spin*, implies that the officials of our government are offering us promises and solutions that they cannot produce; but rather, they are using a public relations approach to convince us they are very necessary, and should be kept in power to solve problems, real and imaginary. Do you think this is the most wonderful country in the world? I do. Do you think the federal government can solve every one of our problems? I certainly don't!!

We are the oldest democratic republic on earth, based on a constitution created by fifty-five brilliant people meeting in Philadelphia in 1787. In one hot, unairconditioned summer they created a flexible document that overcame the objections of thirteen individual confederated states, allowing the most livable democracy in the world, and the most powerful. Those men could not have anticipated the myriad changes to come in the next two-plus centuries, but the original instrument they crafted allows the flexibility to solve problems. However, that flexibility is being undermined by a proactive federal judiciary, in which federal judges are now running prisons, school districts, and other institutions, exercising power never really granted to them under the Constitution with accountability to no one. The carefully balanced division of power between the three branches of our government is gone, without stirring up a fight from the legislative branch, in fact with their apparent acquiescence. All this in the past thirty-five years.

What needs to be understood is the intent of the framers of the Constitution in each area of intended compromise in the Constitution. Differing political philosophies were melded together, to give satisfaction to everyone. The intents were universal and for all time. Where we have strayed from those intents, we have seen the creation of an inability to solve many of our modern problems. The compromises created a system of checks and balances that allowed the three branches to maintain balanced power. Attention to the strict construction of the Constitution would have maintained the balance. There are other changes. The Framers could not have foreseen the type of Congress we now have. They anticipated a Congress in which the members would offer to serve for up to six years, and return home to manage their business or farm. They could not afford to stay away longer; there were no professional politicians, and the profession was not imagined. Now we have politicians who are difficult to remove from office with the campaign rules they have created in self-protection, and the popular attitude they have propagandized: the federal government has a never-ending supply of money to bring home "pork" to each local district and money to take care of everyone who wants or needs to be taken care of.

How can we expect voters (remember, that's ourselves!) to vote out of office folks who promise and bring home all those goodies? So let's do some simple arithmetic and you will really understand my point: Roughly three million people lived when the Constitution was framed. There are almost 270 million citizens now, ninety times more; 90 x 55= 4,950 brilliant political theorists who should exist in our country, if our population is equivalent to that of 1787 (and we probably are). They should be in Washington creating the latest miracles to solve our current problems, but where are they? Those brilliant people have to be somewhere. There are a few in Washington, but the majority are in business, the professions, and other endeavors. They are very cynical about the current political processes in Washington, but read the books they write, the letters to the editor, the columns in the newspapers—the ideas are out there.

But they are not in Washington. We have an overwhelming need to get founding-father-like people to Washington, people who are more concerned with the future of the country than how to get reelected in two or six years. Ideally we can vote out the present congressional members, but that is like "taking candy from a baby." They have convinced us we can "have our cake and eat it too." WE CAN'T!! We must demand to change the system, remove the cynicism, and attract to our federal government a more idealistic quality of representation from people who intend to stay just a few years, and make a valuable contribution before leaving.

To find answers to the way we voters think and act, we need to look to our evolutionary past. Our founders developed an extraordinarily ideal form of representative democracy. They anticipated our representatives would be statesmanlike and the voters who elected them educated and informed. With the unanticipated appearance of career politicians spinning their PR, statesmanship and a well-informed electorate have both largely disappeared. The psychology we have brought with us from our recent hunter-gatherer (read savage) past creates a major part of the problem. We have suddenly entered a complicated civilized world in a brief moment in time, when compared to the hundreds of thousands of years of evolution it took to get us to this stage. Our motives for voting the way we do, and the motives of the members of Congress all arise from the same evolutionary psychology. We are all the same under the skin, no better or worse than our governmental representatives.

Ever since the New Deal in the 1930s the federal government has attempted to step in and solve all our problems, local and national. It started with national concerns, but gradually, using the commerce clause in the Constitution through the courts, the Feds began to dictate events at the county and city level, damaging the protections for the States purposely put into the Tenth Amendment, which specifically left to the States all powers not enumerated in the Constitution as being awarded to the federal government. Notwithstanding the impossibility of it all, Washington rhetoric tells us that all problems can be solved and perfection guaranteed, if enough money is thrown at each problem. But lo and behold, studies now show that although there have been some advances in improving some problems, in general the trends reach a plateau, and even if more and more funds are expended stagnation continues. Trillions have been spent during the thirty-plus years since the

"Great Society" of L.B.J., and finally we are trying a new approach to one aspect—the welfare program.

Naturally, the result of a central Washington control has been a growth of a huge bureaucracy, a group of people consumed with their own self-importance, dedicated to growing larger in numbers, and acting as "experts" to convince Congress that further growth is the "solution" to all problems. The same psychological mechanisms that makes voters vote as they do, makes Congress members act as they do, and drive bureaucrats to try and grow bureaucracies as they do—we all have the same software in our brains.

Along the way we citizens have forgotten one important fact: everyone working in Washington in the government, whether congressional members, their staffs, or bureaucrats, are our employees. But we have let ourselves be seduced by their guarantees of a perfect birth, a perfect life, and finally a perfect death. With Medicare, Grandpa dies sterilely and unnoticed in the back room of an intensive care unit, and his grandchildren don't know that death exists at all!! We hired these people to represent us, not to seduce us. What has been the result? As of 1998 five and a half trillion dollars of national debt exists, and they are trying to tell us the budget is balanced by using smoke-and-mirrors accounting, when in fact unfunded future government obligations are rising! After sixty-plus years of social experimentation we are beginning to allow ourselves to notice that it is not working as well as they claim, and the perfection, guaranteed by the Feds, is just pie in the sky.

This book is an attempt to explain why we all act from the same motivations, why we must understand this to change our perceptions of this country, to understand how our country currently works, and how it can work in a much better way. We must remember that except for Native Americans, we all came from somewhere else. We came (and by this I mean for most of us, our ancestors) and took a raw wilderness, granted with wonderful resources, and made it into the richest and most powerful nation that has ever existed. Other countries have the resources, but they never became as powerful, rich, or as democratic. Why did we do it? I have a theory.

And finally, an important reminder. We are one population with many different subcultural backgrounds. We are only as strong and as safe as our country is. We are only as strong as the sum of all of us. Any group that cannot advance, for whatever reason, weakens all of us in that we are stronger if we are all together. That group must be helped. Even if current policies have not worked, or have not been completely successful, we must not stop trying. As a population we present two opposite aspects: we are the most kind-hearted and charitable people in the world, and yet the most selfish. Our national debt is creating an enormous mortgage on the future that our grandchildren will have to face, while currently giving us the highest standard of living on Earth. How fair is that? We are but four-plus percent of the world's population, going into debt each year to use forty percent of each year's available resources. We must understand what we are—the most privileged of people through the country we have created, and we are sending it into decline if not disaster. We are the ones doing this, not the governing folks in Washington, because they are our employees: they are only doing what we want, what we have allowed them to do, whether we realize it or not. We need to understand ourselves, and to see that we are allowing them to fool us.

If you disagree with me, yes, I am attempting to change your mind. But I am also attempting to make you think. To understand any problem in society, you must study what the other side is presenting as reasons behind their solutions. Study opposing views, research the approaches on both sides, try to remove the emotion within yourself, difficult as that may be, and be independent in your thinking. Forget what your family taught you in childhood. It is not sacrosanct. Use Occam's razor in your deductive reasoning. Sir William of Occam, about 1330, stated the following: "If you can conceive of a simple solution to a puzzle or problem by being able to put all, or almost all, the related factors into one logical basket, your conclusion will be correct 90% of the time." I used this method with great success reaching diagnoses in my medical practice.

Think about another rule I follow: If a series of events seems ludicrous, they have probably been planned purposely, and perhaps with the intent of fooling you. Look for logic.

And one last rule I have found very valuable: If you discover a philosophic principle that appeals to you and makes you consider living by it or using it to understand life or the positions of others, try carrying it to logical extremes in all directions. If it works at the extreme, that tends to prove its validity for you. Look for logic. Read the book, think, and challenge my reasoning. I look forward to the debate.

Chapter One

"Fool Me Once, Shame On You; Fool Me Twice, Shame On Me"

Imagine that you are one of 535 trustees, hired to control the spending of $1.7 trillion. Think of the power and prestige you have. To what lengths would you go to maintain that position, considering that you are working for an organization that can fire you? Obviously I have just described the U.S. Congress and the people of the United States. How often do you think of Congress this way? Perhaps not at all, but this is exactly the way Congress should be viewed by the citizens of this country.

Let's carry this approach further: we allow them to set taxes that pay to run the country at the federal level. Then, aside from the money that gets trapped in Washington to inefficiently run the programs, that huge pile of money is carefully parceled out to keep Congress in office. The office holders in Washington tell us they are making our lives as perfect as possible, by the ways they spend our money. But because they are primarily professional politicians who want to stay in office forever, what they really are doing is buying votes and campaign contributions from special interest groups, from voting blocks and from powerful organizations and people who want favors. The rule in understanding all of this is: "follow the money."

Further, Washington controls a huge propaganda apparatus through their press releases. This material presents one viewpoint, despite "freedom of the press" that might allow enterprising reporters to research and print the opposite side of what is being presented. The people in Washington make much of the news, and the news they make very often is deliberately directed at telling us how to think. They want us to think that they can come up with all the solutions to our problems, much better than we can: they tell us they have a better overall view of everything than we have. They control in large measure the "facts" we get about our government, and the "facts" that are presented on both sides of debates about new and old programs. What happens is that impressions are purposely created, but true facts are hard to dig out and just often enough the impressions and the facts don't match.

This all makes me sound very cynical, but actually I think most people, when first arriving in Congress, are primarily honest, trying to do a good job, and therefore have our best interests at heart. They go to Washington full of good intentions and good works. And gradually the current system gets them. It is very hard for anyone to resist the feelings that the power gives to them: the self-importance, the implied ability to help everyone in their district or state, the way the lobbyists stroke their egos and even the way we stroke their egos. When reelection becomes more important than taking tough, unpopular stands, they turn into professional politicians, whose political careers are more important than steering the nation properly.

The best example to offer is the Social Security mess. And it is a crazy mess. Both parties have voted in so many benefits, it is estimated that the system will begin to lose money by 2013, and will run out of money by 2032, unless the system is "rescued." It has never been run as any proper private investment fund is run under current laws and accepted rules. If you had an investment account run privately by a bank trustee, and he handled it like Congress has handled Social Security, you could sue him for lack of proper care in managing your funds and easily win your case. If handled properly from the beginning, no rescue would be needed. It has always been run as an income transfer between generations, magnifying the importance of Congress as it rescues the system for our "benefit". The rescues so far have been to raise taxes, to plan on raising the retirement age, but the solution of "privatizing" social security, which has worked beautifully in Chile, has been resisted. Why? Controlling the distribution of money means power. No money, no power. Follow the money! I will discuss this in depth later, but couldn't resist making the point here that Congress finds it very hard to resist giveaways if the members think they will buy votes. No money to give away, no votes.

But we, the citizens, the true bosses and owners of the country, are just as much at fault. Half of us don't vote and that may hold a clue as to how people feel about their government: powerless to do anything about it, or too cynical to try. Or the following: Taxes draw money from us in many hidden and in some obvious ways. It seems we can't stop giving money to Washington. Once the money has gone off to Washington we then play the game the other way around: Try to get back the money that is being given away by supporting the giveaways, by backing the representative who is able to arrange for more federal spending in our area, or by arranging some special deal through lobbying. It is as if we forget that the money taken from us is *our* money. When it gets to Washington, everybody grabs for it. No wonder the politicians can get re-elected by using our money.

A 1997 movie, *G.I. Jane,* points this out and demonstrates just how cynical the whole country is about their relationship with Washington. Demi Moore tries to become a Navy Seal to help the feminist public relations of a female Texas senator. The "macho" male commanders try to flunk her out, but she survives! So a deal is cooked up to close five military bases in Texas, damaging the senator enough so she will lose her next election. The senator then tries to blackmail Moore's character to shove Moore out of the program. Obviously, Hollywood can't allow the blackmail to work, and Moore conquers in the end. Thus, Hollywood uses the country's perception of their government to make a perfectly "believable" movie!

An even more egregious example of an "unbelievable" movie which was rapidly accepted by our cynical public as being entirely possible is the 1998 *Wag the Dog.* With Clinton in deep trouble over the Lewinski scandal, the Cruise Missile attack on a chemical factory in the Sudan and terrorist bases in Afganistan was immediately questioned as *Wag the Dog:* an invented incident in the movie to divert attention from the

movie president, brought to real life in the Lewinski affair!
And what is worse, follow-up investigation of the missile attack strongly supported the contention that it *might* have been
partially or wholly a politically-driven diversion (New Yorker,
12 October 1998). Without question, Washington creates the
public cynicism.

Another way that money plays a major role in maintaining
more than 90% of Congress members in office is the collection
of enormous amounts of campaign contribution money by both
parties, under a set of complicated rules. The money is used to
buy huge amounts of TV time, presenting spots that give
impressions about candidates, but few hard, verifiable facts.
There is "hard" money and "soft" money, money collected by
the candidate and money collected by his party. There are
limits a candidate can spend of contributions received, but he
can spend all of his own money he wants. The party can
produce TV ads with party philosophy, but technically should
not help the candidate spend more than his limit. The rules
are so confused that the money sloshes around, out of control.
Citizens are part of this problem also. Private contributions,
when large, are often suspected of being connected to a favor
that is needed, as newspaper columnists tend to point out.

The information fed to the country by the professional
politicians just makes the Washington image even worse.
Research the facts behind the slick slogans from the two parties, beyond the 15-30 second news spots fed to the TV news
programs. The truth about the national budget gets totally
obscured by the propaganda put out by both political parties.
An example for each side: The "Reagan Deficit" of the 1980s
was an invention of the Democrats, parroted by the national
press. Under Reagan policy during his eight years, revenues
almost doubled, but the Democrat-controlled Congress went
on a wild spending spree that increased the yearly deficits.
Reagan tried to impound some of the appropriated funds, that
is, not spend money authorized by Congress; the Democrats
took him to court to force the spending! On the other hand,
the Republicans, who like to talk about reducing government
spending, carefully protect tax breaks and government subsidies to big corporations that really don't need the help.

The news media are no great help in the problem of Washington propaganda and neither is the public's desire for quick bits of news. Until the Great Depression, the newspapers were primarily quite conservative in their opinions. Radio was new and not very opinionated. TV arrived right after World War II, and along with radio, gradually developed what we hear/see now: opinion shows, talk panels, along with the sound bites and the instant fifteen-second news spot. Public opinion is easily molded by what is presented as newspapers are read less and less, and a busy public grabs for quick slices of news on TV or radio. And the lost art of carefully reading a newspaper isn't too helpful anymore. Journalists admit in polls they are eighty percent liberal and the stuff they put out comes across that way. The shift in political opinion within news sources is not surprising. Democrats were in power for forty years. It is natural for journalists (or anyone) to get close, read as "friendly," to the hand that feeds. Since the public seems to want its news on the quick, "don't confuse us with too many facts" fills the citizens needs, and allows a lot of impressionistic half-truths to go sneaking around, without the journalistic challenges that did occur years ago.

The bureaucracy (a word invented during FDR's time), is another major aspect of the problem. Congress writes laws in a general way, demonstrating intent, and it is left to the bureaucrats to write the regulations to cover the administration of those laws, and to administer the laws themselves. The regulations produced create volumes and volumes of dense prose that attempt to cover every contingency or possible human act under the law. Congress uses its powers of "oversight" to keep track of this, in the hope that all is done correctly. One result is that all of the federal law suits you hear about, in which the courts are requested to interpret the intent of Congress by citizens who run afoul of the regulations, read the intent in the law differently than bureaucrats do. And of course, there are those who look for unintentional loopholes in the regulations, to sneak through their own schemes to work around the law. The system is so cumbersome, it sets us fighting among ourselves, creating more cynicism about Washington.

It makes more money for the lawyers; but then, who is running the federal and state legislatures but the lawyers!

The best example of regulations-run-amok is the five foot shelf of IRS tax code that is needed to contain them. Each taxpayer "relief" or "simplification" act of Congress adds inches of regulations. Those regulations are now approaching 9,500 pages, contain 7.5 million words, and the latest law takes the capital gains form from nineteen to fifty-four lines, and creates four different tax rates, where two had been present before. There has been a recent campaign by politicians (in both parties) to "reform" the IRS. Despite the fact that the IRS at times has handled taxpayers terribly, I feel sorry for the agency. Can you imagine trying to administer this tax regulation monstrosity? The real culprits are your congress members who try to micro-manage our society for everyone's "benefit" through taxes on one hand, and then turn around and give some favored groups special tax breaks in the bills they write. The IRS bureaucrats are probably doing the best they can, considering the mess Congress forces them to administer.

Which brings me to the next point, implied by most of what I have written so far: in Washington reality is twisted to hide the truth. Perception is reality: We are told the national budget is now balanced! In fact this smoke-and-mirrors approach achieves balance only by including Social Security receipts on the income side of the ledger, and those receipts are promptly spent, not saved to protect the future. In 1993, unfunded money obligations of the Federal Government for the future (such as Social Security) totaled over 22 trillion dollars! ("Annual Report of the United States of America, 1996," by Meredith E. Bagby, HarperCollins Publishers, 1996). No private corporation is allowed by the SEC or by national accounting standards to run account books this way.

At this point I need to stop presenting examples of why we are so cynical about Washington. You might become so discouraged that you'll quit reading this book and simply decide nothing can be done. Go back and read the Introduction if you haven't, or reread it. In the first paragraph I tell you that this is the most wonderful country in the world. It is, but it can be tremendously better. Here is a story from my life to illustrate this point:

In the late 1970s and early 1980s, over about a four-year period, my neighborhood in southwestern Houston, Texas flooded as never before. Our little bayou had been deepened, straightened, widened, and concreted by the Corps of Engineers in the mid-1950s to prevent this, but no one foresaw the exponential growth of Houston. All those new concrete roads poured water into the bayou. I asked my local Congressman, who happened to sit on the House committee that handled flooding, to see what the Corps could do again: they offered to deepen and widen again, at a cost to the Federal government of $2 billion. They did not account for the fact that the outlet of the bayou was only two feet above sea level. Locally, we put together a group of neighbors with engineering and science backgrounds. We went over the problem with hydrology professors at our local universities, and with local engineers who had worked in the recent past with some of the local flooding streams, and had corrected one of them. A plan that included retention ponds, shifting from wells for drinking water to surface (reservoir) supply, changing bridge supports by taking them out of the waterway, and shifting some of the watershed back to a neighboring bayou from which it had been moved by the Corps in the 1950s, was presented to the local flood control district and accepted. Stopping the usage of ground water would stop subsidence of the land in our watershed, which had already dropped 6-8 feet, thereby creating a bowl effect on our flat coastal plain, increasing the water that ran in. The plan in 1983 was estimated to cost $250 million (not $2 billion!) in locally spent money. Because local funds are small and had to handle several streams, the plan for our bayou has not yet been completed, but has been implemented enough over fifteen years so that the bayou has not flooded since! Local initiative can handle local problems—Washington is not needed for everything.

The more we do for ourselves, the less it will cost, the better we will plan and understand what is going on, and the less power will be concentrated in Washington. But not without a fight: the Republican Contract with America based the "devolution of power" from Washington by granting money from the Federal income back to the states. Why does the money have to make the round trip from the states, through Washington, and back to the states, losing a sizable amount on the trip? This happens so the congressional politicians can maintain control over the money and over being reelected. It is slightly more complex than this. State governors are also politicians and will have to be willing to raise state taxes while federal taxes are lowered. We citizens have quite a task ahead of us, decentralizing government and exerting more of our own control. Entrenched politicians will find excuses and reasons to fight that kind of change. They will continue to claim that Washington can guarantee perfection, and we the people can't possibly learn or understand enough to play a major role.

Chapter Two

Medical Adventures and Learning to Reason

I was determined to become a doctor from the age of three. The changes in medicine since I entered medical school in 1950 are absolutely amazing. I could not have predicted them when I graduated from medical school in 1954. Most changes are good, even miraculous, but some are bad. We will discuss these changes as we go along. As I noted in the preface, this book comes from logical reasoning I developed, aided by conversations I had with my patients. Before proceeding, we must stop and describe the type of reasoning a diagnostic physician has to develop in order to help his patients. The thinking behind the philosophy of this book comes from that type of reasoning. Clear deductive reasoning doesn't appear automatically when the acceptance letter to medical school comes, although my excited and proud relatives started asking me medical questions the moment the letter arrived, as if somehow I had been magically imparted with a physician's wisdom. Far from it, deductive reasoning takes much practice to do well and requires that any emotional agenda must be removed. One enters medical school thinking like a lay person, and leaves, hopefully, reasoning as a physician. Med students are literally brainwashed to accomplish this goal, perhaps one of the few forms of brainwashing that is for the good.

It is important to point out that much of medicine is taught at the bedside of the patient. It is an apprenticeship with the master teaching the student and the patient is the object of the lesson. Remember the "practice" of medicine is the practice of the "Art of Medicine." It is not a 100% exact, black and white science, something I wish the tort lawyers and the courts would recognize. A diagnosis is a professional guess based on probabilities. A diagnostic physician is playing the odds! Before I have you thinking that doctors go stumbling around making wild guesses, lots of exact science gets taught in the classrooms. It is the application of those facts and the use of very careful history-taking from the patient, physical examination, and laboratory work that then have to be combined into a decision as to a diagnosis (what is wrong with the patient).

Studies have shown that a carefully obtained complete history alone will provide the competent physician with the correct diagnosis eighty percent of the time. That's right! The physical exam and the lab work add only twenty percent to the accuracy, and of course help confirm the eighty percent. Way back when I was in school, lab work did not provide the magical aids that are present now, and history-taking was taught with a vengeance. The physical examination was also very carefully taught. Before I left practice, while working with medical students and house officers (medical residents in hospital training), I found less emphasis placed on expertly getting that very complete history, and more reliance on the lab work. That approach costs more. I'll discuss the reasons later. Very good history-taking requires getting rid of common cause-and-effect notions. Just because event B follows event A does not mean they are related. Time relationships must be taken into account, but it must be proved by other means that A and B might be related. Timing of events is important, but possibly not the whole story. A far-fetched example just to make the point: You see me go to the light switch and the room we are in goes dark. You assume I turned the light off, but perhaps a colleague of mine peering through a peep hole did it; or perhaps the bulb burned out just at the moment I passed by the light switch. And we haven't even considered the circuit-breaker in the basement. The human body's organs are inter-related—this is the type of convoluted thinking a physician must perform. First the doctor must know what to look for, and then put the findings together. Sometimes the road to follow is very easy, at other times it is full of curves and branchings. Every conceivable interrelated fact must be obtained and then deductive reasoning takes over to find a solution, a diagnosis. This is where Occam's razor comes into play. If an answer appears that will explain almost all (if not all) of the findings that answer will be correct about ninety percent of the time. The trick is to be knowledgeable enough to pick out an answer, or to know how to use the textbooks and journals to help you. One definition of an expert is to know where to look it up. Sometimes it takes luck. I took care of a woman with very strange spontaneous swellings in and on different parts of her body occurring over a ten-year period. I had only known her as a patient for a very short while when I saw her with one of these reactions. I had never seen the condition before or heard of it, until I read a case report in the *New England Journal.* There was a perfect description of my problem patient, and I wasn't so dumb after all. It was one of the first reports in the medical literature, and it showed me how to help her.

An example of using Occam's razor is the following case. One evening a patient of mine brought her somewhat rebellious fourteen-year-old son to the ER for me to see. Putting aside his fairly obnoxious behavior, because he was obviously quite sick and needed immediate help, I found out quickly by history that his lower abdomen felt very painful to him, and he constantly had the urge to urinate, although he produced only tiny amounts of urine. He previously had an appendectomy. My examination of him found a mild fever, confirmed pain in the middle of the lower abdomen, above his pubis bone, just above the penis. His muscles in the abdominal wall were tense, protecting the painful inflammation that seemed to be present. A finger exam in the rectum was normal. I ordered very simple laboratory work, a blood count and a urine exam, expecting to find a urine infection. The urine was absolutely clear: no bugs, no pus. The white blood cells showed a pattern of mild infection, just like in appendicitis, but his appendix was gone. In this detective story the key clue was that his bladder was being irritated to make him want to urinate constantly, but his bladder was not infected on the inside, or the urine would have shown pus. I could think of only one diagnosis that fit all of this, and called a surgeon around midnight to come in.

"I've got a hot belly, here, that I think you will want to open. Please come and look," and told him my findings.

"What do you think it is?" he asked.

"It's a Meckel's diverticulum that's inflamed."

"Come on, that condition is so rare, what made you think of it?"

"It is the only thing I can think of that fits. It affects only two percent of the population, but this is one of the presentations in teenagers," I replied. The surgeon came in, agreed that he had to operate ("crack the belly" is the way he put it), and I went home to catch some sleep and await his phone call. "You're amazing. He had a Meckel's diverticulitis, lying on the bladder and irritating it!" I fell back to sleep, smiling; just as I had put the story together a few hours ago.* Another Occam's triumph! Is it any surprise that a physician, Arthur Conan Doyle, wrote the Sherlock Holmes stories with their fabled deductive reasoning?

There is another part of the lesson which should be repeated: to reach the right conclusion, you must have the facts in hand, or have done the research to get as many facts as possible. In political campaign sound bites, fifteen-second television spots offer perception, not reality. Facts are few, and everything depends on personal appearance, and on statements that appeal to the emotions and are not factual at all. This is the way most of the American citizenry researches a campaign and makes up its collective mind. Campaigning is now reduced to how many TV spots can be paid for, and what twist or spin can be used to sway people. Most people will not take the time to do the necessary research and apply logic, using Occam's razor.

Being brainwashed in medical school paid off for me. I was taught to think this way by the wonderful professors in medical school who pounded the technique into me. The previous story shows how to think to reach valid conclusions. I

---

* A Meckel's diverticulum is a two-inch long appendix-like object formed by mistake in the fetus, and comes off the edge of the lower small intestine about two feet before the large intestine. This is in the middle of the lower abdomen.

wish I could teach each reader of this book to use this same depth of reasoning when studying the problems of this country. I feel confident that my conclusions are based on this sort of reasoning; facts and interpretation, research and not emotion. There are no preconceived notions allowed. Take the facts as they come, and study opinions carefully. Opinion must always be open to interpretation.

This is how money is saved in working up a patient's problem. A good history will provide an excellent guide to which laboratory tests to employ. The laboratory tests must be done to confirm the diagnosis. Logically starting with those most likely to be on the mark limits what is done, as compared to a shotgun approach which covers everything at once. The proper sequencing of lab tests saves money.

Coming of age in medicine, growing from student days to being in private practice offered many experiences and events that can be applied today. There were three individuals in training who were handled by very concerned medical superiors in a way that cannot occur today, with our preoccupation in protecting the self-esteem of individuals, allowing individual freedom, and either protecting victims or creating them as the busy bodies see fit. The first person was a senior when I was a freshman. He was in his sixth year of school and had passed them all! Why? He was brilliant. He had gone to college at sixteen and in the accelerated college schooling of World War II, had arrived in medical school at eighteen. He passed his first two years with "gentlemen C's," and was told by the school to repeat those years; he was not working up to his potential, and unless he did so they would never let him graduate! The school wanted him to graduate with maturity as well as knowledge. Are we allowed to be that judgmental these days? The school's decision created a sub-specialist who had a brilliant career in private practice.

The second person finished medical school with passing grades, but had made the mistake of getting a student nurse pregnant. The school took a dim view of this, and he had to repeat his senior year again to gain maturity. The last fellow, while in residency, showed himself as a brilliant medical scholar but a klutz at the bedside, somewhat uncoordinated in per-

forming physical procedures, and a little erratic at bedside
decision-making. He was taken aside and told he would make
a wonderful research physician on a medical school faculty and
that is exactly what happened.

Medical faculties have always considered learning and
maturity equally important considering the seriousness of a
doctor's work. Today they have to tread very carefully. When
black students were brought into Baylor Medical School in the
1970s, their pre-med schooling was obviously deficient. Many
had trouble keeping up and had to be held back to receive
remedial training. It wasn't their fault, but the fault of sepa-
rate-but-equal policies in student education. Baylor, to my
knowledge, was not challenged about this policy, but I wonder
if they can do it today.

In Cleveland, Ohio, where I trained after medical school,
I found a medical insurance concept that might help today's
problems in controlling medical costs. All the hospitals in the
city had gotten together with Ohio Blue Cross, and had worked
out an average daily charge per patient that would satisfy the
yearly budget for that hospital. That meant each patient, in
private care or on a charity ward, paid the same for each day
in the hospital, no matter what the illness, no matter how
complicated the care. The private physicians charged separately for their services. Contrast that with today's convoluted
mess. DRGs, diagnosis related groups, catalog every conceivable condition or illness, are given computer code numbers,
and billings are controlled by the numbers sent to the insurer.
This is a wide-open invitation for fraud: Obviously, illnesses
have degrees of severity and degrees of difficulty in treatment.
Those variations are covered by numbers also. A whole industry has sprung up of experts who teach how to push the numbers to receive the most income from the insurer. The private
physician submits charges under the same system, and there
are experts and courses to teach them how to push their DRG
report numbers.

When I entered private practice, it was on salary in a small
clinic. During the eleven years after college, nine of medical
training and two years in the Army, I didn't have to charge for
my services. I could follow what I had been taught. Do what-

ever lab work and procedures seemed necessary to prove my diagnosis. Cost was never a consideration. But in the clinic, patients were being charged for every little thing I decided to do. At the end of the first month I went into the business office and looked at the bills I had created. I was aghast. To my eyes they were huge. I was going to have to reconsider how I practiced medicine! I discussed this with the senior doctors, and they reassured me that my bills were right in line with what was to be expected. That did not reassure me. I made two decisions: first, never to look at bills again, and next, that I would always work in a clinic with equal salaries for senior partners. Physicians have different styles of practice, attract different types of patients, work at different rates, and produce different yearly totals in gross receipts. My decision would allow me the freedom to practice as I wished, never driven by the idea that my medically important decisions were driving my personal income.

This leads us to the core of today's problem in medical care: money. Everyone should receive good medical care. Human ethics demand it. Because of the expense of modern medical care, an alphabet-soup conglomeration of federal and corporate organizations have been created to impose cost controls on individual doctors. But it is the physician working with the patient, in an intimate relationship that the outsider cannot fully judge, who must make the medical decisions, and therefore the costs. It is the outsider judgment that is causing so much trouble.

Shortly before I retired, an elderly patient of mine ran afoul of Medicare. She arrived at the ER with her very devoted family on Sunday, when I was off and covered by another physician in my group. She was about ninety years old, blind, had high blood pressure, was mildly diabetic, and had severe bronchitis with a moderate fever of 102 degrees. She was also in a low-sodium coma, because her devoted family had continued her medicine even when she quit eating, driving down the salt level in her blood. The coma was corrected overnight by giving her a high salt intravenous. An x-ray of her lungs did not show pneumonia which would have granted admission to the hospital under Medicare rules. When I arrived on Monday, I discovered the nurses committee governing Medicare admissions to the hospital trying to follow their book of regulations. They wanted her to be kept in provisional care, stabilized, and then sent home. I saw how sick and weak she was. It took me until Tuesday to get her properly admitted to the hospital, at higher charges to Medicare, which is what the regulation committee was concerned about. The patient seemingly improved for two days, and then suddenly died. What the Medicare regulations did not take into account was her age. People that age are very fragile, and don't tolerate much stress. That factor, which played a large role in my concern for her, was not considered in the regulations. The nurses who reviewed the situation were doing the best job they could, but were short-changing the patient.

When I started at my first clinic I watched the older, founding doctor of the clinic for whom I saw some of his patients on afternoon hospital visits, adjusting his fees Robin-Hood style. He didn't "rob the rich to give to the poor," but he took from the rich to give the poor. In those days a heart attack earned you a month in the hospital. That was current medical teaching. The charge was $5 a day for hospital care for a coronary and the total charge was simply $150 for the month. There might be a charge added for extraordinarily complicated care. The older doctor would look at the preliminary bill for the heat attack, and if the person was very rich that bill became $450, less well-to-do $300. The patient whose income was barely getting him by might be billed $50-75. Occasionally there was no bill. I did a house call one night for him, and sent a patient of his with a severe stroke to the hospital. I followed the ambulance and spent the whole night in the hospital at her bedside, trying to save her. To no avail, by morning she was dead. She was quite well-to-do, but he would not charge. My care had failed, and in his eyes had no value to the family. He didn't blame me. I had done the best I could, it just wasn't enough. Compare this with today.

When Medicare arrived in the mid-1960s I was thrilled, considering my own psychological problem about proper medical care and resulting charges. Now we could charge reasonably to each item performed. No more making up fees. A business-like approach, without the responsibility of covering the poor by over-charging the rich. This was my first experience with exploding government regulations. My income hadn't yet grown to the point where I had run into the IRS regulations. Over 30 years have passed and we are now hearing about Medicare going bankrupt, about Medicare fraud, and about the morass of medicare regulations. Bureaucrats cannot be relied upon to write the regulations to run systems like this. They try to sit and think over every last contingency, every possible situation, every twist of human behavior. What they end up with are linear feet of bookshelf of regulations piled on regulations, complexity on complexity, confusion on confusion.

I think my personal answer to the doctor/income problem leads to one possible way to help control medical costs. Keep doctors in charge of decision-making and totally separate from money considerations. For purposes of Medicare billing, DRGs were developed in a pilot study using physicians and insurer groups working together to arrive at reasonable charges for accepted, standardized procedures and for time limits allowed for specific illnesses requiring hospitalization. In general, they provide a good method. The problem is that they try to be too exact and too confining, as my case of the comatose ninety year old demonstrates. I think one possibility is to develop broader characterizations and to allow individual physician input in the billing process for the hospitals, letting him define the finer details of each case since he is the only one with intimate knowledge necessary. An alternate approach is the Cleveland method of the 1950s which could be spread across the country with each hospital being paid by the patient/day to cover their proven budget. This would solve the current teaching-hospital problem, that is fighting Medicare to get enough extra funds to cover teaching embryo physicians.

Those hospital budgets must be real and not represent excess beds. This country reached an over-bedded hospital capacity of at least thirty percent before the recent push to reduce medical costs. The excess capacity was partially due to one of Congress' well-intentioned giveaways. In the 1950s, the Hill-Burton Act provided funds so every little community could have its own little facility, a very inefficient way to offer medi-

cal care. Larger hospitals can offer more services on site. The
patient may drive farther, but the care he gets is better. The
medical insurance companies are also to blame for the excess
beds. Years ago they defined compensible illnesses as those
requiring hospitalization. Out-of-hospital work-ups for illness
or for good preventive medicine were not covered. I can remember patients demanding to go to the hospital to have the
studies paid for by insurance.

Hospitals are very expensive hotels. If you really don't
need to spend time in bed because of your physical condition,
it is a lot cheaper for everyone if you do your work-up as an
out-patient. Remember we all pay for the insurance pool of
money that pays for our care. The decision on the part of
insurance companies encouraged the building of excessive
hospital beds. I have a theory as to why the insurance companies did this. One clear reason is actuarial: the fear of fudging.
A patient is really sick if the patient requires the hospital. The
claim is real. The other theory is money. Insurance companies
are generally regulated as to profit margin. A ten percent profit
margin of $10 million gross volume is much smaller than a ten
percent margin on $100 million! Demanding hospitalization
created more hospitals.

Reducing overall hospital bed capacity has been going on
for several years now. Patients stay in the hospital for much
shorter periods than before. Closing hospitals, or contracting
beds by combining rival hospitals, has resulted in community
fights rivaling the congressional fights over closing military
bases. Jobs are lost, community pride is hurt, and everyone still
wants an ER around the corner. It just can't work that way.
ERs are very expensive as HMO fights about allowing those
visits shows. We only need a certain number of beds for the
country, but I would not look to Washington to make those
decisions. It should be accomplished at the state level. Different states have different population mixes. Look at all the
retired people in Florida, Arizona, and south Texas. Low density
populations in the north like Montana or the Dakotas have
entirely different needs. The local governing bodies will know
best how to do this with the input of the local citizenry.

Another major step in saving medical expense for the whole

country is to separate physician decision-making from his net income, as I did. How to accomplish that is a tough problem to solve. Doctors won't want to give up control over their incomes, and they don't have to, if they would be willing to work in small groups or large groups with equal salaries. I think that approach should be encouraged among medical students and residents-in-training. Physicians in groups can set their own salary. I do not favor socialized medicine. I have seen that while in the Army. While I was in service, there were twenty-two two-year doctors, as we were called, at the base where we worked. In those days we were threatened with being drafted as privates, if we didn't join up as Captains to serve our time. Three of us worked as if we were in private practice, and the others took advantage of the situation and treated their work as if they were on an eight to five job. The profit motive cannot be removed. In private practice, a doctor has to win the confidence of his patients to build a large practice base. He has to sell himself. In the protected environment of socialized medicine, he just has to fill the time required. He may practice an acceptable standard of medicine, but it will not be inspired medicine. The solo practitioner who resists joining a group must be allowed to do it his way, but he will end up under much closer and onerous scrutiny.

By scrutiny I am talking about "peer review" (doctors studying other doctors' methods of practice). For a number of years I was head of an internal medical department in a small hospital. The staff was made up primarily of board certified specialists, but our bylaws allowed non-certified general practitioners to join the staff on a provisionary basis. Their first ten admissions to the hospital were studied to determine if they matched the standards we had set. I particularly remember one incident in which the nurses from the intensive care unit (ICU) rushed to me to report such a physician. Yes, nurses should question how a doctor conducts his cases. I assigned a committee of three physicians in my department to review the questionable cases, and based on their decision, and my own opinion, he was asked to leave our staff. In this day and time he might have sued us in order to stay on, but luckily he didn't. Doctors can be vigilant and police themselves, and this is standard practice in every hospital and clinic.

Of course, we must get the personal injury lawyers under control. Effective tort-law reform will allow doctors to stop practicing so much defensive medicine. Proving something over and over by medical laboratory testing to seek protection from malpractice just adds tremendously to cost. Peter W. Huber, in his book *Liability, The Legal Revolution and its Consequences,* 1988, estimated that out-of-control tort cases were costing the country $300 billion a year. Imagine what that estimated cost must have grown to over the decade since. As a Doctor of Mechanical Engineering who taught at M.I.T. and with a law degree from Harvard, his books are authoritative and eye-opening. In the book he did not separate medical malpractice costs, but he quoted a study that found the average physician practiced $3.50 of defensive medicine (excessive tests to pro-tect himself) for every $1 of malpractice insurance he paid. The following example will help demonstrate how this hurts you. In 1992, a neurosurgeon I know paid $140,000 for mal-practice insurance, just to cover that one year. An obstetrician-gynecologist spent $120,000 for the year. Each of these spe-cialists makes almost all his gross income from procedures he performs, that is, surgery, and of course deliveries of babies for the OB. If the neurosurgeon did 300 surgeries a year and the OB-GYN had 200 surgeries and 100 deliveries, simple arith-metic tells us that the neurosurgeon added $467 to each bill and the OB-GYN tacked on $400 to cover their insurance premiums. The patients paid that extra amount. The insur-ance companies didn't pay. They had increased their premium charges to their customers, the patients. Notice, the doctors got their income, the insurance companies got their income, the lawyers got their income, and the public paid. Yes, mal-practice insurance must exist, but it should not have to survive frivolous suits or massive class-action suits based on "junk science."

In 1997 Huber did publish a thoughtful column (*Forbes,* 27 January 1997), and estimated that medical tort reform would save the country over $50 billion a year, without resulting in negligent medical care. He quotes a paper by Kessler and McClellan in the May 1996 *Quarterly Journal of Economics:* None of the liability reforms studied led to any consequential differences in mortality or the occurrence of serious complications. The study compared medical costs in states with tort reform limits compared to states without such limits. The reforms do not limit the right to sue. Rewards are reasonably capped, and there are no punitive awards, doubling or tripling the demonstrated value of the injury. Remember, the doctor who makes a mistake is covered by insurance. It is the insurance carrier that pays the award and passes on the cost through higher doctor premiums to the patients themselves. Yes, doctors are human and they make mistakes. Yes, some doctors are lazy and do not keep up with the latest teachings. The medical profession has set up watchful committees of physicians who review hospital charts to catch these physicians. Those "peer review" systems at times are not strong enough, but lining the tort lawyer's pockets are not the way to improve peer review. Peer review itself must be put under tight scrutiny, which is exactly what has happened in recent years.

Here's an example of the need for tort reform. One suit filed against me was absolutely frivolous. Luckily my lawyer and I got it withdrawn rather promptly. I cared for a man for many years with very severe high blood pressure. I saw him yearly to review his situation and condition, and to scold him for not taking his medicine. His exam always included a chest x-ray from the front and side and an exercise stress test. One night he was rushed to a distant suburban hospital with severe chest pain. He died within a few hours of a ruptured aorta (the main artery from the heart) in the chest. I was immediately sued by his wife's lawyer, under the presumption that as carefully as I had followed his case, I should have caught this in advance. Perfectly true, if we had spotted his aorta enlarging before the mortal event. We checked the admission chest x-rays taken at the ER. They were just like mine. I had done nothing wrong, but her lawyer had. He had not checked the facts before suing me. I asked my lawyer to legally attack that lawyer. He refused. Lawyers protect lawyers.

My chief suggestion for tort law reform is to adopt the English system: loser pays. Now anyone can concoct a legal theory and run it through court. Judges rarely apply sanctions against lawyers who bring stupid, far-out cases to court. Worse than that, under the philosophy rampant in our society, that somehow the poor injured victim must be given some money, we have all heard of jury awards that are ridiculous. Our newspapers and magazines are filled with examples, but as the legal profession runs the courts, the federal and state legislative bodies, there is much discussion, sound and fury, but the mess continues.

Preventive medicine is another major way to lower overall costs. Find a private doctor and stick with that person. You need a long-term personal relationship with your physician to receive the best, and probably least-expensive care. A doctor who knows you well will spot shortcuts that give you excellent care and save everyone money. Those shortcuts involve knowing areas of your health that need not be explored when a problem pops up. A new doctor may range too far afield because of what he does not know about you. The knowledge your doctor has about you leads to good preventive medicine, and even to an unexpected saving of your life.

I took care of a lady for many years. A physical exam one year when she was in her late 60s discovered a murmur in her neck. She had a ninety-five percent blockage of her left carotid artery that fed her brain. Surgery fixed that problem, and we well may have saved her from a very disabling stroke, if not death. A few years later during a routine checkup, I noted that her hematocrit (the volume concentration of her red blood cells) had dropped from forty-one percent to thirty-five percent. Her records with me, going back many years indicated that forty-one percent was her usual level. A small alarm bell went off in my head. First thing you do is recheck the result. The lab or the collection method could be off. I got the same result, and the alarm bell was louder. She had not noticed any unusual bleeding or blood loss. She felt fine. Hidden blood loss (the usual reason for a drop in red blood count) is usually intestinal, and her other red blood counts suggested blood loss. Some stool samples for hidden blood were positive. An upper G.I. series (swallowing barium and having the radiologist look through an image-intensifying fluoroscope) was normal. A flexible partial colonoscopy was normal. A barium enema (barium in the colon looked at with the fluoroscope) showed the bleeding cancer over in her lower right colon, or caecum, and it looked small. Caecal cancers are usually slow-growing. Hers was removed with no sign of spread. She was alive several years later at my retirement, as I write this, and I believe she is still alive. Think of how much good preventive medicine saved this woman in human terms of suffering. Think of what was saved in monetary terms.

Preventive medicine, as we all should know, can be presented as national programs. Pap smears are a case in point. I can remember a lecture in my sophomore year in medical school describing how the program would work when set in place. It was still under development. In my first six years in practice I discovered early cervical cancer six times. In the next twenty-four years, only two more, and they were in the first fifteen years of my practice. Where did they go? I didn't quit doing pelvic exams, but doctors screened the country and found all that was hiding out there, and after that, discovery of cervical cancer was at the rate of occurrence. We got rid of the "overhang." I remember one of those first six cases vividly: A recently married woman turned up pap smear positive. She wanted to have children. Her gynecologist did a procedure called a "conization" which removed the tiny area of bad cells. He followed her very closely; she was able to have the two children she wanted, and then she had a hysterectomy, because it was well-established that her tendency to develop cervical cancer would always be a threat.

Back in the late 1970s one of my partners and I, following the medical literature, realized that doing certain studies on our patients' colons could theoretically prevent colon cancer. We embarked on this approach and started to do limited colonoscopies in 1981, long before it was standard practice in the country. We knew that colon cancer was theoretically 100% preventable, and decided to protect our patients by starting our own screening program. It is the second most common cancer, falling between lung and breast, and in 1992 was killing 55,000 people a year, when screening for colon cancer finally became accepted as a standard of practice in the medical community. It took until 1997 for Congress to pass a law allowing colon cancer screening for Medicare starting 1 January 1998! Several years after screening mammograms were allowed to prevent breast cancer. In 1998, 131,600 new cases were anticipated with 56,500 deaths. The old philosophy that affected insurance company thinking years ago, requiring that only bona fide illness be covered, still exists in Washington. "If it ain't broke, don't fix it," and "if it ain't found don't look for it," doesn't work in medical care. Preventative maintenance saves money and human suffering. What took the medical community so long to accept colon cancer screening was not lack of knowledge about preventability, but the need to do cost/benefit studies to find the best way to screen. This results in spending the least amount of money for the country, and at the same time discovering the largest number of cancers by the methods chosen. The doctor organizations are very sensitive to cost/benefit. I wish Congress was.

Why is colon cancer theoretically 100% preventable? Almost all of them are preceded by polyps, little finger-like growths inside the colon. They can be seen by a fiberoptic scope. Some of them bleed and can be detected by testing the stool for blood. Remove polyps and prevent cancer. I wish it were just that simple. Over a ten-year period I performed slightly over 1,900 limited colonoscopies, reaching the upper part of the left colon ninety percent of the time. Five stool samples for blood were obtained by the patients and returned to us for checking. The blood testing was to screen the right and middle portions of the colon, which I had not seen. If the blood tests were positive, a full colonoscopy was performed by a gastroenterologist. This technique found five cancers and thirty atypical polyps (growths headed for cancer). Since repeat exams were performed on many patients, the actual number screened was about 1,000 people. Think of the value in human terms to these thirty-five people in whom I found cancer or potential cancer. Think of the money saved. I've forgotten the number in whom we found totally benign (safe) polyps, I think it was around seventy people. Even those folks showed a benefit. I had identified them to be followed more closely in the future. Those polyps could change and head toward cancer.

The national cost/benefit studies eventually concluded that eighty percent of colon cancers could be found by the screening method chosen. It is not surprising that the screening method we chose was very close to the method finally recommended as the national practice standard. Medical research is very efficiently spread to the doctors of the country. We know what our researchers and teachers are thinking. The newly-established national screening under Medicare is recommended to start at age fifty, be done every four years, and uses a flexible sigmoidoscope. We started at age forty, did it every three years, and used a longer limited colonoscope. By the way, Medicare guidelines are generally followed by the private insurance programs.

I wish we could find or prevent 100% of all cancers. During the ten years I did this screening before retiring, I missed two cancers. One was in a fellow in his fifties who had been screened regularly, but who had a wide-spread right-sided cancer when the symptoms he developed caused us to find it. The other was a fifty-year-old lady who had lower abdominal symptoms. We did a full colonoscopy, which sees the entire inside of the colon, and nothing was found. Six months of treatment for spastic colon was to no avail, and at that point a repeat full colonoscopy then found a cancer on the right, which from its position at discovery, appeared to have been initially hiding under the inner lining of the colon. Nothing in medicine works 100%. In the established national screening method growths on the right side are searched for by testing stool for blood. This option works because left-sided cancer lesions are sixty-five to seventy percent of the total, and very sensitive blood tests may pick up approaching fifty percent of the cancer lesions. The national screening method plays the odds, resulting in the best return for the money, but not trying to achieve 100%, which is impossible anyway. To try for ninety to ninety-five percent would increase costs tremendously, since it would involve direct visualization of the right side of the colon using the very expensive full colonoscope.

The following woman, who was visiting Houston from the Northeast, would be missed under the currently accepted national method. She was forty-two years old when her problem was found by my partner. She had no symptoms; she was screened as part of a thorough physical exam. Seven polyps were found on the left side, of which one had a tiny area of "pre-cancer" in its tip. Removal by colonoscope ended the immediate danger of cancer without the major surgery that would have been required if the dangerous polyp had not been found. She required follow-up colonoscopies that removed other polyps, which developed during the years. That was fifteen years ago, and she still is a healthy person. By the way, she discovered that a grand-aunt had died of colon cancer (it can be an inheritable problem). Family history acts as another warning for screening. When this woman returned to New England fifteen years ago, her local doctors wanted to know why she had the colon test. She had no symptoms! They were so narrow in their concept of medical practice that preventive medicine had no place in their approach. Since that time, several large medical centers have devised studies to teach reasonable time rates for screening physical exams. Obviously, preventative medicine can be overdone by screening too often (i.e., checking the colon by a flexible scope every year). Blood testing the stool yearly is enough.

This young woman's story sells preventive medicine but raises the issue about the age to start screening—it cannot be absolute. Her family history, although not known at the time of discovery, dictated screening her at an earlier age than the new national Medicare guidelines. By the way, know that Medicare coverage starts at sixty-five, or earlier if you are declared disabled, but Medicare acts as a guide to all the other medical insurance programs and the HMO rules. All the programs, Medicare included, demand rigid guidelines for control of costs. Morality and ethics don't take a back seat but they do get in the way of clear decision-making. It raises the issue of how much perfection can we afford.

Before I get into the issue of what degree of perfection in medical prevention is possible, I need to stop and make a philosophic-political comment about my reason for using the colon cancer prevention program to sell preventive medicine. After all, we all know about the dangers of smoking, primarily due to American Heart Association and Cancer Society public education programs, and the recent intervention of the federal government against the tobacco companies. The demonstration of the success of mammograms has led to national guidelines as to screening age, and women have flocked to do just that. Colon cancer prevention is relatively unknown and is being pushed by the American College of Gastroenterology. Why relatively unknown? Special interest groups, public and private, have made sure that their representative segments of our population get the messages about health patterns associated with that segment. The women's groups made sure that Congress heard the loud complaints that mammograms, as preventive medicine, were not covered by Medicare. In our culture women are a special voting block in the eyes of Congress. As a result, breast cancer, number three in total deaths, got its preventative medicine test years before colon cancer, number two. There are private organizations that literally represent every illness and condition known to medicine. AIDS gets a tremendous amount of publicity and enormous amounts of federal funding for research; the American Heart Association has to attack smoking, the major enemy to cardiovascular diseases; American Cancer seems to have concentrated on smoking because it is so visible a habit in society; and both American Cancer and the various women's groups have championed mammograms. Colon cancer, the second most deadly cancer we have, doesn't affect a segment of the population. It affects our whole adult population. It starts in the late thirties, does become more common with aging, and occurs equally in both sexes, and equally in all races, and we don't seem to be represented by anyone who wants to teach us outside of the most interested physicians. This is such an obvious side effect of the victimization culture of our society, splintering us into special selfish segments, with the do-gooders watching out only for the favored segment and not for the good of all of us. This is the wrong type of competition in health care. It took twenty years from the time that medical research indicated colon cancer screening was feasible for the Medicare program to accept it—much too long for the second most common cancer in our population.

The National Kidney Failure/Dialysis Program is a very clear-cut way to point out how difficult it is to reach perfect care, despite being extremely successful. The current guide for accepting a patient into the program is straightforward: the patient is admitted to dialysis at any age, and the only requirement is that kidney failure has appeared. This is how the program was developed. In the mid-1960s there were several pilot programs in the VA system and through medical schools. The Seattle Demonstration Project was a major influence but not the only center used. In general, the various dialysis centers limited patients to intelligent contributors to society, age twenty to fifty-five, with stable marriages. Keeping them alive to pursue their professions (medicine, law, ministry, engineering, etc.) would compensate for the cost of three-times-a-week dialysis. Also, as it turned out in Seattle, the vast majority of this carefully picked group could be taught home dialysis utilizing their intelligent wives, further reducing costs. In 1967 an expert committee, chaired by Dr. Carl Gottschalk, was arranged for by the federal government, and they concluded that a nationally funded kidney failure program was reasonable. Based on the way the pilot programs picked their patients, they estimated that one person in 50,000 would require this care, and if the program was run through government clinics with doctors on salary, it would eventually cost no more than $800 million a year (in 1967 dollars, I assume, to be later adjusted for inflation) when fully implemented.

It didn't work that way. In 1972 Congress set up a National Kidney Failure Program attached to Medicare but open to everyone, at any age, not just those over sixty-five-years-old, and run by private doctors. A morally correct decision, but no one was prepared for the flood of money that rushed out to cover the program. One person in 50,000 became 27 people! The costs for Medicare climbed past $6 billion in 1995, and since Medicare reimburses for eighty percent, total national costs were in the $7 billion range. Home dialysis was rare. Kidney transplant could cut costs, but there are not enough kidneys out there to fill the need. The administrators in Washington tried to stem the money leak, but that didn't work, even though they cut the payment for each dialysis by forty percent. In any field, medical or otherwise, techniques advance. The dialyzing machines were improved shortening dialysis time, allowing more patients to be done a day, more volume per dialysis center. Continuing research showed that starting dialysis earlier was better for the patients. A very expensive hormone-drug was found to improve the anemia that accompanies dialysis and was authorized by the federal administrators to be administered to dialysis patients. And then there was the technique of doctors beating the bushes to find even more patients who might be hiding from care. Some patients have been included who have another terminal illness, and coincidentally also developed kidney failure. With such an open-ended arrangement, what would one expect? Income still generates invention, just as invention, in the form of better machines, increases income.

The reduction in payment for each dialysis treatment in constant dollars was sixty-one percent, dropping from $138 in 1972 to fifty-four dollars by 1995. Sixty percent of the dialysis centers are for profit, so the squeeze on payments, as a means of cost-control, has raised the specter of inadequate care as a way of cutting costs. It was reported in 1995 that the mortality rate for the United States program was twenty-three percent, whereas in Western Europe and Japan the rates were about ten percent. These are gross numbers, but after correction for our more liberal limits, age, presence of other illnesses, etc. the difference is smaller, but not eliminated. Care in this country may not be as good as it should be. The moral dilemma is obvious. Should we be less generous in offering kidney care to everyone, or should we increase payments? Should we totally nationalize the system into government dialysis stations with physicians on salary, as was originally suggested?

In Great Britain, because of more limited resources, dialysis is limited to those under fifty-five, although that is a flexible limit, and people who are more valuable to society are chosen over others for the spaces available. As a result, 7.7 persons out of 50,000 are treated compared to our twenty-seven. In Canada, with limited financial resources as in Britain, many patients are placed on the cheaper treatment, ambulatory peritoneal dialysis. This involves putting a large amount of fluid into the abdominal cavity then removing the fluid filled with waste products which the kidney should have removed. It is generally considered an inferior treatment to the kidney dialysis I have been referring to, where the patient's blood is passed through a dialysis machine and waste products are pulled from the blood across a plastic membrane or sheet. I doubt that the moral climate in this country will allow the dialysis program to use shortcuts like this.

Should we use a totally nationalized kidney program with government dialysis stations and salaried physicians? My experience as an Army physician warns sharply against this. During the two years I served, I had to become Acting Chief of the Internal Medical Department of the base hospital at a time when the new yearly budget was being submitted. I looked over our department and its equipment, and submitted a request that was the same as the year before. My superiors jumped all over me, and made me find reasons to increase my department budget by ten percent. That is the smallest amount they would allow. It was unheard of in their thinking, as doctor/ bureaucrats, to ask for less! I was left to assume that all government bureaucracies act like this. That was 1959, and in Washington they are still doing it: all programs have built in automatic increases unless specifically stopped by Congress. Also, please remember my comments about the two-year temporary Army physicians I saw while I was in the Army. They acted like eight to five employees, did good perfunctory work, but not much that was inspired.

My memories as a student learning at a VA hospital, and also as a teaching physician in the VA system, do not bring me to recommend government medicine in any form. A 1993 General Accounting Office (GAO) study of the VA frightens me. Patients wait hours for care. Patients in need of specialized consultations may wait sixty to ninety days to be seen. Hospital stays are longer than need be. I know why: if the beds in VA facilities are unfilled in large enough amounts, the facility could be possibly considered for closure. Instead, under political pressure from powerful veterans organizations the system expands and expands, despite the fact that our armed services are smaller and the number for "veterans" in the future will be falling. Closing a facility is like closing a military base: an inconceivable wound to the local VA bureaucracy, with the loss of jobs, and the overall economic loss to the local community. More than likely the VA is over-bedded like the civilian hospitals, but the VA is not about to let anyone find out. Admission to VA care involves service-connected illnesses or conditions and the connections are loosely interpreted. Worse than that, for years any veteran who claimed he could not afford medical care outside the VA was admitted to care. Years ago that claim was never checked. According to the 1993 GAO report, now any veteran can receive free medical care on an "as available" basis depending on the local case load. Based on the VA I have known, a nationalized kidney dialysis program will be a bureaucratic costly mess.

And finally, one last unholy mess. Within the Congressionally-mandated national dialysis program, weird inequities pop up. Seven percent of U.S. citizens are not eligible for the program! They have not worked the required forty yearly quarters (worked for ten years with Social Security payments from themselves and/or their employer) to be eligible! And yet political refugees from places like Vietnam or Cuba can come to this country, find they have difficulty working here, apply for Social Security Disability, and if they are found by medical examination to be disabled they are eligible. I was a Social Security medical examiner for the disability program. I have seen these "political refugees" and examined them. Often they couldn't speak English, had no particular job skills and were somewhat elderly and worn out. Do the members of Congress really know what is hidden in the laws they pass? This arrangement is totally unfair. If Congress is willing to vote for giveaways like this, can we ever expect cost controls? My answer to cost control is the same as I stated before: private groups of doctors, on equal salaries, and with very stringent peer review is probably the least of all evils. This country does not have the moral make up of Great Britain to withhold care from certain groups of people.

Here is one last example as to why medical costs are almost impossible to estimate in advance. Recently an HMO decided to take advantage of the new laparoscopic surgery for gall bladder disease. This involves using amazing fiberoptic scopes through a few small incisions to remove the gall bladder. Because the patient does not have to recover from the trauma of a big gash in his right side, he is discharged from the hospital in a brief time. As I noted before, hospitals are very expensive hotels. The cost of this surgery is much lower. The HMO offered this new surgery, and budgeted much less to cover it, assuming that the same number of gall bladder removals would be performed as in previous years. They did not count on human behavior, which is always the confounding factor. Four times as many gall bladder procedures occurred during the next year. Did they ever lose money! Why did this happen? The HMO did not count on those people with mild gall bladder trouble who had learned to live with it. The easier-to-tolerate style of surgery enticed these people to ask for it. Obviously, in subsequent years, gall bladder surgery should drop back to its usual levels for this HMO, as the hidden "overhang" disappears.

Concerned as I was about the cost of medical care, I was startled to see reports in the mid-1980s which estimated that two-thirds of all Medicare funds were being spent on the last two years of life. The implication was obvious: physicians, trained as we were to save life, to extend life, were not saving or extending very much, and at tremendous cost. Then I realized what had happened. When Medicare appeared in the mid-1960s, intensive care units had not yet developed. Neither had CAT scans or MRIs. Oxygen tents were still being used, not ventilators. Blood tests were simple: blood samples from arteries to obtain blood gas levels were still research procedures. Back then we could take x-rays and see two-dimensional pictures of parts of the body, which were of course, three-dimensional. Everything was compressed unto a flat photographic sheet. The CAT scans and MRIs give slices of the body, clearly showing all the organs in three dimensions. The use of TV screens to allow image-intensification fluoroscopy had just arrived. Looking at a functioning organ like the stomach filled with barium, which blocked x-rays to outline the walls of the stomach, could be done much more accurately and more safely with one-twentieth the x-ray exposure. These techniques and many others appeared one by one and rapidly were put into use. They gave us much more information, much more quickly, much more safely. We could treat in a much improved fashion. We fell into the trap of seeing the techniques, being captured by how wonderful and ingenious they were, and we lost sight of the patient. We lost sight of the ethics involved in a patient reaching the end of life. We were not asking what the patient and his family wanted.

My own immediate response was to take two courses from a psychologist on the issues of death and dying. These courses began to appear as soon as it became obvious that doctors could sustain life artificially, and raised the issue of when and for how long that was proper or improper. I saw death starting in medical school. I gradually grew accustomed to dealing with it as a fact of life. But I received no training in medical school or my post-graduate years in how to talk with patients who were about to die. No one gets out of this world alive. And it was becoming difficult to die with dignity. Physicians were taught to fight for life, we did not learn to accommodate or become comfortable with death, which is inevitable. We were not comfortable in talking with our patients about their impending deaths, but as the courses showed, the patients wanted to talk with us and express their wishes. We had to learn to overcome our reluctance, and to discuss with them their wishes.

A woman in her seventies was dying of progressive heart attacks. She did not want to consider heart transplant, and she didn't want to die, antiseptically separated from her family in the back room of some ICU. She had several very caring sisters. I discussed her wishes with family and with her: We rented a hospital bed, oxygen equipment, and other items, literally setting up a hospital room in her living room. Her sisters and licensed vocational nurses watched over her. I made house calls at appropriate intervals, and finally pronounced her dead in her own living room. Her family was profusely thankful that they could spend so much time with her. The value of those conversations they all had cannot be measured!

Another woman in her seventies with a very long history of severe ulcer disease which I had followed for many years, finally had to go to the hospital with very bad abdominal pain and obstruction of her stomach, which was blocked where it entered the small intestine. She had surgery, and during the procedure, frozen sections were taken of the mass of tissue found, as a routine to rule out cancer. The frozen sections were read as okay, and the surgeon did a simple intestinal bypass adjacent to this mass of tissue. The permanent microscopic tissue sections showed an aggressive cancer. As with everything else in the practice of medicine, no test is perfect. Frozen sections are flash-frozen bits of tissue, sliced thinly, placed on a slide with a stain to bring out cell components. There is some distortion of cell architecture, and the slide can be misread.

The surgeon and I faced the patient the next day and asked what she wanted to do. We could reoperate, to move the bypass further away, and give her more time to live if she wished. The entire cancer, wrapped as it was around everything, could not be removed, and it was not a candidate for chemotherapy or radiation. She chose to ask us to let her die. At this point the surgeon abruptly asked us to excuse him. He was not emotionally prepared to continue the discussion. I agreed to help her. She had never been married and had no children, but a close relative was her executor. The situation was presented to him by both the patient and myself. Nurses were brought in to witness her thinking, and proper notes were entered on her chart. I asked for an oncology (cancer) consultation on an informal basis, as a favor to me (no charge), and she was allowed to be admitted to the oncology floor under my care, where the nurses were accustomed to giving hospice care. Hospice care is for comfort only, not the prolongation of life. She passed away in comfort over a three-week period. At the time hospice care was not available in a formal institution outside the hospital.

I didn't always avoid having the patient die in the ICU, no one could. A ninety-three year old man had a massive stroke, which destroyed all of the thinking part of his brain. Some of his automatic centers were present running his heart pulse rate, his blood pressure, and other vital functions, but he would never think again. By the time the neurologists and I reached this conclusion, he was being kept alive by machines, IVs and medications in the IVs in a neurological ICU. His large family was very religious and church-going. A disagreement developed. Only his wife wanted us to continue all treatments although there was no hope. About twenty family members, their minister, and his wife all crowded into my office to hold a discussion. No amount of persuasion on the part of the minister, from me, or from the children and grandchildren could change her mind. One of the grandchildren escorted her out of the office when she became obviously emotionally exhausted. The family and minister asked me if there was something I could do without her knowing, and yet continue some treatment, since she would not allow us to "throw switches" and shut off support machines. I felt comfortable with stopping the medications in the IVs and letting "nature take its course." The family gave me permission to do so, and he died two or three days later, unfortunately still in the ICU. But at least we had helped his wife become a little more comfortable in her loss. I'm sure she felt that she would be killing him by giving me permission to turn off the life-support.

I treated this family as if they had a living will and a health power-of-attorney from him. They did not, but this shows how important such documents have become. I could do this in Texas, but I could not have done this in New York State, where my aunt was in a coma from respiratory failure and brain damage due to emphysema. She was being kept alive on a respirator with no hope of recovery. Her family asked to have the machine turned off. The hospital refused. While on a visit there, I asked her physicians if they could order the machine turned off. They could not. The nurses would report them to the district attorney for murder! There was no living will.

In dealing with ICU patients, I have been guilty of being unreasonably overaggressive also. There is no way that I should picture myself as the paragon of ICU practice. I literally tried to be the perfect doctor, which made me very tense while I was in practice, despite knowing that perfection is impossible. A patient from thirty years ago still haunts me. ICUs had just started. The woman in her seventies had developed left lower abdominal pain and constipation. Before she called me she made a fatal mistake. She took a very forceful enema, and blew out the inflamed pouches on her colon that were causing the trouble. This is called diverticulitis, which the body can usually control, unless something like an overexuberant enema is employed. Her reaction to her change in bowel function is easily explainable. In my experience, older women monitor this elimination process very closely. Besides hearing worries about constipation, over and over I was told, "I'm passing too much gas." Finally I found a way of handling that complaint. Someone reported a study on how often during a day people passed gas per rectum. A research grant was given to fund that study. Probably the researcher was as frustrated as I trying to answer questions about gas. The study found that twelve to fourteen passages of gas a day was average. I sent my patients home to count to see if they were normal.

To continue the story, my house call exam convinced me she now had peritonitis, a badly infected abdominal cavity. The surgeon operated on her immediately, late at night, stopped the leak by removing the bad area of colon, flushed out her abdomen with an antibiotic solution, and sent her to the ICU.

And that is where I messed up. The cultures of the fluids in the abdomen told us to shift to a newer antibiotic, which was excreted by the kidneys. I gave her a large recommended dose, but missed thinking of the fact that her kidney function might have been reduced somewhat by her age. The drug did not leave her body as fast as it would in a younger person, and her blood level concentration went too high. She gradually became stone deaf. She did not survive the infection, but because of my miscalculation she and her family could not say their good-byes properly. The rule in medicine is to treat, but do no harm.

I followed the desire for a dignified death at home if possible in my own family: I cared for my mother with the help of one of my partners. My father was gone, and she had come to live in Houston. She was a severe unstable diabetic on insulin and she was legally blind. She entered the hospital with a series of small strokes, would eat only erratically, which made controlling her diabetes very difficult, and she was very depressed. Her doctors suggested a tube be placed in her stomach to control food intake. I refused to allow that undignified approach, and when she stabilized, my partner discharged her to the sanctity of her apartment where she had live-in help. She died peacefully in bed one afternoon a week later.

My mother-in-law lived for five years after the discovery of her lung cancer. Her last six months were not pleasant, but she was up and dressed until the last week of her life at home with her husband. She and I had an agreement that her death would be comfortable, that she would not be struggling for breath. We had an oxygen machine at her beside, and live-in help. During that last week we let her stay in bed, continued her medicines and whatever food and fluids she wanted. She was given tranquilizers to ease tension and anxiety, and for two days seemed in a semi-coma. Suddenly, without warning, the day before she died, she woke up, sat up in bed and asked for all the family to come. When everyone assembled, she thanked us as a group for our interactions in life with her, and then dismissed us, only to call in each one separately to be thanked individually. She then called me in and asked only "do what you promised." I began her tranquilizers again, and the next day she was gone. She was such a strong woman, she willed herself awake to say her good-byes. This was one of the most powerful emotional experiences of my life and for the family members. I still get chills up my spine thinking about it. If I had hospitalized her that final week, could this have happened? I doubt it.

With the discovery that the end of life was costing Medicare so much, reevaluation has gone on throughout all of the profession. Ethics committees were established in hospitals, Hospices became common, both lawyers and doctors instructed the public to have living wills and health care powers-of-attorney. A study by the Health Care Financing Administration (HCFA) report in 1992 did not offer a great deal of hope that changes in end-of-life medical practice were occurring. Twenty-eight percent of the Medicare budget was being spent on people in their last year of life, and most of that percentage was on the last thirty days of life. A *Wall Street Journal* article, 22 April 1993, quoted Dr. Steven Schroeder, who heads the Robert Wood Johnson Foundation, a charitable organization, as finding things very different in Europe. ICUs were much smaller, "accounting for 1% to 5% of all hospital beds, compared to

15% to 20% in our country." The patients were younger and
healthier, more likely to go back to full, functional recovery.
Dr. Schroeder was told by the European doctors, "I trained in
the U.S. Your teaching hospitals are excellent, your technology
is superb, but you don't know when to stop." Physicians have
to be taught when to stop.

Another view of the cost of dying was presented in a study
of the sex differences in health cost, published in the *New
England Journal of Medicine*, vol. 338, 4 June 1998 (Sex Differences in the Use of Health Care Services), which produced
estimates of lifetime health expenditures compared to the last
year of life. In men, lifetime expense was $59,950 with $15,400
in the final year, 21% of the total. In women, the figures
respectively were $85,131 lifetime, $14,900 in the last year, or
15%. These figures are lower than the 1992 study by HCFA,
just mentioned, but the study approach was different, so it is
like comparing apples and oranges. Both studies make the
same point. Physicians don't know how to let people die without interfering too much.

In 1994 and 1995, Dartmouth Medical School conducted
a study based on 37 million Medicare patient records, comparing how different regions of the country handled the last six
months of life. The study reported, in the *WSJ* 15 October
1997, that average patient bills varied from $11,000 to $16,571
in the highest areas (with the most aggressive medical care)
and compared with $5,831 to $7,000 in the lowest areas. In
Miami forty-six percent of these end-of-life patients spent some
time in an ICU, while in Sun City, Arizona, this occurred to
only nine percent of patients there. Whether patients died in
the hospital or at home correlated with the number of hospital
beds per 1,000 population. Does this mean that if there are
excess beds available, they will be utilized more? Seems that
way. The proper level of care should not be so different all over
the country, and findings suggest that the more aggressive
areas need re-education.

The mechanisms to guide doctors as to patients' wishes,
even when put in place are not followed, or are ignored according to a study funded by the Johnson Foundation, also
reported in the *WSJ*. About 9,000 patients were followed dur-

ing end-of-life care, and at first 4,300 patients were reviewed to establish the customary levels of care. Even though thirty-one percent of the patients wanted "do not resuscitate" (DNR) instructions in their charts, only half had the order entered into their record. Only forty-six percent of their doctors were aware of their preference. The remaining patients were split into two groups for further comparison. One group was supplied with advisory nurses who provided counselling about terminal illness, treatment options, and better communication with the treating doctors. The other half did not have the nurses. The results were surprising: The nurses made no difference. DNR orders were ignored in the same way, days in the ICU were not reduced, and other costly life-support treatments were continued, not reduced as expected. Fifty percent of the patients were allowed to suffer moderate to severe pain. Why? The families and the patient, in my view, received this special approach too late.

Loss of a loved one is too traumatic to expect reason to take over at the last moments of life. Emotions of anticipated loss, of anger at the circumstances, of guilt, all stand in the way of rational thought. It takes education and counselling over a period of time to make the surviving family recognize that trying to keep a very sick, suffering loved one alive is a form of a loving and somewhat desperate selfishness. There is a stress scale used by psychologists, with death of a close loved one, spouse, parent, child rated as the highest, 100. Divorce is in the low 70s, marriage in the mid-60s, with illness, retirement, buying and selling homes rated much lower, to put this in further perspective.

Before I leave this discussion, I need to comment about the problem of "do not resuscitate" orders. I took an open-chest resuscitation course while I was at Western Reserve Medical Center as a Fellow in Cardiac Rehabilitation during 1957. The rule that we were taught to follow at that time was to "restore a heart that was too good to die," a phrase used by the famous cardiac surgeon, Dr. Claude Beck, who ran the course. What he meant was that before resuscitating a patient we needed to consider the chances of that person returning to reasonably good health, a good functional recovery. In the early 1960s closed-chest massage was developed, which made the resuscitation much easier to perform, so that even lay persons could be taught to do it. Then quite suddenly, it was almost impossible for any dying patient, no matter what the other underlying conditions were, no matter what the overall chances of survival after the heart was revived, to escape a resuscitation attempt. And now we find it almost impossible to turn it off even when the DNR order is given. Guaranteed perfection. No one can die without a fight, even if the fight is obviously fruitless from the beginning.

There are three steps to reducing the excessive costs of dying. First, an educational campaign must undo the perception in the country that the magical new medical technology can stop death. I know that sounds facetious, but death has become so sanitized and remote (in the back room of the ICU) that our population does not understand how much suffering a life-sustaining treatment can cause the patient, especially if pain is not covered properly by narcotics. Along with our government, the medical profession seems to guarantee perfection, but dragging out a life with desperate measures is not perfect. With so many people dying in hospitals and nursing homes death seems disconnected from life. It would really help our teenagers, who think they are immortal, to learn to understand death by having a grandparent die at home. Death should not be depersonalized. Dr. Sherwin B. Nuland's book, *How We Die: Reflections on Life's Final Chapter*, (1994), should be required reading for the public at large and for physicians. He concludes that his book is "an unspoken plea for the resurrection of the family doctor." I am suggesting that family physicians, as primary caretakers, initiate counselling in death and dying the moment that it is recognized that a terminal event is approaching, which brings me to my second point. The hospitals and medical schools must stress death and dying courses and require that any physician, whose practice brings patients to the ICU, take the courses. As I have said previously, doctors must learn to see the whole patient, and learn gentleness in their therapy.

Thirdly, with the help of ethics committees, triage criteria for entry and for remaining in an ICU must be established.

"Triage" is a word that appeared with the advent of the threat of atomic warfare: In the event of an attack, a highly trained physician, the "triage officer" is to command the entry point of the treatment center. Since treatment supplies have to be conserved, he evaluates each injured person and sends the probable survivors, those likely to return to full, functional recovery, in one direction for treatment, and the others in another direction for pain relief and other comforting, but not life-saving attention. Triage is a form of rationing, but is a reasonable way to reduce costs until education takes hold with both the public and doctors. Over a period of time, triage of ICUs will become less and less necessary.

The ability to lower medical costs exists within everyone of us, but I am not going to dig into the admonitions we all know: eat right, exercise, don't smoke, don't drink too much. I am referring to the "power of positive thinking." First of all, there resides in all of us the "placebo effect," that is, if we think strongly enough that a pill or a procedure will cure us, we may possibly get well even though that pill or procedure is a fake. This issue is of such importance that all drug treatments and other forms of therapy are subjected to the "double-blind" approach, while being evaluated before release for general use. Neither the doctors nor the patients know who is getting the "real" treatment or medicine, and half the patients are getting the fake. Subtracting the observed placebo effect from results in the patients really treated allows a determination of the true effects of the medicine being evaluated. There is another by-product of such a study: the true side-effects of the medicine as well as the placebo effects are determined. Our minds have tremendous control over our bodies. Do you know that you can be hypnotized to cure the warts on one side of your body, but not the other side? Of course you have to want to be hypnotized and believe in the cure. This was shown to work over forty years ago.

About twenty-five years ago I ran across a study done by M.D. Anderson Cancer Hospital in Houston. They studied cancer patients beginning treatment, and separated them into two groups. The groups were made as similar as possible as to age, sex distribution, severity of the cancer being treated, and all other attributes, except the emotional state of the patient. The two groups were either optimists or pessimists going into treatment. Guess who lived longest? Of course, the optimists—twice as long. Norman Cousins, who recovered from a severe illness which started in the 1960s (ankylosing spondylitis, a relative of rheumatoid arthritis, which causes a fusing of the spine into a rigid "poker spine") by "laughing at it," described his own optimistic approach, discovered at age ten in his book, *Anatomy of an Illness,* published in 1979. As a boy he was in a tuberculosis sanitarium, joined a group of other optimistic boys, and saw how much faster they got well than the pessimists. He then spent twelve years on the UCLA medical faculty, as a non-physician studying the power of mind over body, the psychosomatic effects of optimism and depression. In the 18 June 1990 issue of *Time* magazine, he published a powerful essay, calling us a nation of hypochondriacs. He pointed out what should be obvious: Evolution has given us pain as a friend that acts as a warning that we may be doing something wrong, hurting ourselves, or warning us that something has gone wrong with some bodily function. The body is a mechanism that has amazing powers to heal itself. I might add that the physician would do well to remember that his role is as a helper, the body does most of the work of healing. Cousins goes on to state that panic and depression can set the stage for illness or intensify existing ones. Researchers at UCLA have shown that liberating patients from panic and depression improve levels of vital substances in the immune system, exactly supporting the M.D. Anderson findings. He asks the American people to accept "the concept of a patient-physician partnership in which the best medical science has to offer is combined with the magnificent resources of mind and body."

In the best-selling book from 1986, *Love, Medicine and Miracles* by Bernie S. Siegel, M.D. (a practicing surgeon who taught at Yale medical school), are two vital passages (from the introduction):

> Exceptional patients manifest the will to live in its most potent form. They take charge of their lives even if they were never able to before, and they work hard to achieve

health and peace of mind. They do not rely on doctors to take the initiative but rather use them as members of a team, demanding the utmost in technique, resourcefulness, concern, and open-mindedness. If they are not satisfied, they change doctors.

Notice that this quote is somewhat threatening to doctors. It shouldn't be. We are taught to take charge of our patients and run their lives for them, to the point of having to wean some patients from hospital care, if those patients have become too dependent on us (see page 87, Chapter Three). Dr. Siegel wisely includes advice to physicians, who over the years had become more and more charmed by, and more reliant on, all the new miracle techniques and procedures and had lost sight of the interdependence of the mind and body. He writes, "If you are a physician, I hope this book will give you some strategies for which you may have long felt a need, techniques that weren't covered in your education . . . We must learn to give patients the option to participate in the recovery from any type of disease."

He then points out that he is not trying to tell other doctors he is a better physician, he is trying to teach them a new approach.

My patients taught me there's more to medicine than pills and incisions. I know your offices are filled with people who drain your energy and don't do well. I know the pain physicians feel. We have all of the problems other people have, as well as the one drummed into us in medical school: The role of the mechanic-lifesaver, which defines illness and death as our failure. No one lives forever; therefore death is not the issue. Life is. Death is not failure. Not choosing to take on the challenge of life is. Let me show you the minority of patients who can restore your energy, the ones who get well even when they are not supposed to. Let me show you how to learn from your most successful patients and help the others reawaken the "life wish" within. The process will inevitably help you heal yourself and make you a more successful healer.

I deeply admire Dr. Siegel. Surgeons generally are mechanistic doers, and he is as thoughtful as internists are supposed to be. Note his message to doctors. Learn from your optimistic patients and teach other patients how to challenge their illnesses. Do not be afraid of working with patients at this level of caring. Readers will find many useful methods described in his book in improving your own approach to staying healthy.

From Martin E.P. Seligman, Ph. D., Professor of Psychology at the University of Pennsylvania came his book, *Learned Optimism,* published in 1991. He clearly shows the dangers of learned helplessness, of pessimism, and of depression on both mental health and bodily well-being. He quotes from a fifty-year study of Harvard male graduates (the Grant Study) conducted by Dr. George Vaillant, a psychoanalytic professor in the psychiatry department at Dartmouth Medical School: "Health at age sixty was strongly related to optimism at age twenty-five." The pessimistic twenty-five year olds showed an earlier decline in health and showed diseases with more severity, starting at age forty-five. Study of other factors, psychologic defense mechanisms, physical and mental health at age twenty-five only served to prove that "optimism still stood out as a primary determinant of health, beginning at age forty-five and continuing for the next twenty years." If you want benefit from all the other improvements that optimism brings to life, according to Dr. Seligman's research, read the book.

Not surprisingly religion improves health. Recent studies at Harvard Medical School, discussed by Dr. Herbert Benson at a "Spirituality and Healing Conference" in 1998 in Houston, Texas, showed that churchgoers outlive people with little or no religious faith. Other studies presented strongly supported this contention: At Dartmouth Medical School 232 people were followed after open heart surgery. The mortality rate was twelve times higher in those who did not use religion for social support. A 28-year study from the Berkeley Human Population Laboratory of 5,000 people found a 25% lower death rate overall among the regular churchgoers, and among women the difference was even more striking, a 35% reduction over the 28 years. A Duke Medical Center study confirmed other studies mentioned in Dr. Seligman's book. He cited research showing that optimism was related to the state of the immune system, as measured in the blood. Duke church-goers, over age sixty-five (when the immunity system begins to weaken naturally) had an average interleukin-6 blood level indicating a much higher immunity level than those who attended church irregularly or not at all. It was concluded: "Better mental and physical health are characteristic of frequent church attendees."

You will notice the obvious connection in what I am presenting here to the discussion of victimhood in Chapter Three. Becoming a victim teaches helplessness, a loss of self-reliance. A society that is creating the right to be a victim is creating an enlarging segment of society that will become more pessimistic, more depressed and physically sicker. Not requiring moral standards and judgment may allow more individual "freedoms," but it allows "certain psychological doctrines [which] have damaged our society by helping to erode personal responsibility: Evil is mislabeled insanity; bad manners are shucked off as neurosis; 'successfully treated' patients evade their duty to their families because it does not bring them personal fulfillment." It is not surprising to find this quote in Dr. Seligman's book. We need to be campaigning for optimism, for self-reliance learned from the successful completion of required tasks or self-induced projects. Protecting "self-esteem," as championed by the politically-correct intelligentsia described in David Gelernter's book, *Drawing Life* (1997), may protect one from failure, but it does not build self-reliance, or a feeling of responsibility to self and to society, a responsibility to achieve.

Medical insurance, as an industry, did not grow by any preconceived plan. It just sort of happened, beginning after World War II. Since groups of employees in large industries offer large pools of people within which to share risk, it was logical for insurance companies to accept an employer's group at lower rates than individual policies could be offered. These medical benefits were offered as incentives for employment in the tight labor market after the war. Unions demanded these benefits as part of their employment contracts. Then smaller employers offered health plans. Of course, as a business expense, this qualified as a tax deduction. This is a jerry-built, fragmented system that we all pay for in higher prices for the products or services we buy. The cost of your new automobile is in large part due to the medical care and pension package of the autoworkers.

This system means that many working people have no control over their medical insurance. It comes with the job, and it goes if you leave that company. Problems arise if you have a chronic medical condition, which will cost more for the insurance company over the years. Apply for a private policy and your premiums will jump sky high. Of course they should: the insurance company is betting their money against your health, and they are in the business of making money, not losing it. Their actuaries are wizard odds-makers. This is one of the reasons I said the system was fragmented. Congress has tried in their wisdom to cure the problem with their usual patch-up job, that sounds good but cannot work. It is a 1996 law that forces insurance companies to issue private policies to people who leave an employer or change jobs. Those who have chronic conditions are being charged enormous premiums or are forced to take policies with long exclusion times before particular illnesses or procedures are covered. Congress can't pass laws that force companies to lose money. Or can they?

Congress passed a law in 1997 forbidding Medicare patients from seeking private care outside Medicare. Actually the "forbidding" is accomplished by another congressional back door: if a doctor agrees to sign a private medical contract with a patient for certain services, the doctor must agree to stay out of the Medicare program for two years. No doctor is going to make that financial sacrifice and go out of business. Thank goodness, a federal law suit has been filed to block the law.

Solutions to the medical insurance mess, including Medicare, have been suggested, and some make sense. I have used these suggestions plus a radical approach of my own. Since private medical insurance grew in bits and pieces and ended up as a benefit of employment, with employers managing the establishment of plans, really by default, it is a jerry-built program. Let's scrap that approach and start all over with something entirely new and, hopefully, planned so that there are a minimum of kinks and problems. The following case illustrates the approach. A middle-aged patient of mine had a hysterectomy. Unfortunately, the lower colon was nicked and some very dirty contents leaked out into the abdominal cavity. The large intestine harbors some of the most awful bacteria in the world, but the immunity in the colon's walls maintains a satisfactory control. The Infectious Disease Department was immediately called in to manage the antibiotic counterattack. I didn't find out about all this until almost two weeks had passed and she was still running a fever. Things were getting nowhere, and the family called me to help out. A fresh mind can stand back, see the whole picture, and start over. I wrote a progress note in her chart to stop all antibiotics and reevaluate. I suggested that she might have "antibiotic fever," that is, an allergic reaction to the antibiotics. The other doctors followed my suggestion, her fever disappeared and she was discharged home.

In the arena of private medical insurance, let's start over. I'd take the employer out of the mix. Since he is paying for the plans, it will make no difference to him if he gives the money directly to his employees as an increase in salary. It will not affect the income taxes of the employee, if he can deduct the costs of his medical insurance premiums. Now we have the individual in charge: He can choose to self-insure, pocket the money and pay some extra tax. Younger people who are not married, and not likely to have any serious illness, may choose to have a policy just to cover injury or catastrophic illness. Somewhat older folks, married with children will want more complete coverage. We all know that individual coverage is more expensive, and being in a group with dilution of risk is cheaper. No problem. During the transition period to this approach the groups are already there, established by the employers. The employees, through their union or by forming an insurance association among themselves, can then negotiate with competing insurance companies or HMOs for the best care at the lowest rates. The plans can be tailored to fit the members' desires. Compare this approach with what happens now. They have to take whatever the employer offers. What happens now if someone changes employment? That person already belongs to an insurance association group. Just stay in

the group, even if one moves across country. Now the person
with the chronic illness is protected from loss of insurance. If
chronic conditions are not a problem, and the cross-country
person wants to be at the decision-making meetings, change
to a local group.

There is going to be the objection that the average employee isn't intelligent enough to make healthcare decisions.
That statement suggests the employer is the only one smart
enough to pick out a yearly medical insurance group contract.
The employees aren't going to buy that. Their association can
poll the members to establish group desires, and an investigation and negotiation committee can be chosen. If the committee does an excellent job, the association members may be able
to have a good policy for the year, and pocket some extra
money. Obviously, there needs to be accounting protection
against kickbacks and bribes, much as I hate to throw that in.
The next objection is this: Okay, the employer is now freed up
of his obligation to provide this medical care benefit. What
happens year by year as medical costs go up? Is he going to pay
his employees more? My answer to this is to remember that we
set wages and salaries in a free-market capitalistic society.
Competitive negotiation between employers and employees will
continue as it always has. Each group needs the other. Let
nature take its course.

I have discussed the need for pilot studies in entering new
approaches like this one. In a sense there has been such a
study: Robert E. Moffit of the Heritage Foundation, Washington, D.C., in April 1992, described how beautifully the
Federal Employee Health Benefits Program worked. This
program allows groups of employees from the various departments of the government to pick their own plan. As a result
of the competition, a number of the best cost-saving plans
were in place. There were a variety of companies providing the
insurance coverage for 1.8 million federal employees. The U.S.
Office of Personnel Management administered that program
and described a sizable saving. This program differs from my
suggestion in that the government underwrote sixty percent of
the premium costs. I have one more request directed at Congress: Stay out of the mix! Don't legislate what must be sold.

Let the individual employee groups and the solo purchasers of medical insurance negotiate and buy basic coverage, adding to the basic coverage what they as consumers want. They know what they need and what they wish to afford. They know better than Congress; it is arrogant of Congress to think otherwise.

Private medical insurance is generally free of federal controls, although there have been some congressional attempts to interfere, (i.e., mandating that an employee who loses or leaves employment and loses his medical insurance must be offered medical insurance coverage). Medicare, of course, is a monolithic structure, totally under the thumb of Washington bureaucracy. As mentioned earlier, Congress and the bureaucrats are alarmed at the rapidly rising Medicare costs, and have used their usual band-aid approach. There are absolute price controls, initiated in 1984, with some increases allowed that do not match inflation. I don't see any way to start the system over as I have suggested for private insurance, and introduce real capitalistic competition. Profit-driven aggressive capitalism may be the best economic system in the world but in certain forms may hurt medical care. HMOs have been introduced into the Medicare mix to provide competition. The HMOs have a problem that is open to the realistic moral debate that is raging as I write this. Is it proper to try and seduce their member doctors to hold back medical services in order to reduce costs *and* increase profits? Is it proper for HMOs to deny their doctors the right to dispense a service to reduce cost *and* increase profits? Is it right for the HMOs to key the income of their doctors to the profits the HMO makes? Perhaps the HMOs can find a palatable solution to their dilemma. The solutions to hold down cost increases lie in the suggestions I have been presenting, not in the HMO method of bludgeoning physicians, and denying patients the care they deserve. Another approach and possible solution to the HMO issue is the recent development of large physicians groups, run by physicians, not MBAs (Masters of Business Administration). The groups are operating successfully. The doctors maintain their autonomy, and to my mind can make better choices for themselves and their patients on how to hold down costs. They can compete directly with the HMOs; their more intimate relationship with their patients allows them to respond to patient complaints in a more meaningful fashion, and in a way less harmful to patient care than restricting service. The physician knows best what the patient needs for the illness or condition at hand.

The Arizona Medicaid program suggests that managed care can work. Starting in the 1980s this program got a waiver from federal regulations, and opened it for bids from doctor groups, hospitals, and other managed care providers. The number of bidders to provide service has increased through the years because Medicaid has proven profitable for them. In 1991 a U.S. General Accounting Office study showed that Arizona spent eighty-one percent of what a traditional program would have cost. The amount spent per patient fell eleven percent from 1994 to 1995! Wait, you say, this is Medicaid. What about real medicine? Advocacy groups for the indigent claim that mainstream medicine is provided.

Dr. Jane M. Orient, Executive Director of the Association of American Physicians and Surgeons, has suggested that Congress end the Medicare price controls, allowing the usual market forces of supply and demand to take over, assuming that competition among doctors will cause prices to fall. In the Nixon administration, when general price controls were lifted, prices jumped up quickly to reach the levels they should have reached under the usual inflation that is part of capitalism, then settled back to the usual rates of inflation. But that is not the only reason I think ending price controls won't work. I have seen studies analyzing how "customary and ordinary" doctors' fees are set in a given area. What one would anticipate is not true: more doctors coming into a region may result in more competition, but what happens is that the doctors recognize they are seeing less patients, and gradually respond by raising their charges to hold their incomes steady. Well, how about flooding the country with new doctors from the medical schools to force the issue of supply and demand? There is a problem with that approach that I need to explain.

Medical schools are very alert to the "quality" of the students they are able to admit, and that quality is found to relate directly to the applicant-admission ratio. They have found that the best freshman classes come from an application year where there are at least 2.5 to 3 applicants for each position. When I applied to medical school in 1949, there were so many returning war veterans, who under the G.I. Bill could now try for medical school, that there were 30,000 applicants for 5,000 places, a six to one ratio. That obviously was a very unusual circumstance. The medical schools think this ratio is so important they keep a close eye on doctor-population ratios and population growth. Over the years freshmen classes grew to 21,500 (approximately) to keep up with population growth and demand for services. In the 1980s, with the negative effect of the debate over the future of the medical profession in regards to controlling costs and physicians' charges, and with other enticing professions (space engineers, computer programmers) pulling away bright students, by 1988 the schools had to accept sixty percent of only 26,721 applicants, when previously 45,000-50,000 had been applying. That is an applicant-admission ratio of 1.25. The medical schools, spotting this trend of declining applications in the early 1980s, went on a recruiting program, looking to older people who wanted to change careers, and even sought out liberal arts majors to entice into a medical profession. By 1992 the schools had turned the trend around by obtaining more applicants, but also by reducing the number of freshman places. From 1988 to 1992 there were 3,900 freshman positions removed. There were 37,410 applicants as a result of the recruitment programs, with an acceptance ratio of 2.14. The medical schools are not going to flood the country with doctors. Individual quality is too important to sacrifice. Perhaps one day the law schools will learn this.

Dr. Orient and many other physicians have campaigned to have the Medicare regulations simplified, and to reduce the mass of bureaucracy-mandated record-keeping, which cause the average doctor's office to add extra personnel to handle the clerical load, driving up costs. Unfortunately, this complaint doesn't just apply to medical practice. It pervades businesses throughout the country. Computer generated codes and electronic automatic claims-payment systems have evolved and are estimated to reduce costs by $8 to $10 billion annually, but unfortunately, that approach has opened up the opportunity for massive computer fraud. In August 1997 a grand jury indictment in Miami described charges of a fraudulent home health care scheme that cost $15 million for a portion of the "network" that had been uncovered. It was estimated that one out of every four home health care billings from Florida was either a phony or did not qualify for payment, according to a federal audit. Home health care has been a cash cow, growing thirty percent per year in the 1990s. The idea of offering home health care to cover the chronically ill is excellent. It is cheaper and way more convenient than going to the doctor's office, as long as the system is not ripped-off. Computer experts and fraud experts should work on the software, but I think a simple solution, unfortunately requiring a piece of paper, is a signed statement from the patient validating the treatment, and under the law, making the patient responsible if the patient becomes aware that fraud is occurring. This could also apply in the physician's office. Now the patient is sent an E.O.B. (explanation of benefits) after the Medicare re-reimbursement is sent to the doctor. On the back of the E.O.B. the patient is "encouraged" to contact Medicare, if he thinks Medicare paid for a service not received. I think a signed affidavit from the patient should be obtained at the doctor's office at the time of the service, and faxed to Medicare at the time the bill is submitted, with the patient held liable for fraud, just as the doctor is.

My final suggestion for reducing medical costs relates to the Federal Drug Administration and the mandated expiration dates on medications. Other than the antibiotic Tetracycline, which has deterioration products that may damage the kidneys after a year from purchase, most other medications are safe and effective after those mandatory expiration dates printed on them. There is a program that collects medicine, which is out of date, and sends it to third world countries, where it is used for several years past that arbitrary date. Must we honor those dates, or should research check the medications as to safety and effectiveness, so we may use those medications for longer periods?

I've made a series of suggestions attempting to lower the rapidly growing cost of medical care. I'd like to see something of value to come from my thinking. I know that there will be holes in my reasoning, which will appear as others (interested as I am), debate the issues with me. I look at the profession of medicine and I see a fragmented group of associations. On one side are the medical schools and groups representing them. They develop new medical knowledge and work on transmitting that information to students and practicing doctors. The teaching medical centers have other socioeconomic worries: how to pay for training young physicians working in the hospitals (house officers), how to cover the costs of charity care, and how to cover the costs of research as federal grants shrink.

The American Medical Association presents socioeconomic viewpoints from the practicing physicians, but has a membership of only forty percent of all licensed physicians in the U.S. and its possessions. At the end of December 1996 the total physicians were 737,764, according to Lillian Randolph, Ph. D. of the A.M.A. According to Dr. Randolph, the membership, which was sixty percent a few years ago, has been fragmented by disagreements with A.M.A. policies. As a result, there are now rival organizations: 40,000-50,000 doctors are members of an organization representing physicians from India, practicing here; an overall foreign medical graduate group numbers 169,826; and a women's medical association with 157,387 members. Obviously these totals include many physicians with two or three memberships. Most private physicians join their county and state medical societies, and are indirectly represented by the A.M.A. There are general organizations, such as the American College of Physicians, representing primarily Internists, and sub-specialty groups, like the one I discussed in regard to colon cancer, the American College of Gastroenterology, which finally got Medicare to accept colon cancer screening. Actually there are societies and groups representing every specialty and sub-specialty in the profession. They are mainly formed to teach the newer findings in research, but of course, form opinions about the economics of medical practice.

Nationally, I don't think that the National Institutes of Health or the Office of the Surgeon-General offer help. They cannot represent the private doctor struggling to practice good medicine in his office. The obvious answer to me is the establishment of a non-profit "think tank," exclusively devoted to studying the problems of medicine as it relates to national needs. It must represent all the fragmented areas of medicine, and it must cover the full range of political philosophy, from far left to far right. It should include physicians, in practice and retired, public health specialists, social service workers, economists, hospital administrators. I could go on listing medical service workers with viewpoints, but you get the idea. The conclusions of this group, presented to Congress, could conceivably carry great weight and influence, and lead us to speedier resolutions of the issues. Perhaps we can do away with the patchwork feel-good solutions that Congress keeps producing: all impression, little substance, and of little help.

Chapter Three

A Nation of Victims

The most amazing change in our culture, as I see it, is the appearance of "victimology" as a driving force. It plays right into the hands of politicians who want to maintain control over the government. They claim that they can solve the problems that are making us victims. The word "victim" has several meanings in the dictionary: "One who is adversely affected by a force or agent; injured, destroyed, or sacrificed under any of various conditions; subjected to oppression, hardship or mistreatment; or tricked or duped." Life isn't meant to be absolutely clear of problems. Most of us have been victimized by some circumstance at some time in our lives. Most of us have solved the problem by ourselves.

More and more our society allows an expansion of the concept of victimization. More and more people are looking for something or someone to blame or to sue for misfortune that they brought on themselves, and this is done under the assertion that they couldn't help themselves: They were drunk, they had an addiction. Someone else should have stopped them. Charles J. Sykes, author of *A Nation of Victims: The Decay of the American Character* (1993), tells the following story: a man did a back flip in a bar and hurt his back. He sued the bartender. The bartender should have stopped him! This ridiculous law suit was settled out of court for $5,000. How about the weird suit in the State of Washington, mentioned in our local paper in November 1997: the fellow claims that his hardening of the arteries is due to milk drinking over a lifetime, induced by the dairy industry ads! One obvious problem is that there are unscrupulous lawyers willing to take advantage of a very loose set of controls over tort law within our justice system. No wonder there are now organizations that are trying to stop frivolous law suits, there are so many of them tying up the courts. There has been some effort in Congress for tort reform, but don't bet on it. The tort lawyer (personal injury/liability) associations make huge political campaign contributions. Wrote Peter Huber in a 1995 *Forbes* magazine column: "Americans are living longer and safer than ever before, but prompted by lawyers, we sue more and more about less and less."

Where does all this come from? Everyone would like something for nothing or the facade of something for nothing. Look at how many states have lotteries, look at the numbers who enter sweepstakes contests, which are just a facade to sell a product. How about the coupons you turn in at the grocery? I'm sure you realize that the coupon value is carefully tucked into the price. To drive the economy to greater and greater heights in our capitalistic society, for years Congress allowed the deduction of time payment interest to encourage buying products before consumers could afford them. Once the habit was ingrained to buy now and pay later, once instant gratification became a way of life, Congress took away the deduction. The economy goes charging forward, and we have the worst savings record of any major industrial country. I really can't see if this entire scenario was preplanned, that sounds too nefarious, but the effect is a very bad habit for most people.

Congress still allows the deduction of home mortgage interest, expressing a basic desire that as many Americans as possible should own their own home—a perfectly reasonable point of view. Now look at the flip side. There is an obvious economic reason. It takes a lot of different materials from a number of basic industries to make a home. Home building really revs up the economy, creates more income for many more people, and creates more tax revenues for Congress to suck up. Note the hidden agenda: surface reasons from our politicians never show the whole picture. The something-for-nothing break in taxes encourages the home-buying, and that's fine, but the social habits and attitudes created do not encourage deferred gratification, which may be much better for many people.

Being a victim makes the victim assume a role of helplessness, which may or may not be true. A line of tornadoes hits an area, and there are real victims. That is why we have home insurance, and it is a reasonable event for the federal government to step in and help. But in the court cases mentioned above, victimization is invented. Do we have no control over our own decisions? Or are we so stupid we cannot see the propaganda in ads for merchandise? In August 1991, *Time* magazine had a set of cover stories on this subject. Lance Morrow, in a wonderful lead essay, describes the cry-baby, manipulative and with a lawyer on one hand, and the busybody, who is organizing protests against smoking, eating fats, wearing furs, and generally setting out new "tribal rules." He points out that "Americans operate on a pushy querulous assumption of perfectibility on earth . . . that has led (them) into absurdities and discontents that others who know life better might never think of." And so we have the two groups: victims, who no longer want to be adults in control of their life and its decisions; and the do-gooders, who are out to protect everyone from those nasty causes of victimhood.

What does each group get out of this, speaking psychologically? The victims, either by winning a large liability award in court, or finding some private or government handout, are being taken care of. For the busybodies, the result is the fuzzy "feel good" they experience because they are helping others, notwithstanding that they are inducing more helplessness in the victims they are "helping." That do-good feeling is usually accompanied by publicity about the "good" works. Remember, true charity is anonymous. Please don't assume that I am against all organizations that are formed to help with problems. The March of Dimes did a wonderful job of eradicating polio. As a medical student, I can remember how sore my hand became giving shots of gamma globulin to break up an epidemic before we had the vaccines—true victims with a real problem.

To see another view of this problem of victimhood, read David Gelernter's book *Drawing Life* (1997). Blown up by the Unibomber, he refused to become the victim the newspapers tried to turn him into! He wasn't being heroic, just maintaining his own concept of himself as a responsible adult. A Yale faculty professor, he points out that the intellectual "elite" in the university faculties, starting in the 1960s, have made a religion of civil rights, tolerance and diversity, to the point that evil is not properly recognized, that we are not allowed to be judgmental of others. We should not be judgmental of "victims," but should be willing to help them, apparently without taking note as to whether true victimization exists. Let the "victim" be his own judge! The victim may be his own victimizer. Let's invent a medical addiction term for whatever it is that he cannot help doing. Whatever happened to self-control and self-determination? Gelernter states the use of the word "judgmental," as implying that you are doing something that worsens society, and did not appear in his dictionaries until after the 1970s. My dictionaries agree.

In a 1997 *Wall Street Journal* editorial page article, Dennis Prager, a radio talk show host in Los Angeles, pointed out another aspect of this change in judging morality: "Over the past generation, the idea that a central message of Christianity is to forgive everyone who commits evil against anyone, no matter how great and cruel and whether or not the evil doer repents, has been adopted by much of Christendom." He continues, "This doctrine destroys Christianity's central moral tenets about forgiveness—that forgiveness, even by God, is contingent on the sinner repenting, and that it only can be given to the sinner by the one against whom he has sinned." He quotes Luke 17:3-4, which states exactly that. His conclusions are inescapable: "Today, judging evil is widely considered worse than doing evil," and "the theology of 'forgiveness' is only one more sign of the decline of traditional religiosity and morality." The Judeo-Christian system of values and morals must underlie this country's continuation as a democratic civilization under the control of laws.

The more we set up groups of victims and victimizers, setting people against each other, without allowing the judgments of ethics and morality to analyze the truth or falseness of each individual "victimhood," the more our society will be fractionated, and the weaker we will be as a country. If we are not allowed to judge, it makes the crusade of the do-gooder easier to accomplish, especially if reasonable, clear thinking would have demonstrated the new campaign to be worthless. If a campaign to help a group of victims does not have a carefully conducted pilot program to analyze potential results of helpfulness, it may end up solving nothing, but the do-gooders themselves will feel good, whatever that is worth to the rest of us. There is another hidden result: the founders of such "helping" organizations have created management positions for themselves and jobs for others to run the organization. That is right, the do-good free enterprise entrepreneur! The March of Dimes is a marvelous example of this. They conquered polio, and immediately hunted around for another cause to conquer, in this case, birth defects, although there were other groups already out there. Why go out of business and have everyone in the organization lose their employment? I can imagine them saying, "We have proven how effective we are, let's try it again." There is an organization for practically every disease or condition. Do we really need all this fragmentation of good intentions, with the attendant administrative costs of each group?

There are numbers of non-medical self-appointed organizations, founded to help a specific group of people, or to fill a specific need. For example A.A.R.P. (American Association of Retired People) provides wonderful services for older citizens, and then the organizers suddenly become self-appointed political spokesmen for the members. They do survey members who voluntarily go to A.A.R.P conventions, but that is not democratic representation of members' opinions. The self-appointed N.O.W. group (National Organization of Women) claims to represent all U.S. women, but all they present is their own view, which represents less than fifty percent of the views of women, according to surveys taken. *Domestic Tranquility: A Brief Against Feminism*, a 1998 book by F. Carolyn Graglia discusses this at length. *Consumer Reports* does a marvelous job of product testing, and then presumes to be expert in the political area, and present opinion articles to their members that are slanted, in my opinion, well to the left of center. I am a member of *Consumer Reports*. I have never been surveyed in regard to my opinions.

I'm not arguing against valid self-appointed medical organizations such as the American Heart Association; the death rate from cardiovascular diseases was about fifty-two percent in the 1960s and dropped to approximately forty percent due to funded research and a great American Heart public education program about risk factors. And the civil rights movements of the 1960s accomplished miraculous results for truly victimized people, although in this area we must recognize that it is a "work in progress," with a tremendous amount left to be accomplished. But like the March of Dimes, a somewhat similar problem has appeared in the Civil Rights arena. In Robert L. Woodson, Sr.'s book, *The Triumphs of Joseph* (1998), he states that attempts at continuing a tradition of black self-improvement are being hampered by "powerful social, economic, and political institutions that have a proprietary interest in (the) continued existence of the problems of the poor." His book describes local efforts by true victims, who succeed in solving their own problems. True victims cannot always solve all their problems. Certainly, many situations will require outside help, which should be asked for by the local citizens, not imposed upon them.

Not imposed upon them—this is exactly the point raised by George F. Will, the Pulitzer Prize-winning syndicated columnist. In a column on "victimhood" (*Houston Chronicle*, 20 September 1997), he described a Civil Rights Commissioner, Yvonne Lee, as "seeing people through contemporary liberalism's lens—as members of grievance groups, essentially passive, who need to have their consciousness raised. Their choices result from social pressures, stereotypes and other facets of victimhood, and therefore are not really free choices. Therefore their choices need not be respected, and can be considered ripe for remedial government action." Simply put: we dumb folks at home really don't know what's good for us, Washington has to tell us. Why did Will pick on Lee? She felt "ability grouping" of students based on their aptitudes created a discrimination problem, not only for "students who are stuck at the bottom rung. It also affects students who get labeled as whiz kids, and they get stuck in the upper rank and never get exposed to other opportunities." In her view, these bright students are "shielded from social studies and other courses" and are directed into more technical areas by their advisors. In other words, ability grouping makes them victims. These students have no free choice? Their families' interest, encouragement, and advice is of no value? I was goal-oriented to be a physician from the age of three. I have had a very broad education and a wide range of interests. I have had the right of self-determination all along. We all do.

Another example of the continuing attack on self-determination is the Federal Government's campaign against tobacco. In this case the do-gooders are our representatives in Washington, protecting us against another evil, because we are too weak to do it ourselves. As a physician, I've never smoked, and I've lectured my patients on all the myriad ways that tobacco is harmful. Surveys have clearly demonstrated that the American public is not dumb, and in fact the average layman is convinced that tobacco is worse than the statistics demonstrate. James K. Glassman, a newspaper columnist and a fellow at the American Enterprise Institute, hammered away at the attempted 1998 Tobacco Settlement proposal in a March 1998 column, "Politicians see the $368.5 billion deal as a huge pile of cash for new spending projects. But far worse is the idea on which the settlement is founded: that individuals aren't responsible for their own actions. This view, so satisfying to elitists of all political stripes, is flat-out wrong. The anti-smoking hysteria is laying waste to basic protections and principles. Every individual is threatened too, as the *liberal* ideals on which this country was founded—freedom of choice, personal accountability, limited government—are trampled in a stampede by some to get others to behave the way they want." I couldn't have written it better, and I agree with his use of the word "liberal." These common-sense ideas were called liberal when the country was founded.

Glassman's American Enterprise Institute represents a type of self-appointed organization that contributes to the wide-ranging debate that should occur in this country. There are think-tank groups all over the political spectrum, expressing their ideas, trying to convince you of their point of view. All of their research, all of their articles and press releases open up

the discussion. They only represent themselves, and there are
no hidden agendas. You may not agree with some of them, but
what they are creating is a wealth of research from which we
all can draw facts, study their conclusions, and reach our own
decisions. They are of great value to the country.

I am against the movements invented by zealots that are
really of no value to us. The breast implant mess is one of
those. It is difficult to blame the tort lawyers early on for
falling into the trap. There was initially some medical research
that suggested the development of antibodies to loose silicone
in the body that conceivably could attack tissues and cause a
variety of complaints. There were some physicians who thought
silicone did cause these complaints. Huge follow-up studies
have effectively shown that this scenario is not true. Still some
of the lawyers have tried to push forward with their class action cases. The reason, of course, is "follow the money." Contingency fees could be enormous, if a class action case is won.
"Junk" science in court actions, due to very loose rules of "expert" evidence, has invented all kinds of compensable "illnesses"
or conditions. Finally the courts are tightening the rules to
accept only medical evidence that is vouched for by a group of
recognized medical experts. The so-called expert on horse-
back, traveling from court to court to earn his consulting fee
for testimony, will disappear.

Another ridiculous aspect of the do-gooders touting one
victimizing situation after another are the statistics that are fed
to the news organizations, which duly publish them without
checking the validity of the numbers. Jim Windolf of the *New
York Observer* lists the following in his article: 9.5 million adults
have attention deficit disorder; 10 million of us have seasonal
affective disorder (they get depressed in winter); 500,000 have
chronic fatigue syndrome; 14 million are alcoholic; 5 million
have a severe mental disorder; 8 million have an eating disorder; 2.5 million have multiple chemical sensitivity (of those
listed so far, this is the only one that may be junk science, there
is no acceptable proof at the time of the condition). He goes
on to list fifteen million folks with social phobia/anxiety according to their association! Fifteen million of us are said to be
depressed; 3 million have panic disorder; 12 million have "rest-

less legs syndrome." Let me stop here to tell you that this one is real. I've treated restless legs in practice, but based on the number of patients I saw in 30 years of private practice, 12 million adults out of 150 million people old enough to have it, means one person in twelve! No way! At this point Windolf's added up total is 139 million people. Skipping the mental health numbers that come next (because I think they are a repeat of previous numbers), he next describes a Ph. D's study of sexual addiction: 7.6 million men and 3.1 million women. Please pause to chuckle at this one. Wanting sex is an addiction? By my adjustment of his figures, we now have 149.7 million sufferers. I would remove 10 million to cover overlap and people with multiple conditions. Windolf gives the number of 198 million American adults over 18 years old, as the numbers he supplies for adult illness. 70.55 % of us have conditions or are sick. Do you believe it? I don't.

Bill Coulter, on the editorial board of the *Houston Chronicle* (16 December 1996), doesn't believe it either. He presents another group of weird numbers: twenty million Americans go to bed hungry every night. He doesn't believe it. He writes "more recently we have been told that 50% of women in America have been victims of 'abuse'." He wants to know the definition of "abuse" in this study. Further, "The truth is that misery is a growth industry in America. We cannot rely on emotional outbursts and statistical shell games rather than the truth." Basic advice. Don't just accept numbers that tend to be repeated over and over. Ask for proof. Ask why news organizations report stuff like this without demanding proof. They prefer bad news and "advice" news. Good news does not increase readership or capture more TV viewers. TV news today is police blotter stuff and features on advice.

The last place I would expect to find this victim philosophy is in the scientific research papers I still follow, but there it is. The backbone of medical practice is the underlying research, based on repeated confirmed results, and clear thinking conclusions. The practice of medicine on patients is a professional guessing game with an extremely high percentage of correct answers. The successful practice of medicine must be based on solid research results. In obesity, things have gone astray.

First a little background in medical facts about nutrition and being overweight: we burn the food we eat using oxygen, just as fires do. This can be measured as calories of heat or energy. We all know about the calories in food; it is in the diet books and printed on most packages of food we buy. While asleep we burn the fewest calories, a rate called the basal metabolism. Obviously, even in the sleep state the heart needs energy to beat, we must maintain body heat, and there is the work of breathing. The moment we wake up and start activities, the calorie burn increases. Not only do we burn food calories, we can burn fat calories, calories stored as muscle starch (glycogen), and even protein can be sacrificed as calories, if we are too starved. This is a biologic function and people fit into it along the much berated bell-shaped curve. Despite the criticisms of using the bell curve to look at IQ, the curve properly describes the range of variations in biologic activities found in groups of animals or people. For the same size, same sex, same age people there is a daily range of 200-300 calories difference in total daily calories. Men burn more calories than women due to a larger muscle mass. Further, from our evolution, there is the "starvation mechanism," which reduces our calorie burn by 200-300 calories per day when we diet severely.

Despite all of these variables, the whole issue of weight loss and dieting is simple arithmetic. Eat less in calories than you burn and if it is at least 200-300 calories less, there will be a slight weight loss. It will be more difficult for you, the lower you are on the bell curve to achieve that weight loss. And as you lose weight, that weight is harder to maintain because calorie burn also relates directly to total body weight. All of this has been known for most of this century. Now along come the brainwashed young medical researchers. They have found the genes that create the variation in the calorie burn rate in individuals, and I am seeing comments in medical articles and in editorials about these people being victims of their genes. How can they possibly lose weight or maintain a satisfactory weight? No one said life was meant to be fair and equal for everyone in every sphere. Each of us is endowed with some good and some bad biologic functions; no one is perfect. But look at the pictures of survivors of Hitler's concentration camps. Try to find a fat one! If a person wants to be thin and stay thin, proper diet, increased exercise, and old-fashioned self-discipline can do the job, good genes or bad genes. It all depends on your own force of desire.

This is a rich, fat country. We have the fattest poor people in the world. And the do-gooder diet police are out in force. And so is our paternalistic government. In June 1998 (*Houston Chronicle*, 6 June 1998) they introduced the public to another approach to victimhood: figure your body mass index by a complicated formula used in obesity studies, which relates height to weight. You may be a victim of obesity. The index may be of some research value, but it ignores body composition. Bone and muscle weight a great deal more than fat. Skin-fold thickness, measuring the fat component of your weight, still is a major factor. A weight lifter will be considered obese by this stupid approach because our governmental officials must be out there guiding us, because we cannot guide ourselves, and our doctors won't take an interest in how fat we are. So by government fiat, added to the estimated 68 million fatties (twenty-five percent of our population) are 29 million more. Now our wonderful government bureaucrats are concerned about 97 million "obese" Americans, roughly one-third of us. Not everyone needs to be as skinny as the emaciated models in the ads. Not everyone needs to be at "ideal" weight to live a long and happy life.

My grandfather was built like "tweedledum," smoked twelve cigars a day, and died happy in his eighty-ninth year. As I have already implied, the faddish weight-loss programs are out there making people feel guilty, and of course, making lots of money as they "help" people lose weight. They and the "diet" doctors are trying to sell easy and painless ways to lose weight. The doctors created the fen-phen combination of medications that turned out to be dangerous to heart and lungs. Now because of this ingrained belief that people cannot help themselves, a new drug, Meridia, has appeared with risky side-effects such as possibly raising blood pressure or speeding heart rate. Read

Anne M. Fletcher's book, *Thin for Life*, a study of 160 people who maintained an average sixty-three pound weight loss for five years or longer. You can take control of your own body; you must look to yourself for the resolve to do it. Otherwise you accept the helpless position of the victim.

No, we do not need self-appointed organizations or our government creating victims. As in obesity, many people are perfectly capable of creating their own victimhood with its attendant secondary benefits. I cared for an older (sixties) woman who had a moderately severe chronic condition. Her symptoms were much worse than studies of her health indicated they should be. She confided in me that she was carrying a terrible guilt. No one in her family knew what she had done, but early in a pregnancy she did not want, she had taken several different over-the-counter medications trying to abort herself. Abortion was illegal and she wasn't about to find an abortionist, as her family might find out what she was doing. Her child was born with a severe congenital defect, disabling that child for life. I immediately recognized, as I am sure you do, that this patient was punishing herself by creating more symptoms than she deserved, a victim of her own guilt. I learned an important lesson from what I did next. I thought that our relationship was intimate enough, in view of her admission to me, that I could point out the connection between her guilt and her unwarranted symptoms. Did I get a bawling out from her! She and her entire family immediately withdrew from my care. I knew that she was "grandma-in-charge" before all this happened. Grandpa was a great guy, but he was laid back, and she was the boss. In no way was she going to remove those symptoms: she was both punishing herself, and at the same time using her self-victimization to keep the family in control.

How did this victimization culture get started? From a time standpoint look to the 1960s. As a primary group of people, Gelernter names the intellectual elite in the leading universities. My classmate at Bates College, Charles W. Radcliffe wrote in our alumni magazine (Winter, 1998), "To a great extent, the political and social radicals of the 1960s have captured academia and turned all intellectual inquiry into issues of race, gender, class, in which there are groups of victims and victimizers, chief among the latter being white males and Western civilization itself." There was the "hippie" movement that celebrated individuality outside of societal norms. There was the war in Vietnam that was so confusing because it was so unpopular and fought as a containment of communism, rather than a war to be won. It caused huge groups of people to question the principals governing the policies of our country and our leaders themselves.

Look to the Warren Court that protected individual rights so much that clearly guilty criminals go free because the evidence collected was "tainted" by improper collection procedures. A New York appeals court in June 1996 voted four to one to suppress the confession and most of the physical evidence, including the dead body murdered by a convicted murderer! They concluded, according to the AP report, that the search of his van, agreed to by him when he was stopped for speeding, violated his rights. I presume because his rights were not properly explained in advance. His lawyer moved for dismissal of the charges with no evidence left to bring to court (*Houston Chronicle*, 7 June 1996). Let me tell you about my uncle, the federal judge, a true liberal Democrat, appointed during LBJ's administration. On this subject of Warren Court rulings, we asked the following hypothetical question and were astounded at his answer. If we had a house, in an area with a fairly high burglary rate, surrounded by thick shrubbery, and we hid bear traps in the bushes under the windows to protect our home was that okay? He told us it was not legal because it was unfair entrapment but that visible burglar bars were allowed! He felt the burglar could sue us for his leg injuries!

The victimhood culture has also being growing alongside this country in Great Britain. In a *WSJ* column (20 July 1998), Frank Furedi, a sociologist at the University of Kent in Great Britain, describes the outburst of public emotion over Princess Diana's death as representing "the emergence of a new secular religion, with a distinct set of values and attitudes. The new religion celebrates emotion, deplores reason and above all reveres the victim. In contemporary Britain as in the U.S., victimhood and suffering represent a claim to moral authority.

Lost is an important distinction: While suffering can be character forming, it does not by itself endow an individual with
any special knowledge or virtue." I might add that the victim
seekers and "helpers" sure feel virtuous, whether they end up
really helping the victim or not.

The overly maudlin emotional outpouring over Princess
Diana's death is an example of how taken western society is
with a truly pitiful victim. This poor little rich girl came from
a dysfunctional family. She was figuratively seduced as a nine-
teen-year-old virgin by a king-to-be, who needed a consort
(like her) to go with his kingly future: she imagined he loved
her and wanted her one day to be queen. All the while he had
his mistress, whose history dictated that he could not marry.
As a result, we are exposed to Diana's railings in public about
her bulimia and other problems. We openly hear about her
liaisons with lovers, and finally fed the agonies of her divorce,
with her two sons forced to watch all of this. The public is
given an excuse for Diana's failures as an adult: just look at her
childhood which did not prepare her to cope with adult challenges. And then her estate, busily arranged to profit from the
sale of Diana memorabilia. No wonder her eldest son William, shortly after her death, declared he does not wish to be
king. The same week Diana died, ironically, so did Mother
Teresa. Mother Teresa got about ten percent the press coverage Diana got and about as much public interest. But jump
ahead 100 years and imagine how the historians will have
interpreted these two women. Mother Teresa will have sainthood and an outstanding evaluation as a contributing human
being to the good of the world. Diana will be a disturbing
footnote to the dissolution of the British monarchy.

The culture of victimhood began in the 1960s and went
hand in hand with the celebration of individuality, and of
individual diversity strengthening society. Diverse individual
ideas, by broadening public debate, do strengthen society. Yes,
individual rights need protection against society smothering
them. But there is the old saying about throwing out the baby
with the bath water! An individual is only as safe as his society
is strong. Denouncing moral judgments about people to allow
more ethical latitude in individual activity weakens society.

Societal rules of behavior at the moral/ethical level maintain the society's strength. The more individual freedom approaches anarchy, the weaker the society and the more dangerous life becomes in a civilized country. Look at the gated and walled communities we have now, the bars on windows of private homes. And recently we learn that in those states where citizens are allowed to carry concealed weapons, crime levels are dropping. Do we have to become an armed camp before we realize that much of the 1960s effect has to be reversed?

I cannot fault this country in its constant striving for perfection. Simply, we must realize that perfection is unattainable. View the solution-finding as a pendulum. Very often we shove the pendulum too far in its arc in trying to correct perceived problems. And then it takes decades to get the pendulum back to a middle position, where all factors are taken into account. I don't feel as harshly toward the "busy-bodies" as you might think. They start off meaning well, but what they do not take into account is a system in Washington-speak called "dynamic scoring." This is a study of how the public at large, responding to self-interest, will react to a given program within the framework of individual human behavior. It is applied generally as an approach to tax changes, but should be used to study proposed social programs as well. I discuss this in Chapter Eight. Let me restate what was presented earlier. Helping the helpless victim may make him more helpless, unless a way out of the victimizing situation is offered. Don't just give out food stamps to the poor; help them find a way out of their poverty. Help the children of unwed mothers, but don't run the program in such a way that out-of-wedlock pregnancy is encouraged. Congress should not jump into massive well-intentioned expenditures without the results of carefully controlled pilot studies run by researchers who have no self-interest in the program.

This brings me to the politically-correct concept of the preservation of self-esteem. My 1971 dictionary defines self-esteem as having a good opinion of one's self; by 1983, another dictionary states that it means belief in one's self and self-respect. It does connote all of those meanings, but note the subtle change to a more forceful concept of how one should feel about one's self, as our society proceeded to increase the glorification of self. Although I have never been in a situation where others are trying to preserve my self-esteem, I keep reading about the attitude that self-esteem must be preserved at all costs. Don't make a task too hard; don't allow someone to ever experience defeat; don't allow failure. What happened to the old saying: "Success is never final, failure is never fatal"? In working with people, in guiding them, there should be the goal of the development of self-confidence and self-reliance. Self-esteem will follow from that. Failure can be a teacher, if the failed person is not condemned for it, but instructed in how to achieve success, and with each success receiving some praise and a sense of accomplishment. If the only result of a failed attempt is praise for trying hard, without the encouragement to try again, nothing is gained. If tasks and challenges are made easy to create success, that is fine, as long as the next step is a more difficult task until the person has reached the limits of his capacity. Limits to capacity are individual limits. We are all different, with differing abilities based on innate inherited physical and mental capacities, combined with the psychological encouragement we received in the expectations of our families and communities. If people are treated as victims who cannot help themselves, and their helplessness assumed to be irreversible, while their self-esteem must be protected at all costs, there will never be true self-esteem.

This protection of self-esteem, without really creating any valid reason for having self-esteem, has resulted in some pretty strange thinking. There is actually a move afoot in various areas of the country to not keep score in Little League games in a variety of sports. We shouldn't bruise the egos of young children by having winners and losers of the games. When do children learn about competition, the basis of our capitalistic society? How can it be avoided when it forms the basis of our evolutionary past, challenged as we were by our enemies in our Stone Age past? Why avoid it, when the sports games on television make it obvious that winning and losing are a part of life? Who is kidding who? This has roots that come from almost fifty years ago. I was a camp counsellor while in medical school at a camp that preferred the fun of playing to winning. They did not like the attitude I generated in my kids to win.

Grade-creep in all levels of schooling is another form of this softening of life's challenges. I have heard of schools that give nothing but A's and B's. How about those programs that allow students to earn extra credits so that their grade-point average is above 4.0? How can you be better than perfect? The reason this is done is that there are so many 4.0 students, a result ridiculous in itself, extra work for differentiation is allowed. My eldest daughter is a Ph. D. and teaches in a university. She never received less than an A in her entire education career. I only had a 3.6 coming out of Bates College. I considered us equally intelligent and assumed it was grade-creep. We both took the Graduate Record Exam, obviously years apart, before starting graduate studies. The test reports each person's result as a percentile standing against the entire country. We had the same percent. Must we falsify life with grade-creep?

We all need to read William Ernest Henley's poem "Invictus": "I am the master of my fate, I am the Captain of my soul." We must say, "I can control my own life, or I can find the help to regain that control." Children are born with the drive to become independent adults. However, adults can revert to dependent children—we were taught this in medical school. After a lengthy hospitalization, where medical folks ran the adult patients' life, we were cautioned to help the patient regain his willingness to control himself. This was usually easy to accomplish, but with the occasional patient who was afraid to resume decision-making, a little understanding and counseling would get him back on track as an adult. I never met a patient who did not strive to return to adult control of his life when encouraged with optimism and empathy. Softening the demands of life to protect children, or to "help" adults, produces weak children and dependent adults. The tenets of "tough love" do not require harshness, but only to impart the demand that each individual develop the discipline to face life as it truly is, with challenges that each person is required to face. Life was never meant to be entirely fair. We learn to judge our own feelings of self-worth by evaluating the ways with which we meet and conquer life's challenges.

Chapter Four

Victims with an Attitude

The American Population until the Great Society

With two exceptions, everyone who lives in this country is a voluntary immigrant or the descendent of voluntary immigrants. The exceptions are the misnamed American Indians, the indigenous Stone Age inhabitants, who were unceremoniously shoved aside by the invading Europeans, and the Africans (who were captured by each other, and then sold as slaves by African chiefs and Arabs to the slave traders), ending up here against their wills. I will discuss these two groups, but first, I want to explore the character and motivation of the first wave of immigrant groups that settled the nation and then look at the second huge wave that arrived after the nation was well established. All were victims with an attitude, not like the abject victims making use of, or created by, the victimology culture discussed in the preceding chapter.

Grandpa Mike, my mother's father, was a short rotund man, looking much like the pictures of Tweedledum and Tweedledee in "Alice in Wonderland." For his height of five feet, six inches he had a huge head, with a hat size that approached seven and a half. He lived his American life to the fullest. He was shortstop on a sandlot baseball team and had a lifetime love of baseball that led him to have eight seats for his business at Ebbets Field. These were in back of third base, so you could look into the Dodger dugout and follow the activity there during the game, which helped guess the next strategy. He was a deep sea fisherman, with a huge blue swordfish mounted over his desk at the warehouse. He avidly played pinochle, and I think that he bet on it. I know he loved to go to the track and bet the horses, as he gave me the winning tickets to collect for him the one time we went together (I was 30, he was 78 at that episode in our lives). He lived life with tremendous gusto. He brought six children into the world, owned a small farm in the country near New York for the family summers, managed by a tenant farmer. He always had the newest and best cars. He smoked twelve cigars a day. When my grandmother died after two years of a failing heart, he (at seventy-five-years-old) scandalized the family by remarrying a card-playing friend just a few months later. He spent the next ten years traveling the world with her, gradually burning up his fortune of something over a million dollars. He passed away at eighty-eight, with my step-grandmother watching over him very carefully during those last three years of decline. The two of them were like teenagers with a crush, holding hands and gazing at each other love struck, when they visited us after their honeymoon in Hawaii.

He was the eternal optimist. He never had a penny of life insurance on himself while he created that large family. With my uncle he built up a string of fifteen supermarkets, a central warehouse, and a few shopping centers anchored by his stores, Michael's Fairmart Food Stores. I am describing to you a seven-year-old Russian orphan, sent by his uncle to this country to be raised by his older sister, Sarah, married and twenty-six years old. I met "Tanta Sarah" only once, when I was a little boy, and she looked like a little old lady to me. I now wish I knew her better and had a chance to hear her story of how she came to this country. I don't know how Grandpa got here. He never talked about it and when I was younger it never occurred to me to ask. I know he came alone, probably shepherded by a grown-up acquaintance, and undoubtedly in steerage on the ship. He arrived in New York, probably after two weeks of sea sickness at Castle Garden in 1888, before Ellis Island was in use. He learned English quickly, and spoke it without accent. I never heard him speak Russian, but of course, he knew Yiddish. He left school at fourteen, went to work in a grocery store, and was married by seventeen. He became a butter and egg broker, starting grocery stores on the side and selling them when each was a going business. His optimism had its lucky side. When the Great Depression hit

he had two stores making money, but his butter and egg brokerage became a liability. Realizing that people always had to
eat, he stuck with the stores and added more with my uncle
coming into the business. He survived the Depression handily.

He could have viewed himself as a victim, but with his
optimistic attitude, he took full advantage of what he found
this country had to offer in the way of opportunity. He was the
typical rags-to-riches immigrant who seized that opportunity
and ran with it. He is a prime example, from my family, of
how all of us, as immigrants, have created an American population with a character that drove us to develop the greatest
nation the world has ever witnessed. Allistair Cooke, the
Englishman who loved our country and showed it to us on
television in the 1960s, observed in his books *America* (1973):
"While Europeans attribute America's bounty to the luck of
her resources, Americans on the other hand like to ascribe it
to nothing but character. It usually required a combination of
both. As the dramatic history of this country, including the
actual invention of a nation, will show." Paul Johnson, whose
A History of the American People (1997) is another Englishman's
labor of love of this country, concludes after almost 1,000
pages of history: "The story of America is one of difficulties
being overcome by intelligence and skill, by faith and strength
of purpose, by courage and persistence. (It) is a human achievement without parallel. . . . Americans are, above all a problem-
solving people. They do not believe that anything in this world
is beyond human capacity to soar to and dominate. They will
not give up. . . . The great American republican experiment is
still the cynosure of the world's eyes. It is still the first, best
hope for the human race." All of this from an amalgamated
hoard of immigrants who would not remain victims in their
home countries and came here. Victims with an attitude!

I have always thought, perhaps with my personal example
of Grandpa Mike, that the original settlers who came here,
into a hostile new land, selected themselves out from the general population of Europe, Darwin style, to be an unusual
group of people. I believe the later immigrants did the same
self-selection. There has to be a bell-shaped curve for each of
the characteristics of personality that might apply here. Ag-

gressive versus passive; optimistic versus pessimistic; self-reliance versus helplessness; responsible versus irresponsible; leading versus following; toughness versus softness; constructive thinking and studying versus mental inaction; courageous versus fearful; hopeful and forward-looking versus melancholy and depressed; risk-takers versus the risk-averse; entrepreneurial versus a worker bee; caretakers versus the cared for. Obviously, I am describing the extreme poles of each curve and am applying it to both men and women. Generally, the people who decided to come here had to be somewhat removed from the middle ground of each of these pairs of characteristics, and shaded toward traits that would create a more driving, self-assured, optimistic personality. For example, not everyone was a leader, but those who did not lead were willing to be led away from the troubles in Europe. Those who would not be led stayed home. No one was forced to be a pilgrim or a colonist.

In contemplating this book, the particular personalities of the voluntary immigrants forming the basis of our unusual population has been a key issue in my mind. I hoped, in my research, to find some type of comparative study of the personalities of the folks who came here, and those who stayed home to completely validate the idea. I haven't found such a study, but instead I found a general acceptance among authors that the concept is a truism. Look again at the quote from Paul Johnson with which he concluded his history of our country. Johnson's opinion notwithstanding, he is echoing a French nobleman, Alexis de Tocqueville's amazement at the American society he found when the Frenchman toured this country in the 1830s: highly educated (actually more literate than any other country), an unlimited society (but a competitive society), wedded to the freedom and market system of the secular world, yet moral. He concluded "most Americans held religion 'to be indispensable to the maintenance of republican institutions.'"

To carry this further, Johnson's *History* describes that de Tocqueville noted the government was minimal in its effect on the citizens, and this was "a great source of moral strength." De Tocqueville (per Johnson) stated: "One of the happiest consequences of the absence of government (when a people is fortunate enough to do without it, which is rare) is the development of individual strength that inevitably follows from it. Each man learns to think, to act for himself, without counting on the support of an outside force, which however vigilant one supposes it to be, can never answer all social needs. Man, thus accustomed to seek his well-being only through his own efforts, raises himself in his own opinion as he does in the opinion of others; his soul becomes larger and stronger at the same time." This statement should be read to the entire Congress every day until they understand it. It is the key to what has currently gone wrong in this country. The American syndrome, de Tocqueville's impression in Johnson's book: "Morality/independence/enlightenment/industry/success" was present in our early country because our citizens were a people "whose practical, political education is the most advanced." At the time of this description our country was fifty-years-old, and operating under the Constitution just over forty years.

The population consisted of most unusual people! Who were they? We know about the religious oppression that brought the Pilgrims, Quakers and Huguenots of France here. Not all the religiously oppressed came, but these did and they were different than the people who stayed in the "old country." Adventurers came, of course they would. Ordinary people came, tired of the restrictive governmental rules and taxes in Europe. Some convicts were sent here, but not in the proportions that were sent to Australia. Many came as indentured servants, working off the cost of their passage to America. Others became indentured servants to escape debtors' prison. All of these people were giving up what they knew to risk the dangers of the New World on the chance that might allow them to win a better life. They knew the chance involved. They all knew that early colonists had died, that the Roanoke colony, the first in Virginia, simply disappeared, and the Jamestown colony lost over half its numbers in its first year—still they came. Landed gentry also arrived—not the first-born sons, but second and third-born, excluded by the British custom of primogeniture from inheriting the family estate.

Some of our founding fathers came from the gentry, some did not, but the group of intellectual political philosophers, or philosophical politicians, whichever you prefer, that finally gathered to give birth to this nation was a rare occurrence. At no other time in history have such a group gathered to lead a group of colonies into nationhood: George Washington, Benjamin Franklin, Thomas Jefferson, Alexander Hamilton, James Madison, and John Adams. I urge you to read *Miracle at Philadelphia, The Story of the Constitutional Convention,* by Catherine Drinker Bowen (1966), to fully appreciate how miraculous this was. The men at that convention, led in part by the group just mentioned, fashioned the most advanced and remarkable political document in the history of civilization. Such a document, with its Bill of Rights, exists nowhere else. Even Great Britain had its parliamentary democracy grow by fits and starts, and cannot point to a single set of guarantees for individual freedom as came out of Philadelphia. This same group represents the White European Males, now so denigrated by the American Feminists. Without those political-philosophers there would be no so-called feminists today.

During the early colonization period before nationhood, and during the fifty years until the 1830s, there was a further driving force, and a further selecting-out process molding the personality of our population, and that was the pushing westward of the frontier. There were people who were not satisfied with the life they achieved on the relatively safe east coast. They were driven enough to take on the dangers of conquering the frontier, and possibly make their fortune, or at least a better life for themselves. The frontier existed until the early 20th century, and left a population that is still in place, individualistic and relatively conservative politically. All except California, where many Easterners leap-frogged in during the twentieth century, and turned it much more liberal. I still remember the bumper stickers I saw in Idaho in the early 1980s: "Idaho is what America was," and with the appropriate American flag. The frontier spirit is still out there, and up in Alaska, where there still is some frontier.

As the country successfully managed its first fifty years immigration continued with the "pull" of America's reputation as the place to make a fortune, as well as the "push" of disasters in Europe, such as the potato famine in Ireland in the 1840s. In the old established order in Europe, religious repression continued and heavy-handed government rule and over-bearing taxation had not changed. You might think that with the east coast, a very civilized area, the decision to migrate would be an easier one, but as described by Joe R. Feagin in *Racial and Ethnic Relations* (1978), "Trans-Atlantic crossing was quite dangerous in the 1840s. Few ships arrived which had not lost a significant number of their poorly accommodated passengers to starvation or disease." Push and pull factors are expanded on in his book but need no further amplification here. The idea I am advancing is that the decision to come here still required an individual who was somewhat special. Think of the people you have known who have quietly endured a failing community, and haven't had the drive to leave for someplace better. There is the inertia created by the comfort of what is familiar and pleasant, and even a comfort in knowing how to handle the problems remaining. There is the nostalgia connected with one's hometown. Leaving takes "guts."

In *The Rest of Us* (1984), Stephen Birmingham, in describing the emigration decisions of eastern European Jews coming to this country, touches on a variation of my point:

> Needless to say, emigration was a painful step to take in itself, and an enormous gamble. But decades of persecution had at least one positive effect—a Darwinian principle had been proved, and only the hardest and toughest had survived. (They) had even developed a hard-boiled sense of humor about their situation. But pride and humor were put to the test with emigration. Emigration was an admission of failure. It meant an inability to endure any longer. As a result, some of the older rabbis stubbornly counseled their congregations not to emigrate. The Jewish immigrant had often left behind him a seriously divided family. If, for example, a young man finally made up his mind to leave for America, he usually had the support of his mother, who saw nothing but hopelessness for her son's future in Russia. His father, on the other hand, was often op-

posed. He had heard tales of young Jews losing their
faith in profligate America, and also argued that a son's
duty was to remain at home to help support his family.

The young Jew was made to feel he had abandoned his
home by those he left behind. But leave they did. These eastern European Jews came as a sizable portion of a massive
immigration after 1880. From 1840 to 1880 ten million immigrants arrived, but from 1880 to 1920, twenty-five million
came, nine million in the first decade of the twentieth century
(*The Unmaking of Americans,* John J. Miller, 1998). Of these,
over two million were Jewish (*Migrations and Cultures,* Thomas Sowell, 1996), with an explosion in Jewish population
from 250,000 in 1880 to 4.5 million by 1924 (Allistair Cooke's
America, 1973). Sowell comments in the same vein as Birmingham: "Among the heaviest costs of all (in migration) are
the severing of personal ties in familiar surroundings to face
new economic and social uncertainties in a strange land."

They came because of the severity of the anti-Jewish discrimination and the pogroms: cossacks descending on villages
to rape, pillage and kill were an enormous push to leave. But
another finding by Dr. Martin E.P. Seligman, in his book
Learned Optimism (1990), again fits my theory that certain
personality types emigrated, while others didn't. The Russian
Orthodox "Slavs lived under unrelieved, crushing poverty, poverty of a degree unknown in this country. The Jews lived in
poverty and under religious persecution and the threat of pogroms. Yet the Jews emigrated and the Slavs stayed." A study
of Jewish and Russian Orthodox liturgy found that "the religious material of the Russian Jews was noticeably more optimistic than the Russian Orthodox material." Seligman specu-
lates this helped the Jews to leave.

My impressions as a child, a later member of this sub-
group of American culture, may help to draw the picture of
immigrant groups. We were told of how terrible things were
in Europe, and how lucky we were to be here, and I felt very
lucky that my grandparents had made an effort to be here,
although they never described the journey. They all tried to
Americanize as quickly and as much as they could. They all
spoke English perfectly, they were well-read and understood

the politics of the day. Grandpa Mike was probably the most American of them all. They were Americans first and Jews second. They and my parents taught me that success lay in education. This was a time of strong anti-Semitism in the country. Climbing the corporate ladder in a gentile corporation was unheard of. Certain hotels, resorts, residential subdivisions were "restricted"—no Jews allowed. The way "up" was to have your own business or to succeed in the professions. At the City College of New York in the 1920s and 1930s (Thomas Sowell, *Migrations and Cultures*, 1996) "eventually nearly three-quarters of the students were Jews. By the late 1930s, more than half the physicians in New York were Jewish, as were nearly two-thirds of the dentists and lawyers." My father, born here, was an uneducated success. His motto was: "You make your own luck." He dropped out of high school in his junior year to help support the family, and eventually help send a younger brother to college to be an engineer. Before his life ended, he had founded his own business, and his net worth exceeded a million dollars. There are other examples in my family: two uncles of mine achieved millionaire status, one born here, one a teenage immigrant. Immigrant families often succeed beyond their wildest dreams, as ours did. It should not be implied that immigration success must be measured only by the accumulation of individual wealth. Becoming part of the American Dream involves becoming a knowledgeable citizen, an active participant in American politics, and a contributor to the overall advance of the society of the country. My grandfather, father, and two uncles created hundreds of jobs in the businesses they developed. They and my other aunts and uncles sent their children to college and I now have cousins, nieces and nephews, and a sibling scattered from Vermont to the Chicago area, from California to Florida, representing many professions, and corporate positions. Each is a productive member of the American society. All this from four plucky folks who came here between 1880 and 1900. I am thrilled they came.

My personal history made me a graduate of the State of New York Medical School, Syracuse, 1954. Twenty-two of the sixty-six graduates were Jewish, an unusually large number

for the country at large, but New York State had no quotas
limiting Jews as did other states. Yet we all worried because
the intern and resident programs for our post-graduate training might have quotas. Of the top fifteen in our class, eleven
were Jewish. Was our Jewish I.Q. bell curve better than the
gentiles? No way! We were driven by our cultural background
of the value of scholarship to study and get better grades to
improve our chances against those quotas. And did it work!
Sowell reports "By 1969, Jews averaged 80 percent higher family
income than other Americans. As of 1990 most Jews over
twenty-five years of age had at least completed college, with
about half of these having gone on to graduate study. By
contrast only 12 percent of the corresponding age bracket in
the general white population of the United States had completed college. Not surprisingly, nearly 40 percent of all employed Jews were working in the professions and another 17
percent in managerial occupations." The civil rights movement
had opened up the corporations, the hotels, resorts and subdivisions in the 1960s.

The group that followed the Jews as a successful minority
was the Asians. They faced greater risks than the 1840s Atlan-
tic crossings; as "boat people," they faced the challenge to run
a gauntlet of pirates who raped, robbed and killed, trusting to
unseaworthy vessels, crossing the South China sea to escape
Southeast Asia in the 1970s and 80s. I met a number of those
brave people while doing Social Security disability exams in
my medical practice. The younger members of the families
who came to me all had learned to speak English well. The
Asian group overall are now the star scholars, again driven by
family advice and pressure, and a cultural background of a love
of scholarship, as in the Jewish group. They are also very successful in business. As Miller comments in *The Unmaking of
Americans,* "Asian Americans are frequently recognized as one
of the great success stories of modern assimilation. The Ko-
rean grocery store owner and the Vietnamese valedictorian
have become popular symbols of how the American dream is
still a reality." Miller also generalizes: "In the United States
[the] selection process tends to choose immigrants who are
optimists, risk takers, and entrepreneurs. People who volunteer

to uproot themselves from their birth countries and travel hundreds or thousands of miles across borders and oceans to succeed in America are a special breed."

The point I am presenting is that migrants, whether we are discussing the original settlers, or the immigrants who continue to come, have continuously enriched the population of our country with aggressive, optimistic hard-driving individuals, creating and then continuously reinforcing the most unusual national character on earth. Birmingham, Miller, and this quote from Thomas Sowell's *Migrations and Cultures* confirm my original premise in which I suggested a Darwin-like selection process brought an unusual group of people to this country: "Migrants tend to differ not only from the general population of their respective countries of origin, they tend also to differ from the general population of the countries to which they are moving, as well as differing from migrants from other countries. The selective nature of many migrations is indicated by the fact that migrants often begin their life in a new land earning less than people of the same national, racial, or ethnic background who were born there and yet, over a period of about ten or fifteen years, the migrants rise to *higher income levels than their compatriots.* Such patterns have been found among black, white, and Chinese immigrants to the United States and similar patterns have been found in Canada and Britain" (emphasis added).

Sowell not only agrees with my premise regarding the driving personality of immigrants, but he is suggesting that once the immigrant groups are well-settled, and well-satisfied they tend to lose some of their aggressiveness. A national population personality cannot afford to become too self-satisfied. It can become too complaisant, too soft, and finally lose a sense of the country's purpose, like Rome's fall to the Goths and Mongols. Sowell concludes: "The history of immigrants who began in poverty and achieved prosperity, while at the same time advancing the economic level of the society around them, brings into sharper focus the importance of *creating* wealth, especially important when so many are preoccupied with its distribution. Such immigrants have left a legacy not only of economic examples but also of human inspiration."

Sowell's point must be understood clearly. First create the wealth, and continue its creation, or there is no point in developing programs to redistribute some of the wealth to unfortunate citizens, who need a help up from the situation into which they have fallen and may be struggling. We must continue wealth creation to have the funds to help people become self-sufficient again. The goal of that help must always be self-sufficiency, not the entitlement/welfare trap of the Great Society that we are beginning to undo.

The other corollary of my view of our immigrant nation, the fear I have had for years, is that we may allow ourselves to become too soft, too complaisant. We will Darwin-like select out the characteristics that have made our nation and its population so unusual in the world. For some people it is easy to want to become soft and lazy. Unfortunately, it is easy to induce laziness, and apparently its companion, victimhood. We came here with strong work ethic patterns and a strong sense of independent accomplishment and self-sufficiency. We did not look to others for help. We created a dynamo of a nation. We have no greater resources than the Eurasian continents, but although they are far older in civilization and culture, we have outstripped them in wealth and power. In my comments about our evolutionary past in Chapter 5, what will jump out at you is that we were constantly challenged, had to constantly be vigilant, and had no time to be lazy or laid-back. We deserve the time off because we have earned it after working so hard, now that civilization has advanced to the point that we don't always have to be on guard. Rest and vacation times are never harmful. It is the lack of challenges that is bad. From an evolutionary standpoint life was meant to be a challenge, bringing out the best in us. Theologically, the same point is made. Think about it. If life were the Garden of Eden, in a short time you would be bored to death. Unless there are challenges, obstacles to solve, difficulties to endure, how do you judge yourself and your ability to handle life? If it is all wine and roses, you can't. You can either grab life by the throat and live it, or you can endure it. The immigrants who came here grabbed life by the throat and shook it. They stopped enduring.

My fears for our unusual population arise from the principles oozing out of the far-left extremist intellectuals in our colleges and universities. These are the people Gelernter refers to in *Drawing Life* as the "intellectualized elite." Competition is to be abhorred, self-esteem glorified. All varieties of victims are to be identified and "helped." White European males and by association, white American males are to be vilified as oppressors. Multiculturalism must dominate our thinking, lest we forcibly remove the inherent ethnicity of our diverse cultural groups and force them to assimilate. I've completely assimilated just fine, and my ethnicity is intact, but no one asked me! Therefore we must have bilingual education, which only serves to slow immigrant students' progress in education. We must be politically correct to protect those folks who are so soft that they cannot protect themselves. To protect "races," the pressure of these intellectuals' ideas has caused our government to subvert the underlying intent of the affirmative action aspect of our laws. We have entitlement by quota. There were not to be quotas, the laws say so. The intent was to draw us together as one society, by giving all of us equal protection under the law. Instead the government has divided us up by races, counted us like beans, and created quotas so the ratios of racial divisions are then forcibly carried out by the quotas. For example, if a racial group is twenty percent of our population, then twenty percent of federal judges should be from that group. Twenty percent of students from that group should be admitted to the "best" colleges. Whatever happened to individual merit and the ability to earn your own way? Governmental lumping of us together in racial and ethnic groups is divisive and antagonistic to forming one cohesive society. It sets one group against another, and loses the individual who is striving to achieve by his own accomplishments and merit. It negates the idea of De Tocqueville, from way back in the 1830s, which is an extremely important psychological principle: self-achieved success is the best success, and makes one's feeling of self-worth much stronger, compared to achieving through an outside arrangement that allows your success by pushing other people aside.

We have grade-creep to help self-esteem. Students who earn more than 4.0—more than perfect! Whatever happened to the saying I've used before, "Success is never final, failure never fatal?" Life is becoming too soft for a successful society. There is no need to return to the harshness of the Stone Age, we have earned our way well beyond that. Within our civilization people must continue to be challenged honestly, and dare I say it, in competition with each other. We are not created biologically equal. We cannot biologically achieve equally, but we should have equal opportunity to be as successful as our biologic inheritance allows. Try to imagine affirmative action applied to the National Basketball Association in quota proportion to our population. I hope you are laughing. That shows you how ludicrous the quotas are.

Concerned as I have been that our society will become so laid back, so entitlement conscious, that we start into a national decline, the arrival of John J. Miller's book, *The Unmaking of Americans, How Multiculturalism has Undermined America's Assimilation Ethic* (1998), while I was writing this chapter, was extremely disturbing. I was blithely going along assuming that the arrival of immigrants of the quality I have described would have an energizing effect, and set an example for those of us who have become so self-satisfied and laid back. Yes, some immigrants will continue to be inspirational, but the same softening and cushioning process is being applied to immigrants, to the detriment of the country. Multiculturalists feel that immigrants have to be protected, while other citizens feel threatened by these new arrivals, not inspired.

Miller points to the multiculturalists as saying "that the immigrants should not have to assimilate. They advance an unsettling agenda of racial and ethnic entitlements, cheapened naturalization standards, foreign language voting, and bilingual education. (They feel) assimilation is nothing but a gentrified form of ethnic cleansing." To me, the permission to become an American citizen is a valued privilege we offer to immigrants, and we shouldn't dumb down the requirements, but continue to challenge them to meet high requirements of citizenship or return home. We must approach each individual with these requirements, not divide the individuals into ethnic and racial groups that may generate special entitlements. Again from Miller, "About 85% of today's immigrants during the 1990s are racial and ethnic minorities that, according to the federal government, automatically qualify as disadvantaged. Immigrants traditionally have been enterprising achievers and they remain so. Now they have a powerful political motivation to boast of their downward mobility, since victim status confers its own rewards." By multiculturalist views, the immigrants are victims the moment they arrive. Victimology by anticipation! They don't have to be actually victimized to be considered victims. Just inviting them here seems to do it.

These multicultural theories of group rights have been taken to amazing legal extremes, now known as the "cultural defense" in criminal law, allowing "immigrants to defy the most basic American legal principles. In 1987, a Chinese immigrant in Brooklyn, murdered his wife with a claw hammer after she admitted having an affair. The defense (presented) an anthropologist who testified that in Chinese culture, the terrible shame of having an unfaithful wife made such drastic action understandable. He was sentenced to five years probation on a manslaughter charge . . . if an action is acceptable in another culture, then it should be acceptable in the United States." This is pure multiculturalism of the worst kind, and must be thrown out of our thinking. If people immigrate here, it is to live by our rules, or there will be no rules. The cultural defense is as ludicrous as the following scenario: let's invite in some tribes from Borneo or New Guinea; if they start up the culturally acceptable headhunting they have enjoyed in the past, we will have to let them do it. Won't we, taking a principle to its logical extreme? I thought the legal examples in Philip K. Howard's *The Death of Common Sense, How Law is Suffocating America* (1994), gave extreme examples of perverted legal thinking.

How badly this nation is influencing our immigrants is shown by the following court case, which contains a number of events illustrating how perverted thinking has become. An immigrant father and son came here from Greece in 1983, and at some point the son bought an Exxon station at which his father worked. A car wash sent over a car with water mixed

with the fuel in the gas tank and asked that the tank be emp-
tied. Unfortunately, the tank was under pressure and gasoline
spurted onto the father, who jumped back, knocked over a
light, which ignited the gasoline, resulting in severe burns over
his upper body. Logically, this was an unfortunate accident
with no one at fault. Workers Compensation Insurance paid
for the father's medical care. But in today's climate of opinion,
the immigrants found a lawyer who found a legal theory under
which to sue: the gasoline vendor, which was the car wash,
should have warned the father and son that gasoline is flammable! Perversion number one, the money-hungry tort lawyer
who invented a frivolous law suit. Perversion number two is
the weak-kneed judge who accepted the suit.

The Greek immigrants won their case, the father being
awarded $125,000 for his injuries, and the son $39,000 to
cover fire damage to his Exxon station. Actually the awards
were double the figures just given, but the jury felt the father,
was fifty percent at fault, cutting the awards in half. Perversion
number three is this typical jury award in this country: An
accident happens and someone must pay. There are "deep
pockets" somewhere to make up for every accident in life.
Unforeseen accidents must always have compensation; someone must be found guilty. Why didn't the Greek son have
liability insurance on his station? Wasn't he "at fault" for not
reasonably covering his station?

Thank goodness, the Court of Appeals threw out the jury
award, stating "that a manufacturer has no duty to warn a
customer of risks associated with the use of a product when the
risks are generally known and recognized. It is indisputable
that the flammable nature of gasoline is obvious and well known
to the community" (*Houston Chronicle*, 12 June 1998). But
contrary to the court's view, have you noted how many obvious
warnings are put by manufacturers on products out of fear of
being unreasonably sued ("Don't let children play with this
plastic bag;" "this is not a step," on the top of a ladder). The
final perversion is the son's reported reaction to the Court of
Appeals verdict. He said that he cannot understand the U.S.
legal system: "I don't know what to say, other people fall down
and get $1 million." Hasn't he learned his lessons well in this

country? Why isn't there a payout somehow? I had been hoping that our new immigrants would revitalize the country. It looks like we are re-educating them in a disastrous way.

Miller explains the origin of the ridiculous multicultural approach: "Many Americans are strikingly hesitant to believe that their country is the greatest the world has known. They would never say such a thing in mixed company without making all the necessary qualifications about how it was wrong to steal land from the Indians, enslave blacks, deny women the vote; . . . sharing America's greatness with immigrants hardly seems like an option when it appears as though there never was much greatness to go around." Our country has made mistakes. We recognize them and we have struggled to overcome them, to make things fair for everyone. Paul Johnson wrote his history of our people because he is so impressed with how hard we have tried to solve our problems. Look at the other countries that ignore their own misadventures.

Politically opposite the multiculturalists are their strange bedfellows, the conservative nativists who feel that most of the current crop of immigrants, of all colors and from all parts of the world, cannot possibly assimilate into a country that once was primarily white and western European. These nativists claimed in the nineteenth century that the eastern European immigrants could not assimilate, and in fact, Chilton Williamson, Jr. very recently, in *The Immigrant Mystique* (1996) is quoted by Miller as claiming that the Ellis Island generation of immigrants never actually became Americanized. Williamson should talk to my family, or he should consider the performance of the Japanese-Americans in World War II. Despite the totally unfair act of uprooting the west coast Japanese and putting them in internment camps after Pearl Harbor, Japanese men volunteered to fight, and were sent to Europe where they acquitted themselves with the most outstanding heroism. Their unit, the 442nd Regimental Combat Team, had a fighting record unmatched by any other unit of the armed services (*American Ethnicity*, pg. 384). Of 16,000 who joined the service, there were almost 10,000 casualties, fighting in Italy and France, proving they were worthy of being Americans. This experience alone demonstrates the value immigrants place on the right to join our country.

Miller obviously advocates Americanizing our immigrants, as I do, by restating forcibly our pride in our country and by re-educating our doubtful citizens that we are the most amazing country on Earth. We should continue to invite immigrants to come, but under the expectation that they intend to become naturalized as English-speaking citizens, who have learned the basic tenets of our democratic principles, expect to obey our laws, and who will be self-supporting on arrival or have supporting sponsors, not being automatically eligible for welfare or S.S.I. (Supplementary Security Income) as has been the case.

Left to discuss are the two groups mentioned at the start of this chapter. First is the American Indian. Overwhelmed by the rest of us, they have always had the choice of staying on their reservations and remaining "tribal," or coming out and assimilating. In 1924, all of them were granted citizenship. In Paul Johnson's opinion, "In material and moral terms, assimilation was always the best option for indigenous peoples confronted with the fact of white dominance. That is the conclusion reached by the historian who studies the fate not only of the American Indians but of the aborigines in Australia and the Maoris in New Zealand." However, remaining tribal, and staying on the reservation must be by individual choice. In recent years some of the tribes have discovered ways to make money and remove their people from poverty. We, who are not Indians, must remember that "The oneness of Indian, Indian land, and the rest of the natural environment permeates Indian thought . . . The tribal-communal way of life, devoid of economic competition, views land as the most vital part of man's existence" (*American Ethnicity,* Bahr, Chadwick, & Strauss, 1979). This book quotes Chief Seattle, whose sentiment has always captured the spirit of the Indian for me: "Every part of this soil is sacred, in the estimation of my people. Every hillside, every valley, every plain and grove, has been hallowed by some sad or happy event in days long vanished. Even the rocks, which seem to be dumb and dead as they swelter in the sun along the silent shore thrill with memories of stirring events connected with the lives of my people, and the very dust upon which you now stand responds more lovingly to their footsteps than to yours, because it is rich with the dust of our ancestors and our bare feet are conscious of the sympathetic touch." The quote is much longer and deserves deeper reading, but this segment makes the point. The Indians have much more to offer in their philosophy of life and the rest of us should listen. For example, this quotation from the Great Law of the Iroquois Confederacy: "In our every deliberation, we must consider the impact of our decisions on the next seven generations." We do have much to learn from the Indians. Perhaps they will join more closely to us, but the Indians will continue to choose, over the years, the lifestyle they prefer. It is their privilege to choose and solve for each the dilemma that is theirs.

The issue of our black population is totally different. They have no reservations to retreat to, no homeland to emigrate to like the Jews with recently reestablished Israel. Some of them have assimilated and appear to be content with that choice. At the other extreme are those who live in rage with the generally white population, and are angry at the assimilated blacks. As a Jew who has experienced discrimination, I have tried to imagine the "Black Experience." I really can't, because I can pass for gentile. But I think I can understand the rage. If I were growing up as an innocent black child and ran into the "caste segregation," as it has been called, a second-rate citizen with implied biologic inferiority, the appearance of anger and rage at the time this unfairness is discovered is not surprising. The books on ethnicity describe stages in the black reaction to being black in a white society, but putting aside the sociologist jargon, it is easy to see it in comparison with the stages we go through mourning the loss of a loved one. There is always a stage of anger or rage that must be worked through, because stagnation at the anger stage is non-productive, and solves nothing. The question is how to bring the black population through this stage to a more productive level that will allow them to lose the rage and find the way to gain assimilation within the general population.

The black minister, the Reverend Jesse Lee Peterson, founder of his ten-year-old organization, Brotherhood Organization of a New Destiny, (B.O.N.D.) has a startling answer. The rage and hatred of reverse racism is continuing because it is being fomented: "It is apparent to most Americans that Jesse Jackson, Maxine Waters, Louis Farrakhan, the NAACP, liberal elite whites, and the Democratic Party are racist." He also states that many black preachers are spreading this racism from their pulpits, "Whenever most blacks hear these pastors blame whites for their own failing, they rejoice because it takes away the responsibility of looking at themselves. The failure of blacks comes not from white people, but from hating white people." He adds, "To blame past slavery for the actions of blacks today is a lie. Blacks are slaves only to their minds in 1998 thanks to these wicked leaders." Peterson's solution is to show blacks that they must stop listening to most of their current "leaders," "drop their anger and find the truth within themselves" (http://www.bondinfo.org).

The approach so far has been to involve all of us with the passage of equal opportunity laws. Those laws must cease being applied with quotas setting one group against another, increasing racial and ethnic antagonisms. We are not going to undo bigotry through law. There will always be bigoted people, but at least the legal playing field can be equal. Working through the rage in the black community can only be done within that community, but not with some of the black leaders who continue to play on the rage and anger, and seemingly do not want to work through it, continuing the inter-racial antagonisms. If Martin Luther King had lived, his non-violent, Gandhian approach would have brought the issue further along than it is now. His original concept was to desegregate public institutions, but he logically advanced to the dream of a "beloved community," blacks and whites living side by side in a racially integrated America (book review by Julia Vitullo-Martin, *WSJ*, 28 May 1998). My Nigerian patients could not understand the attitude of American blacks; that is, retaining the anger, and not putting it behind and taking advantage of what the Nigerians had found to be the opportunities here. The Nigerians felt some of the discrimination, but pushed it aside and were successful in relying on their own merits. Black academic leaders who understand the value of achievement through one's own efforts, that is using merit alone, are Dr. Thomas Sowell, Dr. Walter Williams and Ward Connerly, but they are not national leaders and are resented by many blacks who have been poisoned by the current leaders. Connerly feels that blacks should assimilate into mainstream organizations, stating: "It is not white culture, it's *our* culture" (*Parade* magazine, 31 May 1998). I discussed black issues with my black patients, who by definition, being in my practice were successful and assimilated into the mainstream. They had no answer as to how to bring their entire community past the point of anger and resentment. My suggestion that they go back into the ghetto neighborhoods and act as examples was not well-received. One patient of mine was a prime example. He was one of nine or ten children, and had been helped by his hard-working parents to get a college education, and he ended up in Houston with a good position in a large corporation. A younger teenage brother was sent down by his parents to break up, by the example of living with his older brother, a gang-related set of problems. Younger brother wasn't going anywhere at home and was headed for trouble. It didn't work. After a few months the younger brother went back unchanged, in some way resenting his older brother's middle class lifestyle. Somehow or other the example of successful ethnic groups, culturally pushed to use education for advancement, must be stressed among black people. It works—ask the Jews and the Asians. However, that will have to be accomplished by blacks working with blacks.

A final thought about the value of individual accomplishment from Milton Friedman, Nobel Prize winner in 1976: "The true hope of freedom everywhere is the enterprise, initiative, drive and courage of the individual citizens, cooperating voluntarily with one another, producing the miracle of progress in every sphere that comes only from the achievements of the individual" (*WSJ* book review, 27 May 1998). Individual merit is still the key to a successful society and nation. Whether it is de Tocqueville in the 1830s or Milton Friedman in 1977, the message is the same. It is the individual who is the primary producer. Central government can be a facilitator or a hindrance. In the case of the Great Society, the intentions were good, but the results have been minimal and have hindered the individual by pitting group against group, and piling up regulations which simply get in the way of individual action.

President Clinton, in a commencement address at Portland State University in Oregon, 13 June 1998, (reported in the *Houston Chronicle*, 14 June 1998) pointed out how severe the immigration problem can become, unwittingly undercutting many of the political principles he espouses: "The driving force behind our increasing diversity is a new, large wave of immigration. It is changing the face of America." He noted that in fifty years there will be no majority race in the United States: "No other nation in history has gone through demographic changes of this magnitude in so short a time. What do the changes mean? They can either strengthen and unite America, or they can weaken and divide us. We must decide." Decide what? To continue government-imposed quotas that divide us into groups opposing each other? Continue to weaken our immigrants as we weaken our own population, by telling us that only Washington can find the solutions to help and protect us?

All the while the multicultural intellectuals in their ivory towers have theorized how "bad" our country has been and invented "solutions" that may destroy the innate drive of our society by smothering the very essence of our success, our individuality, and our sense that there is nothing that cannot be conquered. These are far-left extremists, with their feet planted firmly in mid-air. They are protected by tenure, cannot be rooted out, and they dominate the college and university faculties in the country, but they can be shown for what they are and ignored. This is a nation if immigrants, who came here for a purpose, to be free to be successful and they have made a great nation. Those multicultural intellectual elitists have a right to express their ideas only because this nation, founded by immigrants, is wed to the notion of the First Amendment that every idea, no matter how nutty, has the right to be heard and to be evaluated by a clear thinking, educated and informed electorate. The multiculturalists have had their day. The "politically correct" movement is as much a form of thought control as were the McCarthyism communist witch hunts they now decry as an excuse for imposing PC on their campuses. A battle is now being joined—let the most reasoned ideas win.

Chapter Five

"It is Not Nice to Fool Mother Nature"

Human beings are a strange lot. We have been more or less civilized for 5,000-6,000 years, which is as far back as written history goes, and we think that everything on Earth will always stay the same, as it seemingly has remained for those civilized years, a fleeting moment when compared to time elapsed from the Big Bang. The universe goes back perhaps 15 billion years, the sun, 5 billion, and the Earth about 4.5 billion. Tremendous changes have gone on throughout that time. In fact, the key statement for all of us to remember is: "The only thing constant is change." In another 5 billion years the sun is going to blow up, and take the Earth with it. Since we live eighty-plus years, that shouldn't bother us. Until a few hundred years ago all of us were sure that we were at the center of the universe. A few scientists changed all that. The Catholic Church reacted rather violently, history tells us, against Gallileo, Copernicus and Kepler for taking away the Vatican's theologic anthropocentric view of humankind: we were the most significant entity of creation. We may very well be the most significant entity, but not on the grounds that everything seems to revolve around us. Since we see such a little segment of the real passage of time, and since we have never really lost the feeling that we are the center of the Universe, in our self-importance we are guilty of living in the present, as though nothing on Earth can change. We are not taking the responsibility in long range planning regarding our relationship with the Earth, by specifically forgetting that the only thing constant is change.

There is also an even stranger aspect of our self-centered psychology regarding nature and the environment. Not only do we lack insight about constant change, in our egocentric, supposedly omnipotent way we try to stop change and at the same time make huge changes in what Mother Nature has given us. It is as though we refuse to recognize the onward march of fifteen billion years of the universe, and the four billion years of evolutionary progress on Earth. That progress produced us with no direction from us! It also produced an environment with living plants and animals that can take care of themselves and are adaptable to changes that have always been present. In 1988 we tried to stop the forest fires in Yellowstone at an expense of $120 million, despite a decision in the 1970s to let nature take its course and not fight them. The 1970s decision was correct: in 1998 the Yellowstone meadows are abloom with wildflowers and there are carpets of young trees everywhere. How did those forests survive for millions of years without us? They adapted with amazing mechanisms. For example, lodgepole pines seal seeds inside wax-covered cones that open only in the presence of intense heat.

We expect no change, we try to stop change, and at the same time we have created enormous water projects changing the West, impounding water, diverting water, and transporting water, transforming huge areas of our West, and actually creating more change and more problems than were foreseen. One of our responsibilities to the Earth is to realize that we are not more powerful than the mechanisms inherent in nature and our climate. We need to learn to work with the Earth, not with preconceived notions of what the Earth needs, but only after careful scientific study of what is necessary to do to help us and the Earth be cooperative partners. The Earth, with built-in mechanisms of its own, will fight us unless we study those mechanisms, understand them, and undertake projects that conform to them.

I grew up in the east and the furthest west I got was to Chicago for my brother-in-law's wedding, and then finally to Texas to practice. I had always wanted to "go west," and finally got my chance when I began to take long vacations from the clinic I worked in. My wife and I took car trips of two, three and four weeks in length, hopping from national park to national monument, day-hiking down the trails, picnicking at an overlook that made us feel we were living in a postcard or "Kodak moment." I lived the National Geographic travelogues that popped up on television: we'd been there. When you see the Grand Canyon, or go to Yellowstone, you see the immense energy and power that made the Earth as it is today. No one believed the trappers who first came back and described Yellowstone. They were thought to have made it up, perhaps in a drunken stupor. To say that some of our national wonders are awe-inspiring short changes the actual experience. Words cannot really transmit the feelings, the emotional responses I have felt when I look at these natural wonders, when I hike through them, or raft a river.

Not everyone has the responses I have. I am not a "greenie," tree-hugging environmentalist. I don't worry about the tiny snail-darter fish threatened by the TVA dams. Worries about the Houston Toad losing its habitat, as Houston grows, slide right by me. I am much more concerned about the gross misuse of our national resources, currently, and what will be the result for this country in the future. Studies have been done of the bus tours that take people to the rim of the Grand Canyon, stopping there for just an hour or two, before moving on to another natural wonder. Probably the vast majority of people who experience the canyon come in on a tour bus. A much smaller number stay in a hotel at the rim for a day or two, and even less hike, camp in, and/or raft the canyon. Those bus tourists have been timed to spend twenty minutes staring over the rim, and forty minutes in the gift shop, in the hour they have to walk around before having to reboard the bus!

No wonder our Washington folks have been able to so abuse the natural wonders and resources of our country, with only a minor ripple of response from an outraged citizenry. As you will see, the uses and abuses by the Washington politicians and bureaucrats of our national resources all look good at first blush. They do increase our immediate general growth and prosperity. However, there is a conspicuous lack of long range planning. If it works well now, why worry about 150-200 years from now, especially if those considerations might stop the planners from achieving the current show of good works. The advocates of nature do rage on: The Sierra Club, American Rivers, and others. Most of the rest of us are not informed enough to pay attention.

I had no idea of the problems in our western states related to water until I began river rafting as a summer vacation. Spending a week on a river seemed like a delightful idea, after my wife and I had done some river day trips during those driving and hiking vacations. Her idea of camping out was the Holiday Inn, so the first big trip was eight days in June 1982 on the Grand Canyon with my son and another doctor friend. It was a blast and I was hooked. How to get my wife to go the next summer? I spoke with George Wendt, president of O.A.R.S., a wonderful river company with whom we had done the first trip. He suggested the Rogue River in Oregon, staying in riverside lodges at night. He would rent the lodges and run the trip if I set up a group of twenty people or so. Never being faced down by a challenge, and wanting my wife to have a similar experience, that is exactly what I did. The trip was full of adventure, and we slept in cabins at night. On the final night the group asked me where we were rafting next summer. I had a new side job, and every year through 1991, I set up a trip for a group of people on various rivers, coming back to the Grand Canyon every four years, giving newcomers to the group the greatest rafting experience in the country.

If you never have rafted a river, I suggest you try one of the day trips available all over the country. With some adventure in your soul, try and find a trip with paddle rafts. That way you participate with the river guide, and get more of the feel of the river. Next try the Rogue as a four-day lodge trip, if sleeping bags on the shoreline are not appetizing. Actually they are very comfortable with an air mattress underneath. The rapids are quite mild and the scenery is great as you travel between the mountains. For anyone who would like to camp out, six days on the Middle Fork of the Salmon is an ideal beginning. There are outhouses all along the way for the squeamish. They are all two-walled for some privacy, and you can't beat the great scenery. In the middle of the trip there are campgrounds with hot springs, for a little alfresco bathing. Imagine fifteen folks in bathing suits drinking their sodas or beer and passing around a tray of snacks at the end of a fun day on the river. The trip starts up in the Sawtooth mountains of Idaho, around 7,000 feet, loses about a mile in altitude, which means the first nights are crisp and gradually get warmer. The rapids are class two to four, but the fours are all in the lower section allowing you time to train in the paddle raft for them. Rapids are graded from class one, with some ripples, to five which require extreme skill. Class six implies not only the requirement of extreme skill but introduces the moderate chance of injury. The other attribute of the Middle Fork is the opportunity for some good trout fishing. In picking a river company, ask if they take their passengers on side hikes. These are not arduous but open up even more scenery. This is the reason I like rafting over back packing: the rafts carry all the equipment and food, and a side hike only needs a day pack for lunch, your canteen or water bottle, and your camera.

A river trip has another aspect that might not occur to you. There is the enormous silence of the wilderness, except for the creaking of the oar locks, the occasional command of the paddle captain, the time to think and to exchange ideas with each other. People relax, let their civilized guard down, and open up to each other as the days pass. I mentioned earlier that ideas for this book came from discussions with my patients. Other ideas developed on these trips we took together: my patients, my friends, other doctors and the river guides having conversations on the rafts as they drifted along. In the evenings lying out under the stars, staring into that brilliant smog-free sky at our galaxy, the Milky Way, and the Universe, counting satellites as they quietly passed over us, there were more very meaningful exchanges of ideas and ideals. Stress disappeared quickly. A psychiatrist who came on these trips year after year with me recognized that these river floats could be organized for stress-management training. We talked about trying it out, but unfortunately never did. We were both convinced that it would have worked better than group therapy in the cities.

I would not suggest doing a rafting trip on the Colorado River, through the Grand Canyon, until you have tried out a shorter river. You can tour the canyon, as if you are a passenger on a Greyhound Bus by signing up with a company that runs G or H rigs, giant thirty-five-foot rafts made of long pontoons, with a big outboard motor. You will bounce through the rapids, have great meals on the river banks and dash through the inner gorge with that noisy motor in five or six days. If that is the only way your body condition allows, do it. The experience is like nothing else you can do as a tourist. If you want a greater sense of adventure, find a company with oar rafts (also called oar boats), paddle rafts, dories, and tahitis (inflatable kayak-like one- or two-person boats), and make sure they take time for hikes into the side canyons. Some of the most exquisite jewels of natural scenery are hidden there. A Grand Canyon trip is a multifaceted experience done this way. The photo opportunities are endless. The guides will explain the geology, the plants and animals, and they will teach the theory of how to run the rapids, if you ask. They need to know the theory and the practice to handle those rapids, some of the largest ones in North America that can be run. They even teach how to make wonderful meals in a Dutch oven, over carefully counted-out charcoal pieces. They will tell you all about the water problems in our western states.

Elves' Chasm is a little side canyon that looks like it was designed by a leprechaun landscaper: delicate waterfalls, artistically placed rocks, lots of greenery with wild flowers scattered throughout. At one time it had four levels, each different. A flash flood washed out the upper two after my first visit. Havasu Canyon, part of the Havasupai Indian Reservation, was like the Garden of Eden on Earth. The creek arising miles away from a spring at the Indian Village at the East end of the canyon, had three major sets of falls, and a series of travertine falls one to three feet tall, one after the other like a group of wedding cakes, made of crystal clear water, running down the center of a red-wall canyon several hundred feet high, perhaps 100 yards wide, covered with lush vegetation, wild grapes that ran up the canyon walls, flowers everywhere and trees that formed a canopy over your head as you hiked back in. Too hot? Stop and take a dip in one of those wedding-cake pools. The last time I saw Havasu looking like this was late in June 1990. One of our group had a gimmick thermometer to pull the zipper on his shirt. It read 127 degrees. No wonder we spent a lot of time in the pools while hiking three miles to Beaver Falls. When we got to Phoenix to fly out after the trip, we heard that the 737s had been grounded in Phoenix the day we were hiking Havasu. The temperature on the Tarmac was over 135 degrees, and fully loaded 737s were not rated for that temperature. The air is too light when it is that warm. Three weeks later a huge thunderstorm dumped enough water above Havasu Canyon to completely wash out one of the most beautiful spots on Earth. I saw it two years later. It looked like an army of bulldozers had torn their way through. Gone was most of the vegetation and the wedding-cake falls. It was almost bare from wall to wall. Nature does not play favorites.

In July 1984, an O.A.R.S. river trip was derigging at the usual take-out, the normally dry bed of Diamond Creek. Bill Brisbin, who was with us on our 1986 trip, described the scene: They were ready to start the trip up the dry creek, bounce along the dirt road, then through the village on the Hualapai Indian Reservation and onto U.S. 66 for the trip to Flagstaff. A large truck was stacked with deckings off the rafts, which were deflated and on the truck along with the kitchen equipment, the folding tables, camping gear and the very large coolers. The passengers had already left on the old school bus driven by an Indian from the reservation. The crew from another company's trip were just ahead and ready to leave in their vehicle. There were clouds overhead as everyone boarded the vehicles to leave. The sound, like a freight train, suddenly sounded through the canyon: "Flash flood. Run for the canyon walls and climb." Everyone ran to both sides and climbed and clawed their way up about twenty feet. Just as they got to that level, a twelve to fourteen foot wall of water swept by, carrying the vehicles into the river. Several hours later the passengers and crew were able to climb down and find that everyone was okay. The truck was spotted months later during low water downstream. Mother Nature is never fully predictable. The depressions in the plateau above the Grand Canyon collect the thunderstorm rain, which travels slowly downhill until it reaches a side canyon scoured out of the earth by past flash floods, and in that canyon it is funneled into a dangerous flood.

Bill Brisbin was the one reason that the 1986 Grand Canyon Trip was very special for me. Bill had been a guide on our Delores trip the year before (southwest Colorado into Utah). He was a Ph.D. geologist who had studied the Grand Canyon for about twenty-five years, and had become Chairman of the Department of Geology, University of Manitoba, Winnipeg, Canada, with a large bibliography of papers on Earth-formation. He loved rafting and in his mid-50s was trying to become a licensed river guide. What great luck to find him. He was invited to be a guide on the 1986 trip, and he lectured every day on what we were seeing. He took us into Blacktail Canyon where we could touch what was *not* there, the "Earlier Great Unconformity," 450 million years of missing layers in the Canyon. Those layers are found elsewhere in the world. What happened to them in the Grand Canyon? No one knows for sure, but the theory is that there was a prolonged period of erosion. There is also a "later" Great Unconformity, covering about 250 million years of layers, which lies well above the floor of Blacktail Canyon. The Grand Canyon is a mile deep and the lower layers of Vishnu schist along the river are two billion years old. If you hike down from the rim, you are gradually going back in time two billion years, and about every hour on the trail, getting to warmer and warmer micro-climates, all semi-desert until you find water, and then there is lush vegetation.

In Blacktail Canyon he showed us intrusions in the schist that he estimated were 2.5 billion years old! In Deer Creek Canyon, back of Deer Falls, he pointed out fossilized worm borings from an ancient sea bed. He was very circumspect to tell us that the science of geology was about 100 years old, based in great part on the Grand Canyon, and he told us to remember that the scientific material he was presenting represented the academic geologists current thinking, and fifty percent of it would be wrong in ten years, as new discoveries replaced old ones. He also lectured on general topics such as continental drift, plate tectonics, theories on continental changes, and the probable effects of damming the Colorado River on California and the Gulf of California. I asked him when the eight-day trip was over how much college-level geology he had taught us—about three semesters worth: nine hours of geology, right in nature's laboratory, discussing the formation of the earth as we understand it.

The Grand Canyon demonstrates, like nothing else I have ever seen, the power of the geologic changes on Earth combined with a scouring river like the Colorado, carrying its load of silt, which grinds away at the soil and rock. The power of wind, of erosion, of rain and flash floods cutting out side canyons is very apparent. Formation of the canyon started twenty million years ago with the uplifting of the Colorado Plateau and the rivers of the region beginning to slice through forming the eastern portion of the canyon. The western portion started its formation about five million years ago and joined the Gulf of California, which had appeared 5.5 million years ago thanks to subsidence along the San Andreas Fault. That well-known fault is still as active as ever: Western California up to San Francisco and Baja California are headed north toward Alaska, and fifty million years from now will lie as an island off Western Canada, caused by the sliding of the Pacific Plate past the American Plate. As those plates bump and grind, the California earthquakes will continue.

Twenty-five percent of this country is semi-arid desert, one half of our Western States, with most of it in the southwest. The only major surface water source in the area is the Colorado River, which handles the runoff from the western slopes of the Rockies south to the Gulf of California. Seven states have been using the Colorado, recycling the water up to three times, so that by the time it reaches Mexico nothing but a brackish tired little stream is left. Mexico screamed loudly at the unfairness—they were not getting their allotted share and it is salty. We have had to build an expensive desalinization plant to satisfy our treaty with them. In California and Arizona deep wells are supplying water also. The aquifer under Maricopa County, think Phoenix, is being rapidly depleted. The aquifer in California may well last longer, since that state has so much surface water to use. Further east the Ogallala aquifer, the largest in the world (stretching from a couple of hundred miles east of El Paso in Texas to the northern boundary of Nebraska), has made the "dust bowl" of the 1930s into extremely productive farm land. Farmers may pull five feet of water a year out of the ground, while natural replacement is about a quarter of an inch a year. A reservoir of water in the aquifer that took a half a million years to build up is being allowed to disappear. From the time they started pumping in earnest in 1960, the states in the area have regulated water consumption so the aquifer would last thirty to one hundred years. Early in the next century, either there will have to be enormous river diversion projects completed to keep that farm land from going dry, and to supply water for the rapidly growing populations of the southwest or the growth has to stop.

The U.S. Census Bureau announced, in March 1998, the fastest growing counties in the country from the 1990 census to 1 July 1997. Despite the problems with water supply, seven of the top ten were in the dry southwest: Maricopa in Arizona was number one, Clark (Las Vegas) in Nevada number two; southern California had five. The other three were Harris in Texas (Houston), Broward in Florida (Fort Lauderdale), and Dallas in Texas (Dallas). The growth in Maricopa, 574,097, far outstripped Clark, 364,679, which was just ahead of Harris, 339,994. Obviously the common factor is that these locations are all warm weather destinations.

The federal government, through two of its bureaucracies, the Bureau of Reclamation and the Army Corps of Engineers, has impounded and redirected surface water all over the west to help create this population growth. The mission of the Bureau of Reclamation is just what the title suggests—create reservoirs to supply irrigation water for land that could otherwise not grow crops, due to lack of rain. Along the way they added hydroelectric generating power, which is the product that really pays for the dams. The Corps of Engineers have as their responsibility flood control, and the creation of navigable waterways along rivers, digging canals, and dredging harbors. Note that both agencies have to build dams to accomplish their missions. The bureau started as the Reclamation Service in 1902, and became a Bureau as its responsibilities grew with the number of projects it created. The Army Corps of Engineers was officially begun in 1794, with military and civilian branches, the latter responsible for the waterways. The corps concentrated its work primarily in the east and midwest, but in the 1930s moved into the west and developed an intense rivalry with the bureau.

Marc Reisner's book, *Cadillac Desert* (1986), 500 hundred densely-packed pages, representing 10 years of research, is a monumental exposé of our government's efforts to turn the west green, and how this effort has failed to consider the future. His story of what has been done with the available water in the southwest is a macrocosm of pork barrel politics as it is practiced in this country by our politicians and bureaucrats. In short, the water supply has been raped to satisfy large business agriculture, and to seduce folks who are seeking a warmer climate to move into the area. Think how that pleases the real estate developers!

Dams have been utilized in the east since the country began, but the big push to dam the west started with the Hoover Dam, authorized in 1928 and completed by 1936. According to Reisner, as the bureau raced to complete dams, the size of this agency grew from 2,000-3,000 people under Herbert Hoover to almost 20,000 employees by the time Franklin Roosevelt died. In the dry southwest, in the first thirty years of the bureau "it built 3 dozen projects. During the next thirty years, it built 19 dozen more." In the meantime the Corps of Engineers was working in the Pacific Northwest, where there was a good supply of water to control those rivers. The two agencies then entered into an open rivalry. Reisner says that "No one will ever know how many ill-conceived water projects *were* built by the Bureau and the Corps simply because one agency thought the other would build it first." He carefully documents a number of these foolish projects. By the early 1980s just about every available site for a dam or water project had been completed. In 1985 the bureau was operating 333 reservoirs, 345 diversion dams with all the attached pipelines, canals pumping stations, and tunnels. Michael P. Ghiglieri's book, *Canyon* (1992), presents his view as a veteran river guide, and captures the foolishness of the rivalry: "Sev-

enty-four and four tenths percent of the Colorado River water
used in the United States and sold at 10% of its development
cost goes directly into maintaining roughly 15 million cows,
the most expensive cows on this planet." My wife and I have
had the wonderful experience of rafting the canyon with Mike.
The other guides refer to him as "Doc" or "The Doctor." He
is a Ph.D. and a research zoologist, having done his doctoral
work on chimpanzees in Uganda. He is not shallow, or emotional about the environment. He brings a scientist's intellect
to the problems of the west. His book complements Reisner's
in presenting what has happened.

In fairness to the Bureau of Reclamation, those dams are
not just about water. The cheap hydroelectric power coming
on stream in the 1930s is a vital resource for the entire west
that has no important adverse side effects in and of itself. The
Grand Coulee Dam, completed in 1941, played a major role
in winning WWII by supplying huge amounts of electricity to
the aluminum plants and the airplane manufacturers of the
west. Remember that as recently as the 1930s, one of Roosevelt's
important initiatives was the Rural Electrification Administration. Large areas of our countryside had no electricity, strange
as that may seem now. Selling electric power is the major way
the hyrdoelectric projects are being paid for. They are called
"cash register dams," which sounds like a derisive term, but
they should not be considered that way. Electricity is now in
short supply in the west with population growth. Brownouts
do occur, but electric power generating plants of various types
can be added, even if there are no more hydropower sites to be
developed and even if that electricity will have to be sold at
higher cost.

The big issue is water, and the coming shortage of it. Both
the Bureau of Reclamations and the Corps of Engineers knew
years ago that at some point water would have to be diverted
from the Columbia River Basin, Western Canada, and even
Alaska to keep feeding the growth of a thirsty southwest.
Remember the motto of Seattle: Washingtonians don't tan,
they rust. Ketchikan in Alaska gets rain 320 days a year. Reisner
makes the point that many projects appear to have been built
primarily because of the agencies' rivalry, not because they

were economically or geologically feasible: "Had they really cooperated there is no telling what they might have built. Their rivalry prevailed, and grew more intense. The money invested in the dozens of relatively small projects each agency built—in many cases because the other threatened to build first—would have sufficed to build the great works they insisted were necessary. A diversion from the Columbia River to the southwest could have been built for $6 billion or so in the 1960s. Today (1986) the cost seems utterly prohibitive, and Washington and Oregon would probably resist the engineers with tanks." Reisner notes that the seven Ogallala states and the Colorado Basin states all have expected a bail-out by the federal government. That bail-out currently is not in the offing.

The issue is not just bringing in more water. There are major problems associated with dams in the west and using water for irrigation or drinking. Water in the southwest desert carries salt, and irrigated areas in California are being damaged and withdrawn from production, because the style of irrigation has involved flooding water along channels in the fields, bringing in more water than is needed and depositing salt at a higher rate than should be allowed. In volcanic areas the water can pick up selenium, which is a vital trace element, but is poisonous in large amounts. Selenium is picked up by growing plants from the soil. Llamas living in the Andes, where there is a line of volcanoes, have adapted to and need two to eight milligrams a day because of eating plants with a high selenium content, but humans can tolerate only one-fortieth of two milligrams. Another issue: if the water is to be used for drinking is asbestos. The fibers are leached out of rock by surface water and are considered a cause of colon cancer. "Background" asbestos fibers can easily be removed from water meant for drinking by filtering, making that concern a minor issue. A major issue however, is silt. All rivers carry silt, and all dammed streams are forced to deposit that silt in the reservoir. Before the Glen Canyon Dam began trapping silt that was headed for Hoover Dam, Lake Mead had lost 5.28% of its capacity in the first twenty-seven years. Now Lake Mead will last much longer, but the rated life of Lake Powell may be as short as 316 years, according to Ghiglieri, before Glen Canyon waterfall appears. In other words, a tremendous portion of the works created by the bureau and the corps is not permanent. Removing all that silt is way too expensive. In 300 to 500 years all their projects impounding water will be gone, some smaller projects well before that time, and because those smaller projects were built between 1930 and 1970, they are all going to go out together! Quite a legacy for the future citizens of our country.

An example of the "fixes" to come in the future, and poor 1960s planning in the past, during the height of the rivalry with the Corps of Engineers, is a 1960s Bureau of Reclamation project, the Lake Meredith Reservoir, which is the Texas Panhandle's only major lake (*Houston Chronicle,* 13 April 1998). When the Sanford Dam was built on the Canadian River in the 1960s, the bureau knew the water would be salty. The lake water now has about seventy-five percent more salt than allowed by federal standards for tap water. There is a brine aquifer that leaks into the Canadian River close to the Texas border in New Mexico. The cities in the area—Lubbock, Amarillo, Plainview, Pampa, Dumas, have been using part of the Ogallala aquifer. Residents in Roberts County, a rural farming area, have fought, without success, the pumping of their aquifer water to the cities. Now the bureau, in 1998 (over 30 years later), is drilling wells in Roberts County to come on line in 2000 to mix reservoir water with thirty percent well water to lower the salt level delivered to the cities. This is just an interim fix! The bureau recognizes the obvious, that the Roberts aquifer must not be depleted; they must make the reservoir water potable, somehow. Therefore, they are also planning to tap the brine aquifer, to reduce pressure in it by diverting the salt water 3,000 feet into the ground. The lowering of pressure should reduce or stop the amount of salt water now entering the river. Hopefully they know in advance where that salt water will end up. But that is not the end of the story! The salt build up is so big in the lake, they estimate it will take ten years to have enough fresh water flow into the lake to dilute the salt level back to proper levels! At that point they can shut down the Roberts County wells and stop depleting the aquifer. The Bureau estimate of a ten million dollar cost for this rectification project is probably way low, if the past history of bureau estimates is any guide. The problem should have been solved in the 1960s as part of the original project or the dam never built. Excluding the salt issue, the concept at that time was reasonable enough, using surface water in the area rather than depleting the aquifer. The only positive benefit so far is that the lake and some surrounding area was declared a national recreation area for the citizens of the region so they can boat, swim and fish. The negative effects are the attraction of an enlarging population, now running out of potable water, a fight over water between the cities and Roberts County, and a law suit by the Sierra Club which is worried over the loss of a rare minnow. Shades of the snail darter (a tiny fish) and Tellico Dam was another unnecessary mess in the T.V.A. system in the 1970s.

In the southwestern area the weather can be very hot and very dry, which makes the heat much more comfortable. The air is so dry there is no perspiration perceptible on your skin. The guides on the Grand Canyon warned us to watch the color of our urine, and to drink more water if it got too yellow. At the rate that the invisible sweating occurred, one could dehydrate before thirst warned you to catch up. No wonder that one major issue in southwest water supply is loss from evaporation; the large surface areas of the reservoirs increase the loss. There is further loss in the canals and aqueducts that transport water. There is more loss in the style of irrigating, surface flooding of the fields, and spraying water to create artificial rain. Spraying results in a fifty percent loss from evaporation. Our government, by seemingly guaranteeing an endless supply of water, convinced our farmers not to conserve. Conservation measures have been developed in Israel: the Israelis use ninety-five percent of the water that is available each year from Yam Kinneret (Sea of Galilee), a five by ten-mile lake which receives its water from the snow melt off Mt. Hermon in Syria. The water travels under the hills of Galilee in three tunnels to the south, where it is piped to the agricultural fields with drip irrigation, and computer control. Further, they are replanting the cedar and pine forests that were cut down two thousand years ago, and are changing the climate back to what it was. On our visit to Israel in the 1980s, we were delightfully inconvenienced by two thunderstorms in Jerusalem in June. It is not possible, but I wish we could change our southwestern weather pattern like that. I doubt that we can drip irrigate all the golf courses that draw people to Arizona and Nevada.

According to the U.N. Conference on Water and Sustainable Development in Paris, France (March 1998), ten countries, ours included, have sixty percent of the world's drinking water. It is not surprising, considering our lack of conservation, to find that the use of water in this country is 150 gallons per person per day, compared to fifty gallons for Europeans and seven and a half gallons for each African. The title of the conference also contains another lesson for us. "Sustainable development" is exactly what we have not done in our western states.

Dams can be dangerous. The great Johnstown Flood of 31 May 1889, gave way before heavy rains and drowned 2,500 people. From Reisner's book are the following stories: despite presumably improved engineering knowledge as the years passed, Los Angeles lost the Saint Francis Dam on 12 March 1928, drowning about 450 people, and destroying 1,200 homes; in September 1965, Fontenelle Dam sprung a huge leak, but rapid emptying of the reservoir saved the dam which was then successfully repaired; on 5 June 1976, the 305 foot Teton Dam collapsed, and all the water behind it released. Luckily it was day time, warnings went out and only eleven people died. Four thousand homes were damaged or destroyed; 350 businesses were destroyed. Damage estimates reached $2 billion.

This final account told with glee by the Colorado River guides with details added from Mike Ghiglieri's book. In June 1983, the bureau almost lost the Glen Canyon Dam. They had allowed the reservoir to become overfilled, considering they had been warned by the weather department that the snow pack in the Rockies was much larger than normal after the 1982-83 El Nino winter. In a frantic attempt to lower the water level in Lake Powell, they opened wide the spillways, which travel around the dam through the canyon walls, only to see huge sheets of lining concrete spin out. They then opened the turbine channels, slowed the spillway flow and put an eight foot barrier of 4 by 8¾-inch-thick plywood sheets at the top of the dam, which held the water from coming over the top of the dam, as they slowed the emptying through the spillways. If the spillways had become gouged out, the dam might have failed. If water came over the top, the dam would have failed. Luckily by July first the bureau saved the dam. The eight other dams downstream were flooded, causing millions of dollars in property damage. Repairs to the dam cost thirty-five million dollars. Consider this: if that dam had been lost, most likely Hoover Dam and the seven others would have been taken out. It is hard to imagine how southern California would fare after that. As with the Teton Dam loss, no one at the bureau was fired; the news of all this was played down as much as possible, so most of the country never heard of what almost happened, and the fiasco was blamed on a computer program. Humans write the software, humans put in the information, humans make the judgments. Bureaucrats cannot blame themselves— the computer did it!

The river guides tell the Glen Canyon Dam fiasco story with glee because they hate the dam. It inundated Glen Canyon, one of the most beautiful canyons in the country, with a 190 mile lake, and it changed the ecology of the river through the Grand Canyon. At the time the dam was built (it was finished in 1963), there were no mandated environmental protections to be studied. The first Environmental Policy Act appeared in 1969. The managers of the dam dumped water when it was needed and ran the turbines to meet peaks and valleys in the electric power demand. The water in the canyon surged up and down, severely damaging the beaches and the general ecology of the canyon along the river. Years of complaining and an expensive ecologic study finally approved, in the mid-1990s, a much more regulated pattern of release of water. The environmental protections also stopped the Corps of Engineers from draining wetlands all over the west to produce more farmland.

All of this points out that there are short-term and long-term unintended consequences to changing natural resources, a fact which finally occurred to humans more than forty years after we started to change the face of our west so radically.

Only then did we start to demand environmental impact studies (Hoover Dam was authorized by Congress in 1928, and the first Environmental Policy Act passed in 1969). For example, the work done on the Mississippi Basin by the corps and bureau has resulted in cutting the silt load reaching the delta by one-half. The Mississippi Delta, the size of New Jersey, is now rapidly shrinking, according to Reisner, and one-third will disappear in the next few decades. Bill Brisbin, during our discussions of the 1986 Canyon trip, pointed out that the land at the north end of the Gulf of California is subsiding. This is due to the Pacific Plate sliding under the North American Plate, as the Pacific Plate also moves north. It is this process that originally created the gulf. It is this geologic change that destines the Imperial Valley and Salton Sea of Southern California to eventually be taken over by the Gulf of California as it creeps north. Now that Colorado silt is not reaching the north end of the gulf, the northward creep will move faster. Like the Dutch, Californians will have to dike the bottom of their state. Geologic processes take centuries, but that should not stop us for recognizing long term effects. We must stop living in our own little moment of eternity and see what we are doing to the Earth which is to be inhabited by future humans.

Our nation has created an environmental and economic monster out of our western states, all in the name of progress. The cost to future generations in solving the many inherent problems *will* be monstrous. I view what was done as a very high stakes game, with big winners and big losers, involving billions and billions of dollars. Besides the losers of the future, who will have to spend enormous sums just to maintain the west as it is now, there are the current losers: the taxpayers of this country who do not live in the west. The cost of their water supply and electric bills are several times greater than the lucky citizens of the west. Is it fair that general tax funds were used so a portion of our population could move west, while the rest stayed put, and were stuck with higher utility bills at the same time? Congress did pay lip service to the unfairness, and the regional projects were expected to be handled in an economically feasible method, with a return to the treasury of at least the initial costs and the operating expenses. In *Cadillac Desert*, Reisner offers several examples to show that did not happen.

The bureau, in the mid-1950s, charged irrigation farmers water at fifteen dollars an acre-foot (an acre-foot is the volume of a foot of water covering an acre), one-fifth the cost of water for New York City, and Reisner implies that price did not rise by the time his book was published in 1986. An example of his described charges for electric power: "In 1974, $196.01 worth of power from Con Edison in New York would have cost $24 if purchased from Seattle City Light." These low prices amounted to subsidies to the agriculture industry in the central valley of California. In the westlands portion of that valley, from a 1985 economic study, Reisner states that the subsidy amount is "something like $217 per acre per year; the average annual *revenue* produced by an acre of Westlands land is only $290. This means that 70 percent of the (gross) profit on what is supposed to be some of the richest farmland in the world comes solely through taxpayer subsidization—not crop production." As a result of these subsidies, Reisner states that the Central Valley Project of California is "at least hundreds of millions if not billions of dollars in debt." He blames Congress primarily: they authorized the project, they approved the Westlands contract, and they continually allowed the subsidies to be enlarged. The bureau acted with congressional authority and with congressional oversight. Both the Bureau of Reclamation and Congress are at fault with *our* money. In Reisner's opinion, much of these subsidies were illegal: "Illegal subsidies enrich big farmers, whose excess production depresses crop prices nationwide and whose waste of cheap water creates an environmental calamity that could cost billions to solve." Reisner fails to note that the depression of crop prices may trigger price support payments from the government to farmers, the ultimate irony in this ludicrous scenario.

I agree with Reisner that our country should have developed an infrastructure in the west to allow feasible agricultural growth and the growth of population. However, what has happened goes far beyond feasibility. According to Reisner, "We overreached ourselves. What we achieved may be spectacular; in another sense, though, we achieved the obverse of our goals. The Bureau of Reclamation set out to help the small farmers of the west, but ended up making a lot of rich farmers even wealthier. We set out to tame rivers and ended up killing them. We set out to make the future of the American west secure; what we really did was make ourselves rich and our descendants insecure."

All the while, the Army Corps of Engineers is still at it, as pointed out by Bruce Upbin in *Forbes* magazine (23 March 1998). To summarize his article: Pushed by the Midwest Area River Coalition 2000, a lobbying arm for barge companies, the Corps just completed a $49 million study of upper Mississippi River congestion, looking at the need for replacement locks based on projected traffic till the year 2050, each larger lock to cost between 250 million and one billion dollars, with seven locks predicted to be needed by 2025. One problem, as with many of the water projects, is massive taxpayer subsidies: the barge fuel taxes cover only ten percent of the corps annual spending of $674 million of building and maintaining the waterways, exclusive of new projects like the Mississippi locks. In comparison, the railroads cover their own cost of maintenance of right of way, and the trucking industry covers most, if not all, the damage they do to the interstates through fuel taxes and user fees. In the 1940s, the corps made the Missouri River navigable from Sioux City, Iowa to St. Louis, Missouri, estimating an annual river traffic of twelve million tons. Traffic in 1997 was only 1.5 million tons. Upbin describes a 234-mile canal constructed in 1985 between the Tennessee and Tombigbee rivers in Mississippi and Alabama, based on a forecast of twenty-seven million tons a year. By 1997, only nine million tons were carried. Initial cost was 1.8 billion plus $22 million a year for maintenance. There is no clear reason why the taxpayers of the country need to subsidize these private commercial carriers, just because they use the waterways. It is another subsidy primarily for the agricultural industry. There is another approach to this whole project, ignored by the Corps of Engineers, since they are accustomed to an unlimited supply of taxpayer money. Treat the existing locks as airports handle the airlines. Simply schedule the barges going through, instead of the first-come, first-serve system currently used, and according to Upbin, relief of the congestion can be obtained with the current lock system. Minor changes of existing locks would also help.

The big losers of this high stakes water reclamation/electricity production game are the taxpayers of the country, the taxpayers of the future, and the environmentalists who mourn the loss of beautiful areas such as Glen Canyon and Hetch Hetchy Valley. Hetch Hetchy, just north of now crowded Yosemite Valley, is reputed to have been just as gorgeous before it was dammed in the 1920s. There has been serious talk of removing the dam and allowing the valley to return to its original state. At the least it would help the crowding at Yosemite, after all the silt was removed. There have been tongue-in-cheek discussions of blowing up Glen Canyon Dam because Glen Canyon was so beautiful.

Winners in the big water reclamation/electricity production game are many. Representing big business, a *Forbes* magazine editorial in the same 23 March 1998 issue, described the Sierra Club suggestion of decommissioning the Glen Canyon Dam and draining Lake Powell as an "astonishingly goofy idea." The editorial listed the dam's benefits: helping supply water to twenty million people, electricity for 5.6 million, flood control and extra water for droughts. The Glen Canyon National Recreation Area has 2.5 million visitors a year. A caption under a picture of Lake Powell describes its beauty. I'm told the empty canyon was more beautiful in a different way. No, we cannot give in to the Sierra Club and go back. It is too late. But the *Forbes* editorial ignores the problems of the future, looking only at the benefits to the current winners: the real estate developers, the construction companies, the resorts, the agricultural interests, in fact, the creation of the equivalent of a whole new country, and in a capitalistic society the generation of huge wealth. The issue is not whether this is a "sustainable development"; we have the intellect and the driving American character to solve the problems. The issue is the initial lack of future planning and the subsequent costs.

Congress is an obvious winner. They are using our money to create these marvelous projects, which are developing the

country into a wonderland. No matter how harsh the environment, they will see that it is softened for us. We can now move
anywhere in the country, and all the possible problems in that
new region are solved. This is pork barrel politics at its worst.
It brings in big campaign contributions from the corporations
benefited. It sells to the public the impulse to re-elect Congress members who have brought all this largesse to the districts involved. In thinking through the total implications of
what they are doing, the average Congressman appears to have
a time horizon of his next election. Pork barrel politics is
simply a daisy chain of bribery, with the voting public never
fully understanding what the future may hold. Everything is
glorified for today, and again perception becomes reality.

The Bureau of Reclamation and the Corps of Engineers
are also huge winners, but in a way you might not imagine.
Before explaining why I think the bureaucrats of those two
government agencies are winners, we need to discuss human
nature, and I want you to apply what I describe to your own
feelings about your personality, your temperament, your character—in other words, what you think your instinctual tendencies do to control you.

Our species, Homo Sapiens, has been around for about
250,000 years. We threw the Neanderthals out of Europe and
caused them to go extinct about 50,000 years ago. Most of us
lived as hunter-gatherer tribes, in which the men hunted and
the women gathered nuts, fruit, and edible wild plants. Using
western culture for the timetable, about eight to ten thousand
years ago agriculture began, and with the advent of written
language, civilization and its history appeared four thousand
years ago. Civilization hasn't spread everywhere. Head hunters
disappeared during this century. There are still hunter-gatherer tribes in remote areas around the world. For most of us in
the western world we stopped being hunter-gatherers in just a
blink of the eye, when compared to the several million years of
Hominid evolution that produced us. There hasn't been the
time needed to change the genetically controlled parts of our
personality. Our temperaments and our reactions to the chal-

lenges and perceived dangers of our environment have to be about the same as when we were living in groups of twenty to thirty trusted tribe members, constantly wary of trouble and threats. Maasi children in east Africa have a common nightmare that would be rare in this country: dreaming they are being eaten by a lion.

It makes sense to try and study how evolution might have prepared our instinctual behavior and our thought patterns to the problems of living. Evolutionary psychology is just such an approach, and as a science is now in early development, amid much controversy. It is a difficult field of research. There are no fossils of mental attitudes. I think this new science is of value because the science of evolutionary medicine has been around longer and, although also controversial, Evolutionary Medicine, as a scientific discipline, has a straightforward way of checking theories that work. Researchers use studies of hunter-gatherer tribes; for example, diet and exercise patterns, and apply those patterns and diets to current day humans, who, because of one condition or another, might benefit. For example, an eating pattern of a typical hunter-gatherer would be to nibble snacks during the day, usually of high fiber, high roughage, and low in fat. Then, gather with the family/tribe at sundown for a larger meal. When this eating pattern is applied to the diabetic, blood sugar control is better. Incidentally, fruit sugar (fructose) doesn't need insulin to be used by the body. High fiber diets reduce cholesterol and the incidence of colon cancer in modern humans, problems which are due to our current diets. Exercise also has a multitude of beneficial effects such as helping to lower blood pressure. High blood pressure is another modern affliction related to modern diet, which is higher in salt and lower in potassium. It is only logical that evolution prepared our bodies for constant exercise and our digestion tracts for the hunter-gather diet, requirements of life that were present for hundreds of thousand of years.

How long does evolution take to make changes? I have an example from a medical problem that plagues some citizens of our country but not others. There are some biologic differences among the different races. Fifty to seventy percent of adult Americans of African descent have trouble digesting milk.

Thirty to fifty percent of Mediterranean origin Americans have the same trouble. But our northern European citizens usually don't have this trouble (about fifteen percent). The answer to these differences is the length of time milk herds have existed in the given regions. In the hunter-gatherer cultures the babies were weaned by age two. Lactase, the enzyme in the intestine that digests lactose (milk sugar), would then disappear by age fifteen or so, with about fifteen percent of adults maintaining lactase throughout life. But in Northern Europe, milk herds were developed 35-50,000 years ago; I'm told as reindeer, but I have never verified the animal type. Around the Mediterranean, goat herds appeared about 10-15,000 years ago, and in Africa, cattle herds used for milk started 2-3,000 years ago. The adults in these regions, given enough time, gradually redeveloped, through evolution, the persistence of lactase in their digestive tracts since milk was a valuable food source. But it took 35-50,000 years to have eighty-five to ninety percent of Scandinavians reverse the original evolutionary arrangement from fifteen percent persistence of lactase. In the Mediterranean area only fifty percent of the current population can drink milk, and in Africa about fifteen percent of its people can handle milk, essentially no change so far. Milk was a valuable food source, but not absolutely vital. Something of greater importance to the human species might have caused evolution to work more quickly. Note how we can come to understand biologic differences in people from different areas of the world just by looking back at evolutionary history. As an aside, I have to admire American entrepreneurship: there are all kinds of lactase substitutes on the market to add to milk products so everyone can digest milk.

Another example of using evolutionary medicine to explain a medical condition is the problem of heart failure. The term "heart failure" is a terrible choice of words. The heart doesn't just quit in this condition, it fails to keep up the proper pumping volume of blood circulation. The odd part is that the result is the over-collection of fluid in the body. Part of the accumulation of fluid is due to back pressure from the sluggish heart, squeezing water out of the blood through the walls of tiny veins. But the major culprit is kidney function. The kidneys are very sensitive to the pumping volume rate of the heart, and they normally receive twenty percent of the blood pumped each minute. When that volume reduces, the kidneys interpret that as a loss of the total volume of blood in the body, and retain water from urine production in order to increase blood volume by simple dilution, the same trick that is used in ERs. The victim comes in to the ER with blood loss and a very low blood pressure: I.V.s are quickly given to expand blood volume, and raise blood pressure to salvage the patient until replacement blood transfusions can be given. Now think about this in terms of evolutionary medicine. The stone age human is injured and loses blood. Evolution taught the kidneys to be our ER and restore blood volume until our bone marrow could replace the red blood cells. Now we live so long, our hearts fail to keep up, and the kidneys misinterpret the situation, doing what they learned to do, now for the wrong reason.

It does not take a great leap of logic to apply this same kind of evolutionary thinking to our minds and the construction of our personalities. Thus the science of evolutionary psychology has appeared and it makes sense to me to apply it to all of us today. Not enough time has passed to change our brains and the instincts that come with it from our evolutionary background. Four thousand to six thousand years removed from being savages or partially civilized people is not long enough to have changed us much. The Holocaust in Europe and the "Killing Fields" of Cambodia indicate that the veneer of civilization is still quite thin, and human minds can be quite savage. Therefore, I think we each still work with the mind of a cave dweller.

I asked you to think about yourself as we entered this section. I would like you to imagine yourself living in a hunter-gatherer tribe, in a makeshift hut or cave. Your *entire* world is dangerous—not only the flesh eating animals that are wandering around hoping to make you their next meal. There are also rival tribes, and they would like nothing better than taking what you have, possibly killing you in the process. The chief instinct you have is survival, self-protection and the protection of your family, and then secondarily, contributing to the strength and the protection of the tribe. Cooperation with tribal members has been posed by the environmental psychologists as a zero-sum game. You protect them and they watch out for you. You have to contribute some of the spoils of your hunt, but then they give up some food also. In other words, everyone wins and no one loses, although everyone gives up something from individual total independence and total selfishness in order to gain membership in the strength and protection of the group. Don't forget the flip side to this. You are just as much a killer as the folks in the neighboring tribes. You would just as soon take what they have, aggressively murdering if you have to. You will kill to protect your tribe, and you expect the tribe to kill for you or your family. Now come back to the present for a moment: does road rage surprise you? We read about case upon case of momentary rage leading to an unpremeditated murder on or off the road. I have seen the survival instinct at the time of death. I remember the eighty-seven-year-old man struggling to breathe as the fresh heart attack slowed his heart. I was at the bedside in his home as a senior medical student, assisting the private physician. As he was dying he said to me, "I know I am dying, I am ready for it. Why am I struggling so hard to breathe?" Because our mind and body is prepared by evolution to struggle to survive. Our civilized veneer (as thin as it is) is trying to hold back tendencies from the Stone Age. We must necessarily have been very self-centered in the early Stone Age, very self-indulgent ,but the logic of group strength gradually allowed us to work together and the desire to work in small groups has become comfortable, and perhaps to some degree instinctual.

Herding together is certainly an instinct in animals. Take cows for example. They are prey animals and they seem to know it. They group together for strength against flesh-eating intruders and mother cows will bunch as a team to drive off an invading dog. They will cooperatively baby-sit a group of calves, while the mother cows go off to graze. At times they will even allow another's calf to nurse. But put out grain in the feed troughs and they will fight and jostle for position, and woe to the calf that gets in the way, four hooves in the air as it is tossed aside.

Judeo-Christian teachings that we all sin are simply a recognition that we come from a savage background, with noncivilized tendencies that are difficult to control. The moral and ethical precepts of both the Old and New Testaments are summarized in the moral guide to treat your neighbor as you would yourself, the "do unto others" admonition. How successful have the teachings been? To find out, I asked this question of a number of psychiatrists over several years: how many of your patients truly seem to follow the Ten Commandments, exclusively guiding their life by them? There should be basic truths that the patient presents about himself in the privacy of psychiatric interviews, as he opens up his deepest feelings for review and help. The psychiatrists all estimated that only five to ten percent of their patients lived up to my question. Moral and ethical religious principles have not been around long enough for evolution to have a chance to change us. Put in computer terms (and our brain is a fabulously complicated computer), we have been given all the software programs we need, but not the hardware that will willingly accept it. Psychopaths, very dangerous people without a conscience, appear to be that way because the area of their brain, which should have accepted the moral teachings that create a person's conscience by age twelve to fourteen, either doesn't work or isn't present.

Psychologists present the concept that our personalities are forty percent inherited, forty percent learned from family and neighborhood culture, and twenty percent an amalgam taken from the other eighty percent and put together by the individual to complete the job of creating a personality. The inherited part appears to be our temperament, how aggressive or passive we are, how optimistic or pessimistic, how outgoing or reserved, and so on. Our character is the learned part, and how we control or change our temperament depends on how much strength is developed in the character portion, and I think that is a function of the amalgamation process. Each person's control over his baser instinctual behavior depends on how strongly the individual views the value of that control. Even so, our emotions will give us hidden agendas in our decision-making, and we may not recognize or be willing to recognize the slant we are allowing in our evaluations. We all have emotional biases. Polls of the American public demonstrate this all the time. They ask questions of people who identify themselves as republicans or democrats, and find that in presenting issues about Washington "scandals" in which there is much heat but essentially no proven facts, the two sets of party followers will find reasons to accept their side's "facts."

There is one other facet of our evolution from hunter-gatherers, that is tribal group size as it affects our social and business groups now. The Stone Age tribe was generally no more than thirty individuals. When professionals such as physicians try to form groups they run into patterns of problems. The individual doctors are stand-alone people. They are self-sufficient and can provide a service and create their own income all by themselves. In many ways they are like the cave man hunting on his own. In fact, doctors become so sure of themselves they have the worst private pilot record in the country. They can outthink the thunder storms! In forming small groups, each person must be willing to give up a segment of his self-control to the will of the group, as with the hunter. This works fine until the group grows over five individuals. From a size of five to fifteen these groups tend to become unstable, as members with strong egos are added and factions may form. Once over fifteen, a group gains a strength of numbers, and if one or two people leave, the group size maintains the life of the group, as long as efficiencies of size appear to be guaranteeing a stable income for everyone. The group now grows relatively serenely, as the effect of a disruptive member is diluted out by size. But at the size of thirty and above, trouble appears again. Going above this membership size requires layers of command, formation of committees, even communication by memo. Unless this transition is done smoothly, it can be very disruptive, and many groups choose to stay smaller rather than go through these problems. Bigger is not always better.

What this means to me is that we are more comfortable and perhaps more efficient in smaller cooperative groups, socially or in business. We are more comfortable with members of "our" tribe. This has important implications in our country's problems in race relations. We are more comfortable with people of "our own kind." I think this is a very unfortunate holdover from our Stone Age days. Remember the tribal size of thirty. That limiting number appears to have been around for thousands of centuries. And this has important implications for corporate and bureaucratic growth. Size never guarantees the efficiencies of size. A giant corporation can demand a lower unit cost for purchases because of the size of the orders, but the office structure, with echelons of command, may be very inefficient. The same is true in bureaucracies; how inefficient must the business practices be in the Defense Department with those infamous toilet seats, costing hundreds of dollars?

I hope that you have been comparing your own self-analysis of your temperament and overall personality to the patterns I have described. I am completely convinced that all of us have these evolutionary drives as part of our makeup, and we each deal with them in different ways, some of us struggling harder than others to be more "civilized," more moral, more ethical, more caring of others.

And now, why are the bureaucrats of the Bureau of Reclamation and the Corps of Engineers such big winners? Let's imagine the life of a bureaucrat at work, but first by describing the probable attributes of someone who applies for work with our national government. This analysis can also be applied to applicants for corporate positions, with the only major difference being the possible patriotic drive of some individuals who go to Washington with a burning desire to improve the country. I doubt if people who seek work with the federal government consider that the Civil Service Laws make it more difficult to fire an employee than in a private corporation, but that is another difference. At the IRS senate hearings, 1 May 1998, Commissioner Charles Rossotti stated that the entire federal government had fired only sixteen senior managers since 1979, offering that as evidence of how difficult it is under civil service rules to buck the entrenched bureaucracy. Most problem employees are either transferred or allowed to retire. Applicants for this type of work are not risk takers, at least not anywhere near the level of true entrepreneurial people. Otherwise, among them there should be the standard range of optimists and pessimists, aggressive and passive, outgoing and reserved characteristics in the temperaments. They probably like to please, to operate in controlled situations, work within the rules that are set out, and play the game. They do not like making mistakes in general, but especially since they want topnotch evaluations of their work by superiors. They would not place themselves in the constraints of this kind of work unless they felt they were team players when they applied.

Please remember that I am positing a generalization. There will always be individuals who don't fit the mold; humans are too variable for that not to happen, but they will be at extremes of the bell-shaped curve that describes all biologic attributes. There will be some very ambitious people who enter government service, help write laws (while on a congressional staff) or write regulations, and then as experts on the convolutions of these instruments, go out into private practice as consultants, and help their clients either comply with the regulations or find ways around them! It's like the fox guarding the hen house. Think of the incomes they now command. The more you think about it, the more perversions like this will appear to you.

When my patients and I would discuss how tense they were because of their occupations within corporations, I would remind them that they had chosen a corporate nest with all of its benefits and protections, and in so doing had given up a fair portion of control over their lives. As a form of counselling, I asked the question: was that loss of control, and the attendant worry and stress worth it? Did the patient feel he had enough courage to start a business on his own? There is no right or wrong answer for the patient, just some guidance to show him that he must decide which role in life allows him the most comfort.

Everyone who starts out in a bureaucracy wants to travel up the ladder to higher positions, where there is larger income and larger pensions at retirement. How far they want to go obviously will depend on innate temperament. Imagine then a young bureaucrat who is given the assignment to write regulations to bring into practice the principles set out in a new law. He will think of every nuance possible, every variation in approach to cover every eventuality under the law. Necessarily the regulations will cover printed volumes of material far larger than the length of the law itself. In doing the best job he can, he is pleasing his superiors. But he is pleasing them in two separate ways: first and obviously, the quality of his work. There is, however, the hidden part: if his agency administers the law and keeps statistics on the results of the law, they may well have to enlarge their staff to cover this extra work. Since our young bureaucrat best understands the regulations he wrote, he will probably be assigned to manage this new group of employees, and up the ladder he goes. This activity at the lower echelons pushes everyone up the ladder to higher positions, more responsibility, more income, and eventually more pension at retirement. Of course some people are passed over, that can't be helped; but generally bureaucrats want to grow their own agency, if at all possible, as it improves their importance and their position in life (read income).

This comes from the evolutionary development of our personalities. We still carefully look out for ourselves, while meaning to do a good job. The motivations are much more complex within a civilized society, but they are still the same: survival, self-protection, self-aggrandizement, providing for family. The structure of our organizations is a series of piled up pyramids: from evolution we don't like dealing with more than twenty to thirty people we know fairly well, and practically it is difficult in an eight-hour day to interact with more individuals than that. There is nothing wrong with watching out for yourself, if you are hurting no one else. Someone who is so altruistic they never think of themselves is like Mother Teresa, headed for sainthood, need I say a rare individual.

Bureaucracies grow in the fashion I have described, but they also grow by allowing themselves to become top heavy in supervisory staff. This happens also in corporations, and they end up downsizing to become more efficient. Articles critical of our public schools point out the growth of supervisors in independent school districts has wasted public tax dollars, and suggest reducing those staffs. Does this come from a desire to reduce one's own work load, or the work load of others, or is it the creation of new responsibilities which may or may not be necessary? Were the new responsibilities added because they sounded good, or because they were proven to be good? Or are we seeing self-help on top? More employees mean more responsibility, higher rank, more income. If bureaucratic chiefs are considered experts in the business practices of their agency, their testimony to answer my questions is a conflict of interest. It will take careful outside evaluation to get the proper perspective.

Bureaucracies by dint of writing the regulations, administering the laws, and collecting statistics on the results of the laws become experts in the areas covered. They also give out grants to think tanks, private individuals and universities to study the subjects they are caring for. Dr. Thomas Sowell, an economist and senior fellow at the Hoover Institution, makes the point in a *Forbes* column (20 April 1998) that "it is hard to imagine a greater conflict of interest than allowing operating agencies to shape the very categories in which evidence will be sought by the government and also choose the outside sources of supposedly objective evaluations."

Another major factor is the proliferating lobbies in Washington, each interested in promoting favorable measures for themselves. There were 5,000 in 1955, and in 1997 there were 23,000. Jonathan Rauch wrote a book *Demosclerosis* in 1994, in which he asserted that each lobby "cares much more about keeping its little piece of pie than anyone else cares about taking it away . . . ending even the most wildly dysfunctional program takes Herculean efforts. A wholesale overhaul of government is almost impossible." It isn't just the intense efforts of the special interest groups and their lobbyists. Testimony before congressional committees will come from bureaucracies bent on enlarging, or at least holding, their own. Testimony will appear from outside grantees set up by the bureaucracy, and information will be fed into the mix by the lobbyists most interested in and most friendly with the government agency.

Milton Friedman, Nobel Laureate in Economics, and also a fellow at the Hoover Institution, in a *Wall Street Journal* article (12 November 1991), reinforces the idea that bureaucracies do not go quietly into the night: "The basic difference between private and government enterprise is in the bottom line. If a private venture is unsuccessful, its backers must either shut it down or finance its losses out of their own pockets, so it will be terminated promptly. If a government venture is unsuccessful, its backers have a very different bottom line. Shutting it down is an admission of failure. Instead, in good faith, the backers can contend that the apparent lack of success is simply a result of not carrying the venture far enough. If they are persuasive enough, they can draw on the deep pockets of the taxpaying public to finance a continuation and expansion of the venture. Little wonder that unsuccessful government ventures are generally expanded rather than terminated"—especially if the testimony before Congress can be so one-sided.

It appears to me that bureaucratic agencies can be divided into service organizations and manufacturing ones. The service type are just like the service industries in private business, and they have to create report forms to generate the statistics that will support or deny the value of their programs. The Corps of Engineers and the Bureau of Reclamation are manufacturers of projects, and that is why they are the biggest winners in the game of water exploitation, creation of hydro-electric power, and the management of rivers, all the while seducing a huge population into a semi-desert hostile environment. Perhaps three generations of bureaucrats have created what I have described. They have endowed future generations of bureaucrats with the need for enormous projects to bail out the southwest. They have a multitude of finished projects to administer and maintain. They have created magnificent monolithic structures in the giant dams, the huge irrigation projects, and the beautiful recreational lakes. The worth of their endeavors seems to jump out at the observer, and is easy to behold, until you look under the surface and turn up the problems, not so obvious. All the while the smiling congressmen point with pride at what they had the foresight to create for the immediate impression, and oblivious to the future. The Bureau of Recla-

mation and the Corps of Engineers will never have to fight for
their lives, or even fight against downsizing. They will be around
for hundreds of years solving the problems left by their lack of
planning. They have fulfilled the implicit desire of most bureaucrats: they have grown self-perpetuating agencies, that by
force of their errors in future-planning will continue to grow.

It doesn't take much seduction to invite people to buy
homes along rivers or along a seashore, or even out on a barrier
island. To be surrounded by such an environment is very ap-
pealing. Perhaps it is another throwback to our development
in the Stone Age, an atavistic yearning to be back in the forests
or open spaces, or is it a realistic response to living in crowded
cities, piled up on one another, with the dangers, the crime,
and all the other attendant difficulties of living. In the late
1970s an article in *Scientific American* described an experiment
with crowded rats. Papa rats and their families all lived in one
huge colony, but each rat family had just one entrance to their
home. These were tame laboratory rats, and all the families
peacefully coexisted, until the second part of the experiment,
when a back entrance to each family home was opened to the
common runs connecting the homes. All chaos broke loose,
and anarchy took over. Each papa rat could not control access
to his family and could not offer the protection he had provided before. There was fighting, stealing, and attacks on families. Reminds one of the way New York apartments are shown
in the movies, and I assume for real, a solid metal front door
to each apartment with a lock and at least two dead bolts.

James Bovard, a fellow at the Competitive Enterprise
Institute, who publishes newspaper columns on free markets,
feels that the Federal Emergency Management Agency should
be ended. FEMA provides flood insurance for homes and
businesses that exist in flood zones. Premiums are an amazingly low—$300 a year for $250,000 property damage coverage, and of course, FEMA will turn to the taxpayers to make
up shortfalls. Bovard states "Taxpayers face over $250 billion
of exposure from government flood insurance policies." He is
very critical of FEMA allowing land developers to populate
flood plains, since the buildings can be insured against flood
damage. We do not see that happening in our area around

Houston, but we are well acquainted with flooding, and the developers and their customers know better. I think Bovard is wrong to ask that FEMA be ended. Enticing development of flood zones must not be allowed, but he is forgetting our history. Travel on water is cheap and easy. We settled this continent following rivers and putting towns along them. We cannot move entire towns and cities, but we can demand from owners of new developments, resulting in concrete over ground which would normally absorb rainfall, to put in detention ponds to hold the runoff created until the rain is over and the danger of flooding is past.

Bovard is right to be critical of FEMA. In chronically flooded areas, FEMA is required by law to buy out homeowners when the home is fifty percent damaged or more, rather than continuing to repair homes over and over for that $300 premium. FEMA is not following the law as a study by the National Wildlife Federation shows. Over eighteen years, from 1978 to 1995, FEMA, rather than buying and destroying homes that suffered repeated flooding, paid out slightly over $100 million more than the homes were worth. That is not a total for the country, only for the top ten states in payouts. Fifteen percent of those homes suffered more than fifty percent damage when flooded. FEMA has two excuses to defend itself: eighty-five percent of the flood-damaged homes were less than fifty percent damaged, so the law allows them to be repaired; and secondly, many of the repaired homes are outside the 100-year flood plain, and were repaired under the expectation that there would not be a repeat flood. The excuses are valid enough, but this is an egregious example of the principle I have observed about bureaucrats: if your agency is in the business of giving away money, the more you give away, the more important you remain and the bigger you get. I have seen this in the way the Veterans Administration hands out medical pensions much more liberally than the Social Security Disability Program.

All this information comes from FEMA records. Let's look at what FEMA knows and should be acting on, or asking Congress to authorize them to act on: The 100-year flood plain maps were drawn in 1974, when their flood insurance program was starting. Those maps are way out of date. In Harris County (home to Houston) thirty-one percent of re-peatedly-flooded properties are outside the 100-year lines. One Houston property near a river was repaired sixteen times at a cost of $806,591 for a property worth $100,000! Another, outside the flood plain as shown on the maps, was repaired seventeen times for $929,680. This building was not improp-erly built; the flood plain maps need to be redrawn. One final example: a $49,300 home in Canton, Mississippi was flooded twenty-five times and the repeated repairs cost $161,279. To show the magnitude of the problem, ninety-six percent of re-peatedly-flooded properties were built before the flood plain maps were drawn (*Houston Chronicle*, 22 July 1998 and 1 August 1998). This is a taxpayer subsidized program, and was set up that way, since there is no way it can be actuarially sound. It is a great example of how the federal government can help Americans, who through no fault of their own, are in trouble. FEMA should be asking Congress to buy out these properties and stop the monetary bleeding. I have given you the reason why they don't. It might eventually shrink the size of their agency.

Look at this story in a different way. Congress is supposed to oversee the bureaucracy, and make logical judgments to have programs work in the most efficient and least expensive way. They haven't done it here, yet having worked with Con-gress on flooding of my local bayou, I know there is a commit-tee in the House charged with this responsibility. Where has Congress been on this problem? How did this information come out? The National Wildlife Federation used the Free-dom of Information Act to make this information public and to analyze it. They have a vested interest. They would like to see the creation of green belts along the rivers as habitats for wildlife. Opposing them is another vested interest, the engi-neering firms, who would prefer to make money building struc-tural projects along rivers to increase carrying capacity, thereby saving the buildings. Not necessarily so—a Federation spokes-man points to the Mississippi River, which already has levees, but still has had disastrous flooding, " 'Structural methods of beating Mother Nature' often fail and may worsen the problem." Congress needs to provide enough buy-out dollars to allow fair-market purchase of these repeatedly-damaged properties, and bring the problem to an economic solution. Luckily, in these situations local flood control authorities are allowed to take the lead in choosing the properties to be bought. A simple solution: grant the states money and let the local flood-control authorities clear out these properties. The principle of locals know best still applies. Finally, must we have a huge proliferation of privately-funded advocacy and watchdog groups to help Congress keep an eye on the bureaucracy? Why can't we demand of Congress that they perform the function of oversight they are supposed to be doing? The answer is obvious. Congress, as a practical matter, cannot oversee the huge bureaucracy they have created. Those private groups have sprung up in part to answer a need, but as private institutions, they also carry only their own agenda, which may not be in the national interest. Only Congress can debate and find a common ground for the nation. The only solution to the oversight problem is to reduce the size of the bureaucracy by devolving power back to the states, thereby dividing up the oversight responsibility with many locally responsible governmental bodies.

We must use better judgment about the power of nature. There are drought cycle with rainy periods; ask California. By the early 1990s a long drought had the state hunting for more sources of water, and water rationing was common. Then, El Nino returned with heavy rains from 1995-98, and we see the spectacle of large homes sliding down unstable hills, where the homes were built for the view, and with no eye to the stability of those hills if heavy rains developed. Build first and worry about the extremes of nature later. Government disaster insurance will take care of you. The same reasoning drives those people who build homes or condominiums on unstable beaches or barrier islands. Near Oceanside, Oregon, the "Capes" development of thirty townhouses, worth up to $400,000 each and built on a garbage dump and a sand dune, as of February 1998, was about to be lost to the ocean eating away the beach next to them. Since 1977, Oregon will not allow rock or concrete fortifications along shorelines, having learned that such work simply shifts the erosion to neighboring sites. Barrier islands are large sandbars, notoriously unstable, and exist at the whim of wind, water, currents and major storms. Galveston, Texas, built on such an island, sustained 5,000 casualties during a 1910 hurricane. Now the city is evacuated before such storms arrive. The *New York Times,* in December 1997, reported that Wrightsville Beach, North Carolina, a barrier island town with cottages, beachfront hotels, condominiums, and a nine-story condominium/hotel building was losing its north end as the ocean has moved Mason Inlet south. The nine-story building was in immediate danger. The developers were warned by erosion specialists prior to building the structure that Mason Inlet was on the move, and were told by state officials that they could not build a protective seawall. "The great faucet of government disaster aid and cheap storm insurance, and ulti-mately, denial of the obvious—that is that up and down the Atlantic coast, the sea, aided by storms and hurricanes, is slowly but inexorably rolling up and over the beaches." It is not fair to the rest of taxpayers to subsidize this foolishness. We need to protect each other with national disaster insurance. No ques-tion. We need to designate areas that we will not cover, unless people learn to respect Mother Nature.

On April Fool's Day, 1998, President Clinton spoke in Gaborone, Botswana. Here is an excerpt: "There are chal-lenges on every continent. Here in Africa, deserts are spread-ing, forests are shrinking, water is increasingly scarce. Peoples health is more at risk as pollutants poison water and air. And there, as everywhere, global warming threatens to aggravate droughts and floods, and hasten the spread of infectious dis-ease." As a superb politician, Clinton was demonstrating how much he wants to help all of us. However, his comment invok-ing global warming as if it is just around the corner, or already here, is disingenuous. It is a theory that is not proven, al-though it is a highly credible concept. It is not yet happening, and no one knows when it might appear, if it ever does. And if it does arrive, is it really that bad? Politicians love to bring bad news. After all, they are powerful and can find solutions to protect us. Once again we need to look at the whole picture of the Earth's evolution, not just our current moment in time.

We are all generally aware that there have been major fluctuations in the Earth's temperature during its history, and that there have been Ice Ages. Actually, the Ice Ages are a recent event. There were no polar ice caps for ninety-nine percent of earth's existence. There have been seven Ice Ages, the most recent one starting over two million years ago, after a period about four million years when there were no ice caps. The temperature varies during an ice cap episode, with ice sheets advancing south from the north pole in a "glacial" period during the cold phase, and retreat northward, as they are doing now during a warming phase or "interglacial" period. The North Pole is warmer than the South Pole, and the glacials only occur in the northern hemisphere. The recent greatest advance of the ice sheets was eighteen thousand years ago, and they have been retreating up until the present time. But the temperature doesn't smoothly go up and down. From A.D. 1,500 to A.D. 1,850 was a sharply cooler period called the Little Ice Age. In A.D. 1,100 the earth was two degrees Fahrenheit warmer than it is today.

The overall changes in the Earth's temperature appear to be related to changes in sun activity, the possibility of intergalactic dust reducing the heat from the sun, changes in the earth's orbit from circular to elliptical and back again, a changing of the tilt of the earth's axis, and a wobble of that axis, all of these events happening cyclically in individual periods from 20,000 years to 100,000 years. The interaction of these cycles of different lengths results in sizably different ranges of temperature change over 200,000-300,000 years. During the height of the last glacial, temperatures were eighteen degrees Fahrenheit cooler in the American midwest, Britain was 12.5 degrees colder and the sea around Spain had temperatures like Greenland has now. All this, despite the fact that the sun is thought to be thirty percent brighter than it was when the earth formed 4.5 billion years ago. Volcanic activity is the other important factor in cooling the earth. Eruptions of Ghaie and Krakatoa late in the last century dropped the temperature of the northern hemisphere by 2.7 degrees Fahrenheit.

It is estimated by some that we are seventy-five percent through our current warming period, and since these warming

and cooling cycles are averages of the past, cooling could begin
at any time. Not to worry: the glaciers in the northern U.S.
and in Canada are still sharply retreating. Also, there has been
a regional warming in Antarctica of 4.5 degrees Fahrenheit
since the 1940s, resulting in the cracking off of icebergs fifteen
to twenty miles long. We appear to be firmly in the warm
period of this interglacial. The next major glacial peak activity
is probably 100,000 years away. Some people have pointed to
the retreat of the glaciers, trying to claim that the greenhouse
effect is already warming the Earth. Don't you believe it. Yes,
the potential greenhouse effect of certain atmospheric gases is
well-accepted, so let's look at what is proven and what isn't.

First, let's recognize that the greenhouse effect is nothing
new. It came first on Earth, and then life appeared. Our thin
atmosphere contains gases that help hold some of the sun's
radiated heat close to Earth, rather than letting it all radiate
back out into space. Our small range of temperature on Earth
has given us life, whether as a miraculous accident or by de-
sign, according to your philosophical/theological viewpoint.
Without our atmosphere, with its carefully adjusted greenhouse effect, we could be as cold as the moon or as hot as the
900 degrees Fahrenheit on Venus under its very heavy cloud
cover. Greenhouse gases in the atmosphere are: carbon dioxide, nitrous oxide, methane, and chlorofluorocarbons (CFC).
The CFCs are the propellants and refrigerants that have been
banned for harming the ozone layer high in the atmosphere
that shields us from ultra-violet light. There is a dissident
group of scientists who still doubt that effect, but by international agreement CFCs are no longer released into the atmosphere. Nitrous oxide is a minor player in the problem and
comes mainly from fertilizers and automobile emissions. Methane is the most effective greenhouse gas, and it is produced
from intestinal gas. Remember, there are close to six billion
people on Earth, and we pass gas twelve to fourteen times a
day as I mentioned in the chapter on medicine. The animal
herds we grow to produce meat create the same gas. Methane
is also produced in rice paddies, wetlands and swamps from
the decomposition of organic matter in water, and some may
come from leaks in pipelines of natural gas. Methane had been

increasing at approximately one percent per year, but luckily is currently decreasing for some unknown reason and presently is only a small contributor to total greenhouse gas concentration.

Carbon dioxide has received the most publicity and attention, as a by-product of burning fossil fuels. Humans and animals use oxygen in the atmosphere and exhale carbon dioxide as a waste product, and with the exponential growth in human and animal populations we contribute to the increase in this gas also. Carbon dioxide currently is forty percent higher than 2,000-3,000 years ago. This is established by studying air pockets in glaciers of that age. The rise was nominal from 1850 until this century. Two-thirds of that forty percent increase has been since 1940. In 1997 total greenhouse gas concentration was 420 parts per million (ppm), and carbon dioxide made up 360 ppm.

Water vapor plays a major role and has been considered a greenhouse gas until recent findings suggest that it may reduce heat, rather than increase heat by trapping it as cloud layers. The process of evaporation of water requires the use of heat. Lowering temperatures and the cloud layers it forms have recently been found to reflect heat rather than storing it, which was originally proposed. Carbon dioxide works with water vapor to form strong convection currents upward into the high atmosphere, where rapid condensation and rain then occur, thinning the greenhouse blanket and acting as a cooling mechanism. Sulfur dioxide is another gas in the atmosphere, a pollutant placed there by burning coal, and is thought to help create strong cooling clouds: the gas forms aerosols with water vapor, and these result in bright clouds that more effectively reflect sunlight. These aspects of the science of hydrology of rainfall have been studied for twenty to thirty years, but satellite analysis of cloud cover is less than twenty-years-old, and full understanding of these mechanisms is yet to develop. However, in favor of the theory that increasing cloud cover may play a major role in this complex issue is the fact that the slight overall warming of the atmosphere since 1940 is the result of a mix of cooler daytime temperatures and warmer nights. This is exactly what more cloud cover should do: block sunlight and lower daytime temperatures, blanket the earth at night and hold temperatures up. This discussion of greenhouse uses is from a very thoroughly researched article by Warren T. Brooks in *Forbes* magazine, 25 December 1989.

There are many confounding factors to be considered in the issue of the greenhouse effect. Current computer models have not successfully predicted the temperature changes since scientists became concerned about a possible warming trend starting in the 1970s. Amazingly, they were worried about a cooling trend up until the 1970s, as the highest temperatures in this century occurred about 1940 and then began dropping. How times have changed! Neither can the computer models be run backward and successfully demonstrate the past. Any reliable computer model must be able to go in both directions. There are just too many interlocking cycles and interactions that are not yet fully understood for the mathematical formulae fed into the computers to make the models work. For example, carbon dioxide does dissolve in the oceans and is absorbed in land, and both regions account for a total fifty times the amount in the atmosphere. Transfer of carbon dioxide between these areas is not fully understood, resulting in possibly imprecise predictions of rates of rise in the atmosphere of carbon dioxide.

The rapid rise of carbon dioxide in the atmosphere is not disputed; the fear that the temperatures on Earth will also rise rapidly is the issue. Let's look at what scientific observation has found so far. Surface temperatures have been carefully measured since 1750 in this country toward the end of the Little Ice Age. Since 1860 these surface measurements have shown a rise of .9 degrees Fahrenheit until 1996, according to Robert E. Davis, Associate Professor of Climatology, University of Virginia. Two-thirds of the rise occurred before 1940, but when carbon dioxide accumulated so quickly is after 1940. The association of carbon dioxide and warming temperatures does not fit the data. Further, since 1979, satellites have been measuring total Earth temperature and by 1996 there was an observed tiny drop of .09 degrees Fahrenheit per decade, according to Charles L. Harper, Jr., a planetary scientist from Harvard University. These satellites are accurate to .04 degrees Fahrenheit. The computer models in the meantime were predicting a rise in temperature of .36 degrees Fahrenheit per decade during the period the satellites were in orbit. A study in the scientific journal, *Nature*, reported in August 1998, disputes the accuracy of the satellites claiming that a drop of one mile in their orbit confuses the results. Their calculations show a rise of .13 degrees Fahrenheit per decade, less than the computer model predictions. Other scientists agree that the one-mile drop does effect the results, but to much less a degree than the authors calculate (*Houston Chronicle, Washington Post,* 13 August 1998) and still maintain warming is not proven. The debate will rage for years between those who insist we are warming and those who feel we may warm in the future, typical of the scientific method.

The computer models are wrong so far. There is much more going on to control Earth's temperature than the single factor of carbon dioxide, which is why I presented the information on ice caps and glacial activity. Robinson and Robinson, from the Oregon Institute of Science and Medicine, in December 1997, presented material from the *Astrophysical Journal* to show that solar activity and our surface temperatures have marched in lockstep since 1750. We must learn to look at the totality of our existence, and as we learn more in a broader view, the computer models will improve.

So what if the Earth warms? We have been colder in the past and warmer in the past, and temperature will vary up and down over the centuries with and without carbon dioxide effects. Let's assume what will happen in the short range in the next century with some warming of two to three degrees Fahrenheit as the carbon dioxide concentration rises? But first, if your geography is a little weak, look at a globe. Three-quarters of the land masses are north of the equator. Large parts of Canada and Siberia are not temperate enough to have growing seasons. Increased temperature makes plants grow faster and as seasons change in the temperate zones, the growing seasons will be longer. Plant metabolism is run by the green substance, chlorophyll, which gets energy for its chemical reactions from sunlight, and it turns carbon dioxide into plant material and throws off oxygen. The major reason there is twenty percent oxygen in our atmosphere is due to plant activity. Without the production of oxygen by plant life 3.5 billion years ago, we wouldn't be here. Ninety percent of plant activity in the world is in the oceans as phytoplanktons: as the oceans warm these tiny plants will increasingly use carbon dioxide and throw off oxygen. So far ocean temperatures are the same as they were in 1940. Obviously all plants will grow faster with more carbon dioxide available. Robinson and Robinson reviewed 279 research studies, predicting "that overall plant growth will ultimately double as carbon dioxide increases"—more plant food for more people as the planet's population keeps growing. These same authors also state that studies have shown better plant growth in drier climates as carbon dioxide rises.

As the temperate zone creeps north where daylight lasts longer in the summer growing season, plants will grow faster and bigger from that effect. Visit the Matanuska valley just north of Anchorage, Alaska: in just under three months of growing season, warmed by the Japanese Current, and with twenty-two hours of daylight, I have seen the cabbages they grow over two feet across. This agricultural scenario sounds great. All we have to add is rain. But wait. The global warming alarmists have told us there will be drought. Not so: the 1995 United Nations Intergovern-mental Panel on Climate Change Report (UNIPCC), published at the start of 1996, states: "Warmer temperatures will lead to a more vigorous hydrological cycle: this translates into prospects for more severe droughts and/or floods in some places and less severe droughts and/or floods in other places." Translation: the places are not identified, and the rain cycles intensify. This is typical of the usual cautionary scientific writing to mean *no one* knows exactly what will happen. In fact evidence so far does not support the idea of intensification of storm cycles. Starting from 1995 through the three El Nino winters till 1998, the damage each year, according to FEMA reports, is the same, not increasing as carbon dioxide rises. According to Davis, hurricane experts now feel that the increasing concentrations of greenhouse gases may be creating "a significant trend of fewer intense hurricanes and weaker cyclones overall."

How about melting of the polar ice and rising oceans?

There are confounding factors here also. Ice over the oceans is in floating sheets. Try this experiment: fill a glass with water and one ice cube to the rim. Watch the cube melt and you will see that no water spills over the side. Ice expands when it solidifies, which is why it floats. Also, as the ice melts in the oceans it will dilute the salt content in the melting region, slowing melting. Why do we add salt to streets during winter in the north? To make the snow and ice melt. Higher salt concentration, faster melt. The ice caps on land, Greenland and Antarctica will have to melt to raise the oceans. Robert C. Balling, Jr., Director of the Office of Climatology at Arizona State University, Tempe, observes: "The Arctic area, where most of the warming should be taking place, has not warmed over the past sixteen years (written in 1995), according to the satellite record, or over the past fifty years, as measured by standard weather stations. While some glaciers have retreated, others have advanced, including large ice sheets in Antarctica and Greenland." So, it is not clear about how much the oceans will rise due to greenhouse effect.

Rising oceans are obviously a tremendous threat to low lying seaside towns and cities, to low lying islands, especially barrier islands, but that threat exists all the time, if the forces that cause warming and cooling in relationship to our ice caps decide it is time for profound warming and no ice caps! Always keep in mind the bigger picture. We can be a lot warmer, unrelated to carbon dioxide. What if the Ice Age cycles decide to make it colder? We will have less food and less area to grow it. We could well have worldwide starvation. Greenhouse effect at that point is a blessing! This might be one time when it is *nice* to fool Mother Nature.

I hope I have convinced you by this time that global warming, due to greenhouse gases, must be studied and understood, but does not deserve global panic. Scientific opinion is not clear as to the proper course of action, or whether inaction is best. Why are the world's political leaders trying to fool with the work of science, and fool us about Mother Nature? H.L. Mencken observes: "The whole aim of practical politics is to keep the populace alarmed and hence clamorous to be led to safety—by menacing it with an endless series of hobgoblins,

all of them imaginary." George Melloan, a regular columnist
with the *Wall Street Journal* expands on Mencken, in a 12 July
1993 article: "Politicians and government bureaucrats grab more
money and regulatory power. Third World governments winkle
more money out of rich nations . . . Tax-hungry U.S. and
European politicians are trying to keep the myth (the immediate disaster of global warming) alive to justify huge new
taxes on energy." Again, perception becomes reality, aided by
the newspapers, which love to publish bad news and from my
observations, are very poor at understanding and checking facts
on new scientific findings. Brookes, in *Forbes,* is just as forceful: "What drives Washington policy-making is not economic
or scientific realities but 'public choice,' the pursuit of power
and funding. The public choice potential of global warming is
immense. Under a global warming scenario, the EPA would
become the most powerful agency on earth, involved in massive levels of economic, social, scientific and political spending
and interference."

The much ballyhooed UNIPCC 1995 report on greenhouse effect and global warming is a deception. It was developed by two groups: Working Group I were the scientists
reporting the theories and the studies to confirm the theories,
following proper scientific method—only observed facts prove
theories. Working Group II were the economists, social scientists, and politicians who were charged with assessing the "im-
pacts and response options" related to global warming. They
were also responsible for producing a summary of the findings
since the report ran 2,000 pages plus, and was going to be a
monumental challenge for lay people and the press to work
through. When the scientific report did not confirm global
warming had arrived, and had many modifying statements
indicating that there was uncertainty about a time of arrival
and uncertainty about the severity of the effects when it did
arrive, Group II went through the scientific report, removing
some statements that equivocated, and tried to make the document more firmly predictive of the immediacy of global warming and the severity of its effects. The summary, written by
Group II, presented an even stronger view implying a catastrophic scenario of global warming unless drastic action is

taken now.

One way to understand how imprecise and deceptive the UNIPCC report appears to be is to look more closely at their methane predictions. As I have mentioned, methane is the most effective gas in creating greenhouse effect. According to an article in *Scientific American* by David Schneider (June 1998), the "IPCC projected that atmospheric methane would roughly double by 2100." This anticipated that methane would eventually be responsible for twenty percent of the greenhouse effect. However, the one percent per year rise first seen in the 1980s, when comprehensive measurements began, abruptly decreased in 1992 with that reduction continuing. According to Schneider no reason has been established, although an atmospheric chemical equilibrium mechanism has been proposed. The IPCC "regarded the sudden downturn as a short-term 'anomaly' " (meaning: a deviation from the expected) and chose to ignore it in producing their report. David S. Schimel of the National Center for Atmospheric Research, one of the authors of the 1995 IPCC report on the topic, admits that the assumptions used at the time were "based on an understanding of methane that was five to fifteen years old." He, too, notes that *"climate researchers are disquieted by their inability to forecast such changes"* (emphasis added). I wonder how Schimel feels about the deceptive Group II UNIPCC summary of the scientific data and the way it trashes the scientific method.

The scientific method should be very precise. First, a working hypothesis is developed as an extension of previously accepted findings. If preliminary experimentation supports the idea, it becomes a theory, but the theory is not accepted until at least two independent groups present experimental results that clearly support the theory, after careful critical peer review. This approach has been subverted by the Group II policy makers at the UN. This has infuriated scientists who worked on the project, and other scientific scholars very familiar with the work. I have been quoting from some of their articles on the facts of science that have been deliberately ignored. Frederick Seitz, president emeritus of Rockefeller University and chairman of the George C. Marshall Institute, is one of the angriest. When the IPCC report appeared in early 1996 he wrote:

"This report is not what it appears to be—it is not the version that was approved by the contributing scientists listed on the title page. In my more than sixty years as a member of the American scientific community, including service as president of both the National Academy of Sciences and the American Physical Society, I have never seen a more disturbing corruption of the peer-review process than the events that led to this IPCC report." He describes "more than fifteen sections in Chapter 8, the key chapter setting out the scientific evidence for and against a human influence over climate—(which) were changed or deleted after the scientists charged with examining this question had accepted the supposedly final text." Here are three statements in the draft report, approved of by the participating scientists, which were deleted in the published report: 1) None of the studies cited above has shown clear evidence that we can attribute the observed (climate) changes to the specific cause of increases in greenhouse gases; 2) No study to date has positively attributed all or part (of the climate change observed to date) to anthropogenic (man-made) causes; 3) Any claims of positive detection of significant climate change are likely to remain controversial until uncertainties in the total natural variability of the climate system are reduced. Seitz concluded: "Whatever the intent was of those who made these significant changes, their effect is to deceive policy-makers and the public into believing that the scientific evidence shows human activities are causing global warming." I am not so sure that the politician "policy makers" are deceived, but rather the deceivers.

The claim is made, to give the UNIPCC report an aura of great scientific consensus, that 2,500 scientists worked on the report and approved of it. Again nothing is further from the truth. S. Fred Singer, professor emeritus of environmental sciences, University of Virginia, and president of the Science and Environmental Policy Project in Fairfax, Virginia added up all the contributors and reviewers listed in the three IPCC published in 1966, and could count only 2,100. "The great majority of these are not conversant with the intricacies of atmospheric physics, although some may know a lot about forestry, fisheries, or agriculture. Most are social scientists or just policy experts and government functionaries. Most of the several hundred listed 'contributors' are simply specialists who allowed their work to be cited, without necessarily endorsing the other chapters (in which they do not appear) or the summary. The list even includes known skeptics of global warming—much to their personal and professional chagrin." Robert E. Davis, whose article I cited on page 152, is a contributor and reviewer of the IPCC report, and dissents from the conclusions: "The world is not coming to an end because of global warming. Based on climate records from the last 100 years and our current understanding of climate science, there is little cause for alarm over this issue." He proposes that the purpose is to punish capitalist economies for their economic successes, and declares, "Let's stop using global warming as an excuse to promote a hidden agenda." Right on the mark! Charles L. Harper adds the statement, "that committee-based scientific opinion is widely subject to social and fund-based pressures to support politically-motivated mandates, as seen in the UN shepherding of the IPCC."

Singer reports there was another major dissent from "nearly 100 climate scientists who signed the Leipzig Declaration in 1996, expressing their doubts about the validity of computer-driven global warming forecasts. It takes a certain amount of courage to do this, given that it could jeopardize research grants from the U.S. government agencies that have adopted climate catastrophe as an article of faith." The Science and Environmental Policy Project, which he heads, conducted a survey of IPCC scientific contributors and reviewers, and found that about half did not support the policy-makers' summary: "Parallel surveys by the Gallop organization and even by Greenpeace International produced similar results." Thomas Sowell points out the conflict of interest in government agencies awarding grants, primarily to those who agree with their point of view (see page 142). Many scientists receive a small stipend from their institution, and the major portion of their total income is contained in the salary portion of the grants they are able to secure.

In December 1997, politicians and bureaucrats from 160

nations met in Kyoto, Japan and produced the Kyoto Protocol regarding global warming. Under this agreement, if fifty-five nations ratify it, and if the ratifying nations include those industrial nations accounting for fifty-five percent of industrial emissions, then carbon dioxide production must be reduced below 1990 levels by the year 2012, by up to seven percent below 1990 depending on the country designated. The expert prediction is that carbon dioxide emissions in 2012 will be fifty percent lower than now anticipated for North America for that year. There are no restrictions for developing countries, and as a result global carbon dioxide concentrations will still increase sharply! The protocol, if ratified, will require nations such as ours to pass legislation to massively reduce fossil fuel consumption. This may well drive industries from our country to unrestricted countries, dramatically upsetting our economy. Need I remind you of the George Melloan quote about the manipulations of third world countries? Abstracted from the Canadian newspaper *The Globe and Mail* 23 May 1998, "Let's not be stampeded by the tentative science of global warming," by William Thorsell. Frederick Seitz, whose angry article I previously quoted, has attacked the Kyoto Protocol by setting up a petition project, calling for scientists to review global warming research, and sign his anti-Kyoto Petition if they agree (http://www.oism.org). In early 1998, within a two month period, he received over 17,000 signatures from scientists and engineers, including more than 6,000 Ph.D.s in the hard sciences. "More than 2,000 of the signers are physicists, geophysicists, climatologists, meteorologists or environmental scientists with an expertise in climate change," according to Jeffrey Salmon, Executive Director George C. Marshall Institute, Washington (letter to Editor, *WSJ*, 21 May 1998.)

The UNIPCC Report and the Kyoto Protocol may be deceptions to alarm and control us now. It shows how manipulative our so-called leaders can be in leading us by the nose. Another case in point is the book *Earth in the Balance*, published in 1992, by Senator Al Gore. I was curious as to how an ardent environmentalist would view the rise of carbon dioxide and global warming. I found his book to be a long one-sided polemic. The book is meant to show that science is unanimously convinced that global warming will be here shortly, if not already happening. He discusses the discovery of the scientific method, and then condemns it for producing too much information! He criticizes Professor Richard Lindzen of M.I.T. for downplaying the degree of warming which may occur, by commenting: "A few scientists (agree with Lindzen); their views sometimes carry far too much weight." This observation alone shows that he has no idea of how the scientific method works. It is not a group of judges at a beauty contest, expressing opinions about something that is not quantifiable. It is the development of measurable facts that eventually convinces scientific peers that the theory is correct. Critical discussion between scientists is necessary, and may develop anger and heat, driving the process to a conclusion that all can accept. I'm not the only voice to object to Al Gore's book. In their book *Higher Superstition; The Academic Left and its Quarrels with Science* (1994), Paul R. Gross and Norman Levitt observe: "This work manages to create false impressions, e.g., that an overwhelming majority of scientists believe that we are now passing or already have passed the point of no return toward a *catastrophic* global warming due to a greenhouse effect."

As I write this chapter, a whole new exciting approach to cancer chemotherapy is appearing with the success of two drugs in mice, angiostatin and endostatin, which block the ability of cancers to ask the body being invaded to supply more blood to the tumors. There is no new blood, no growth, and eventual death for the cancer. It works in mice, and will work to an as yet unknown degree in humans. But the discoverer of these drugs, Dr. Judah Folkman, is no Al Gore presuming the future. When asked about treatment in humans, he refuses to predict. All he knows for sure is that "If you have cancer and you are a mouse, we can take good care of you." There is a total absence of Occam's Razor in Gore's presentation. There is a reproduced graph on page ninety-six, showing a rise in global temperature from 1975 to 1989 of almost .4 degrees Celsius (.7 degrees Fahrenheit). It is credited to a single scientific paper, but where is the countervailing data, showing the opposite finding? A proper scientific method review of the

issue will present papers from both sides, and will comment on
the validity of the methods used in deciding which result may
be correct before reaching conclusions. Instead, on page ninety-
eight Gore states, "The artificial global warming *we are causing*
threatens far more than a few degrees added to average temperatures" (emphasis added). In his mind it is an established
fact. No it isn't! Do you yell "FIRE!" in a theater on the
probability that one will start? If you do, the law will put you
in jail.

Gore states that global warming definitely will cause wild
swings and disruptions in our climate patterns over the world,
and cites past frightening examples of very severe climate
changes. The UNIPCC report does anticipate changes, but is
not sure how severe. Our civilization has developed during a
period of relative environmental and climatic calm on Earth.
Gore's myopic view worries about a tiny segment of time and
undersells the innate ability of the humans he would lead. If
we are to survive like the dinosaurs for 150 million years,
humans will have to endure ice ages, warming periods with
rising ocean levels, possible flooding of coastal cities, and perhaps asteroid hits (unless the current effort to identify them
and push them off course with nuclear ballistic missiles works).
Humans have a brilliant intellect, and we are marvelous at
problem-solving. Shoot down asteroids, nudge them off
course—of course we can! Feed the human race during an Ice
Age—we will figure a way to do it. This is not because we have
political leaders who sell fright and fear. Our survival instinct
is tremendously strong.

Al Gore has been an environmentalist since his college
days when a professor showed him the rising levels of carbon
dioxide and instilled the idea in him that global warming had
to follow. I cannot know his personal motivations in writing
this book, but he has made it clear that he wants to be president of this country. He sincerely feels he has found an issue
of great importance, and I agree it is. However, his evolutionary psychology is guiding him, as it guides all of us. Using this
issue he can appear as our Savior: apocalyptic statements in his
book are meant to reinforce this. He may or may not recognize
his hidden agenda and that his emotions are guiding his rea-

soning. Politically, what could be better than an issue like this: confusing arcane science, that the lay voter cannot really understand? Let Al Gore and his advisors study it and translate it into action for us.

An issue we can understand might evoke too much opposition. Here he can praise scientists who agree with him, and vilify the others for not being intelligent enough, and the public won't really understand what is going on. Neither will the newspapers, whose science articles are generally terrible, and who love to publish bad news.

These discoveries about the UN and Al Gore, and their manipulations of fact, should not stop us from supporting continuing climatological research to get the true factual answers to protect our earth for now and generations into the future. The issue of global warming is too dangerous to ignore. The magnitude of the danger must be established. What is reassuring is that as new information is found and the computer models are modified, the predicted rise in temperatures gets smaller and smaller. The answers are out there, but political leaders are dangerous to the process if they control the monetary grants to the scientists. Scientists are only human also. They must be free to think independently, and not be threatened by loss of funding.

These descriptions of our political leaders should provide a long-remembered lesson as to the quality of leadership in this country and in the world. This chapter shows how we are manipulated by the monolithic political and bureaucratic organizations in Washington and by the United Nations, often with the best of intentions on their part. However, it is my opinion that our evolutionary psychology leads the politicians and the bureaucracy to self-justification and self-protective actions, causing bureaucracy to grow with the politicians' permission, and become much too cumbersome and finally to lack the proper objectivity to work for us, the citizenry, the way they should. Congressional oversight is obviously lacking. Bureaucrats tell Congress what to think about the water development projects in the west; they sound like great projects that will garner votes, and they are approved. The problems with the projects are never discovered until several sessions of Con-

gress later. Despite their protestations that they have everything under expert control, they don't. Issues are too complex
for citizens to understand; Congress will research them expertly and take care of us. They don't. The country is being
run by an out-of-control massive bureaucracy, which appears
to be running Congress also. There is no other conclusion.

Chapter Six

Simple Arithmetic and Statistics for the Mathematically Challenged

I have always enjoyed learning and being educated, and in turn, I have always enjoyed teaching. I have been horrified reading reports disputing the value of our current public education. Can Johnny read, can he do arithmetic? From what I have seen at the checkout counter, not arithmetic. Unless the register tells how much change to give, the correct amount may not be offered. I hear that students can earn more than 4.0. How does one know more than 100% of what is taught? Is this really needed to create grade creep, so no one earns less than an A or B? Each child in school must feel good about himself all the time? No one should be victimized by school? Everyone's intelligence falls on the bell-shaped curve, as do all biologic characteristics. Someone has to be at the low end and someone at the high end. The dumbing down of America is not going to help us understand how to regain control over the political and bureaucratic behemoth in Washington.

Donald Kaul, a syndicated Washington columnist, while poking fun at Congress in a column as he often does, made a comment that set my teeth on edge. He was describing congressional inability to look into the future, except as it related to their reelection. Worrying about Social Security failure thirty years from now, without reform being enacted, he said: "Thirty years? You might as well be talking about the *next* millennium, the one that begins in the year 3000 (or 3001, if you are one of those)." It is the part in parentheses that got me. Of course it is 3001. Nothing else is correct, and yes, it is a minor issue at which perhaps he meant to be poking fun. But most of our country actually thinks the millennium in our immediate future will start 1 January 2000! And it is simple arithmetic: Count any group of items and you'll find that you start with the number one and end with ten. The *end* of a decade, a century, or a millennium ends with a year with a zero. The next millennium *starts* on 1 January 2001! Therefore, this chapter. If you think you know this stuff, skip to the next chapter, or skim to see if I might surprise you with some concept you weren't aware of.

In order to make good judgments as citizens, we need to understand the reports given to us by our doctors and the physical or social scientific studies that constantly appear in the newspapers. Governmental agencies, university departments, think tanks, and other groups constantly bombard us with data. Polling groups try to make news by constantly questioning us and reporting the results. You need to be able to decide for yourself just how accurate the material seems, and whether it is worth paying attention to. What kinds of material should you allow to influence your thinking? Ones in which you can understand the numbers thrown at you. How were those numbers determined? From how large a group? Percentages are valid results for statisticians and researchers to report but can be very misleading, unless you look at the numbers behind the percentages.

Let's look at percentages first. Based on decimals being expressed in terms of 100 they tend to enlarge the perception of change, if used to express change. Here is a theoretical example: five people out of a thousand ill patients develop a good result being given Drug A; another Drug B provides ten people out of a thousand a good effect. Drug B is mathematically 100% better than A, but neither are of much value, if so few people are helped. Both drugs are worthless! A true story from my own life to illustrate, one I really shouldn't tell, because I found myself acting dumb until I stopped to think about percentages. I was and still am part of a Harvard Medical School study of originally middle-aged physicians testing Vitamin A to prevent cancer, and aspirin to lower the occurrence of heart attack. The study found Vitamin A did not have an effect, but that aspirin lowered the chances of suffering a coronary forty percent in this originally healthy and knowledgeable group. I knew from the taste of the pills I was taking that I had not been given aspirin, so based on that forty percent reduction, I started taking it. Aspirin poisons platelets, little bodies in the blood that help start the clotting process. Within a few days I was bruising easily, which I didn't like, so I stopped to think: Did I really need to do this, and in real person terms, how much was I actually accomplishing? That is the key—real person terms.

I went back and looked at the study results. These numbers are approximations of that study but make the point: there were 17.5 coronaries per 1,000 per year off aspirin and 10.5 per 1,000 per year on aspirin, an obvious reduction of seven heart attacks per 1,000 per year. This is a highly significant result according to statistical formulas that measure whether this could occur by chance. In this very knowledgeable group, without known heart disease, and who knew how to avoid or modify the risk factors, less coronaries would be expected as compared to a lay population, making the result even more striking. Note that aspirin did not prevent all heart attacks, it effected a reduction. At the time, aged fifty-five, with perhaps thirty years to live, if I used aspirin, I was preventing twenty-one chances in a hundred of my having a heart attack before dying of whatever, not worth bruising for, the way I looked at it. I had one chance in five cumulatively over my life expectancy. The odds were in my favor looking at group odds, but I am an individual with my own odds. I fall on the low risk side of the bell-shaped curve when I look at my own risk factors for a coronary. Those odds suggest that my chances are well below twenty-one out of one hundred over a thirty year period. Moral: Percentages exaggerate; look at the underlying numbers, if you can. Get help from your doctor to understand your own risk factors. Your own individuality comes first in decision-making.

Newspapers present medical, political and social statistics taken from press releases, without any apparent thought pattern as to what it all means. It would help if a reporter or an editor would check with a legitimate authority for an interpretation, or two interpretations, one for either side of disputed material if necessary. I am now going to present a series of newspaper articles to show you that you can do this for yourself. These were culled from our local paper (*The Houston Chronicle*) at random over a period of several weeks, while I was writing other chapters, just to demonstrate the kind of material that is constantly thrust at us to influence our opinions.

A major medical finding, printed 8 April 1998 from a *Los Angeles Times* article by Marlene Cimons, describes a major breakthrough in *prevention* of breast cancer in high risk women by giving them Tamoxifen. For about a decade, the drug has been given to women to prevent *recurrence* in women with breast cancer after initial treatment is finished. In 1998, about 179,000 new cases are expected with a current death rate of 43,500 per year. Risk factors include strong family history, pregnancy without nursing, never being pregnant, smoking, obesity, a history of benign breast lumps, and being over sixty years old. There were 13,388 high risk women in this prevention study, half receiving the drug and half a placebo over a six-year period. The result was 154 cases of cancer appeared in the placebo (or "control") group and only eighty-five in the treated group. Sounds great, but the headline of the article tells women they "face tough choices" because of the dangerous side effects of Tamoxifen: uterine cancer, blood clots damaging the lungs (pulmonary embolism), and blood clots in the deep veins of the legs. There were thirty-three cases of uterine cancer in the treatment group, fourteen cases in the controls; seventeen cases of pulmonary embolism versus six in the placebo group; and thirty patients with deep vein clots, compared with 19 on placebo. The article does not interpret or expand on these numbers, but states the side-effects are rare but "life threatening." How does a woman make a decision? How dangerous is Tamoxifen? High risk is 7.1% over age forty-five and rises to 100% risk over age sixty, according to risk criteria used in the breast study as stated in the article.

The article does not tell women that just one in eight will develop breast cancer *if* they live long enough. The overall numbers in the article are quite scary for those that are high risk however. The way to look at this is simple arithmetic: Divide the total study group in half to get the treatment total and the placebo (control) total. Then, for the risk of cancer, subtract the number of cancers in the treatment group from the number in the untreated. The benefit was 10.3 less cancers per 1,000 women over the six year period. Against that was the increase in side effects of 6.1 per thousand during the six years (subtract the Tamoxifen totals from the placebo totals). The article doesn't comment on the side effect of uterine cancer; medical studies in the past have shown that if the women are carefully followed while on therapy, with yearly uterine biopsies (an office procedure), the cure rate for uterine cancer is ninety percent. A blood clot traveling to the lungs, if large enough, can kill, but rarely does so, and deep vein clots can make legs swell, but only if a clot from them is sent to the lungs are they life-threatening. To summarize, there were sixty-nine less cancers, at a price of forty-one side-effects, but breast cancer is a great deal more dangerous than the article would have you believe about the side effects. All drugs have side effects. It is the risk-reward ratio that is most important, how much good the drug does versus the side-effect risk. There is good news on the horizon: new drugs in the Tamoxifen family are in research as I write this, and they are reported not to cause uterine cancer. This is not a difficult analysis for the lay person, but the additional medical knowledge I added is important. In making a judgment about taking medication, you must have an intimate relationship with your doctor, and ask for a presentation like the one I have given.

On 30 April 1998 the *Houston Chronicle* published a Washington dateline article on the pay scales in day-care centers as being "stagnant for ten years." The study came from the Center for the Child Care Workforce, a "non-profit research and *advocacy* organization." The study covered profit and non-profit daycare centers that have been open for at least a decade. Note the word I have emphasized, *advocacy*. The article is filled with quasi-statistical statements, all to set up their recommendation "that in new federal and state initiatives, officials should devote more attention and *set aside more money* to raise wages and safeguard quality" (emphasis added). Nowhere in the article is any negative statistical correlation between wages and quality of care documented, but the tone of the article implies it. They take the average salary of all workers, $12,800 and state it is equal to the federal poverty level for a family of three. It is never stated how many of these workers are the sole breadwinners for a family of three. They found that the top paid employees, "experienced teachers, (usually required to have a college degree)," were receiving an average annual wage of $18,988, and then compared that to the average female high school graduate with a national average wage of $19,656. Nowhere is there a study of why those "college graduates" have chosen such work. Don't those employees have free choice of where to work? They obviously are working in these centers for personal reasons. Similar comparisons to other lower paid jobs are also made. Finally a sentence which states: "Eighty of the for-profit daycare centers hired public-assistance recipients (folks coming off welfare), while 40% of nonprofit centers had hired such workers." Comparing numbers with percentages is comparing apples and oranges. It can't be done. And what is wrong with helping people escape welfare? In my analysis, the article turns out to be pure propaganda, totally a one-sided approach to asking for more federal and state funds. For what purpose? The for-profit centers they studied have survived over ten years, making a profit in a competitive capitalistic arena. They don't seem to need any outside help.

On 5 May 1998, an advocacy group report appeared in the *Houston Chronicle* (AP by Glen Johnson). The National Safe Kids Campaign studied accidental childhood death and found a drop of 26.4% from 1987 to 1995 in children ages fourteen and under, from 15.56 children per 100,000 to 11.45 per 100,000 per year. That is a drop of 4.11 deaths per 100,000 per year over nine years. The group, obviously extolling their own efforts, pointed to seat belts and bike helmets as major contributors to the decline. However, in the bar graphs which showed types of death, over the nine years, automobile fatalities and bicycle deaths both dropped by only 0.31 per 100,000, which doesn't suggest seat belts and bike helmets contributed a great deal. Drownings were down 0.79, pedestrian accidents down 0.81, and fires down 0.90. Suffocation stayed the same.

Other causes such as falls, electrocution, gun shot, and animal attacks were not mentioned.

The article points out that motor vehicle deaths were 1,800 out of a total 6,600 in 1995 twenty-seven percent. It then becomes clear, the 100,000 used as a base for analysis relates to accident numbers, not population, and the small drop in auto deaths per 100,000 contributed a fairly large portion of the overall decline, when all accidents are lumped together. A failing of the article is not to identify the meaning of the 100,000 base. Another failing of the report is the discussion of bicycle death, which fell from 0.75 to 0.44 per 100,000 per year. The article touts this as a forty-one percent drop, which is true, but as I have warned, percentages exaggerate—the real person drop was only 0.31 per 100,000. A major point left out is a study of miles traveled in a car per year to relate the deaths to risk. The same could be said about bike trips per year per child. The final failing is the use of anecdotal material: "In New Jersey, 41 children ages 13 and under died in bicycle accidents between 1987 and 1991 (5 years). The state passed a bicycle helmet law in 1992 and over the next three years 16 children were killed in bicycle crashes." Sounds great? No it isn't; it isn't related to how many bike riders there were in the state, and dividing by the years involved, in the five years before helmets, deaths were 8.2 per year, and afterward 5.3 per year, a good result which may or may not be statistically significant, but a lot more realistic approach than forty-one compared with sixteen. Anecdotes sometimes make good examples, but are not statistically valid, even if a bunch of them are presented. A bunch of anecdotes, if striking enough, demand the setting up of a proper statistical study.

Safe Kids is doing a commendable job, and their results are pleasing, but not as good as they would like you to believe. At least in the article they are not asking for more federal money as in my previous example. The analysis I have given is an example of how a doctor reads a research article in a medical journal. The physician does not trust the results, unless he understands how they were obtained. The 100,000 base number would be clearly defined, and the article would be peer-reviewed before publication is allowed. Many articles are returned for corrections or clarifications. As a patient protecting your health, you should expect nothing less of your physician. Why then, do we tolerate this half-baked material in our newspapers, when we are trying to make judgments to protect our country? Much of this stuff looks like filler to take up space between the ads.

Under the headline "Clinton pushes bill to punish firms allowing pay disparity," on 11 June 1998, the *Houston Chronicle* article said in the first paragraph: "(Clinton) called on Congress to act quickly to pass legislation giving women the ability to punish companies that allow pay disparity to continue." Further on the article told us: "The administration released two reports to mark the 35th anniversary of the Equal Pay Act signed by President Kennedy in 1963. The reports show the pay differential narrowed from 58 cents earned by women to every $1 earned by a man to 75 cents earned by a woman to every $1 earned by a man. 'I think you will be persuaded that there is no explanation for the gap that is complete without *acknowledging the continued existence of discrimination*,' Clinton said after reviewing the reports" (emphasis added). The article does not show how these figures were obtained, or what they really mean, until toward the end of the story the role of Senator Edward Kennedy was revealed: "(Kennedy), a sponsor of the legislation, suggested Congress should increase the minimum wage because that *would help narrow the pay gap*. He noted women account for 60 percent of the minimum-wage earners" (emphasis mine). We finally learn at the end of the article that the seventy-five cents to a dollar ratio between women and men is a lumped sum covering all incomes of all men and women. That doesn't prove or support anything; it has no meaning at all statistically to support Clinton's implication that discrimination still exists, but it sounds good. Again, perception is reality.

Let's first agree that every person deserves an equal opportunity for employment and should receive equal wages for equal merit. No one should question that statement. To study this statistically, the characteristics of a pool of applicants for employment must be established, and then compared to the hiring results. Skill and experience levels must be measured.

Then, advancement and pay scales must be compared. For example, if in a group of corporations of one industry it is found there are 200 vice presidents and fifty are women (twenty-five percent), you can't complain that it should be 50/50, unless it is demonstrated that the pool of employees for advancement was 50/50 by sex. It may well be that the pool was 75/25 in the beginning and therefore was fair.

By the same token, applicant ratios cannot be the only criteria for advancement. Government quotas now demand that type of approach. The other necessary measurement must be individual merit. Just because the applicant ratio is 75/25 doesn't imply that the hiring ratio has to be 75/25; it may be 80/20 or 70/30 depending on individual merit considerations, somewhat difficult to test or measure, but which has to be accomplished to be fair to each individual. By comparison, salary scales are easier to compare. Therefore, the bill that has been proposed to "require companies with more than 100 employees to report in general terms their pay scales for women and men" is an excellent idea to provide reasonable statistics, not the lumped mathematical garbage presented.

If the only statistics available are the seventy-five cents versus one dollar, women versus men, we have no idea if job discrimination is rampant or if it even exists. Clinton concluded, "Therefore, it is ludicrous to say that 75% equality is enough. I wouldn't like it if someone said you can only pick up three out of every four paychecks. But that is, in effect, what we have said to the women of America." Once again, here is a politician talking with nothing real to back up the point he is making.

This is what we are given constantly by the propaganda machine in Washington. The newspapers swallow this without presenting a fair appraisal. It is a well-known fact that over eighty percent of Washington reporters are pro-Democrat, but the point of freedom of the press in the first amendment was to allow full dissemination of both sides of an issue for the public to digest. According to deTocqueville's description from the 1830s (*Victims with an Attitude*), we were at that time a population "highly educated . . . and politically most advanced." That education came from books, newspapers and debates by political candidates. At the present time, the pap presented in the papers and on TV educates and informs no one. Our current population's general knowledge of politics, political philosophy, and its ability to reason is not equal to the citizens of this country in the 1830s. What could the reporter have done within journalistic ethics to improve the article? He could have pointed out the true origin of the comparative figures, and asked a Republican to comment. This balanced approach helps one to think and make judgments. Instead, we are spoon fed the slant that is desired.

The final *Houston Chronicle* news article appeared 2 May 1998, as a *Washington Post* story by Peter Slevin. I've saved it for last because it is not a statistical piece, but raises an important mathematical concept that helps everyone in their own investment program and in understanding why spending in Washington grows and grows. The article spends twenty-seven column-inches poking fun at Haley Barbour, who headed the Republican National Committee during the 1995 campaign. That the *Post* pokes fun at Republicans is no surprise. The issue is simple enough. In the 1995 campaign, the Democrats accused the Republican budget proposals of "cutting" important entitlement programs like Medicare. Cutting what, cutting how? In the Alice-in-Wonderland accounting in Washington, there is a concept called "baseline budgeting." This means that entitlement programs, for example Medicare, have a planned or anticipated growth of six to eight percent per year as a built-in factor, which, of course, can be changed by Congress. This is a concept developed over forty years of Democrat control of Congress until 1994. The growth covers added participants in the program, enlargement of benefits, inflationary pressures, and bureaucracy enlargement (always a part of bureaucratic planning). As my sojourn in the Army Medical Corps showed me, a ten percent increase in yearly budget is mandatory.

The Democrats in 1995 called the Republican suggestion of three percent growth per year for Medicare a "cut," when, in fact, it is a reduction of the rate of growth. Haley Barbour, in a much-publicized ad offered a million dollars to anyone who could prove he was wrong in his assertion: "In November

1995, the U.S. House and Senate passed a balanced budget bill. It increases total federal spending on Medicare by more than 50% from 1995 to 2002." With a million dollars in the offing, folks did their calculating and Barbour found himself in federal court with several people suing him for the million dollars, basing their claims on a seven-year total expenditure, which does not go up fifty percent. The group included one claimant, who used the Democrat approach of a baseline budgeting "cut," and his math demonstrated a reduction in spending of $265 billion from the previously anticipated total. Barbour's claim is that he meant *yearly* spending would rise from $178 billion to $289 billion over seven years, a sixty-two percent rise on the yearly basis. Since his assertion in the ad did not specify total expenditures for seven years versus a comparison of the yearly rises, no one is right or wrong, and I view the law suit as frivolous, and politics as usual.

The *Post* reporter was having so much fun, his article did not bother to fully explain the differences in interpretation of the assertion by Barbour and his opponents in court. The article also clearly demonstrates how confused the general public is in regard to the sleight-of-hand accounting in Washington. A three percent per year increase in Medicare expenditures is considered a "cut," and made to sound like a reduction. The article brings up the need to discuss the mathematical "Rule of 72." The Rule of 72 is a tool used by investment advisors to figure out how soon a money account earning interest will double in value. One simply divides the yearly interest rate into 72. The answer is the doubling time. For example, an eight percent rate will double the original amount in nine years, a six percent rate in twelve years. That is the power of compound interest: Put $2,000 away at age twenty at eight percent; at sixty-five it will have doubled 5 times and be worth $64,000. Let's get back to baseline budgeting and use the Rule of 72 to look at federal spending in entitlement programs. It works the same way as in investment planning, but in this case the rule shows why we have had runaway federal spending: Six percent yearly baseline increases will double program expenditures in twelve years; eight percent doubles the program expenses in nine years.

This now leads us to solving the Social Security problem currently worrying the country. The origin of the program was deep in the Depression of the 1930s. Roosevelt's New Deal devised the plan as a safety net to provide a subsistence program to underlie the retirement savings that everyone was expected to provide for themselves as we worked our way out of the Depression. Subsequently, bipartisan fiscal irresponsibility by Congress expanded benefits way beyond actuarial estimates of what Social Security was really capable of paying out. Congress took a program that was fairly sound, if kept as a bare subsistence income, and turned it into an income transfer program, from a younger generation to older generations. The congressmen were just buying votes with our money, as usual—they would set up our retirements for us. It would no longer be a safety net, but a full-blown retirement fund. It was safe enough to do that when over forty-two workers were paying in to the Social Security fund to cover one retiree at the beginning of Social Security. Congresses since the 1930s have covered over the mess they created by simply raising the Social Security tax taken out of paychecks, and raising the amount of salary which can be taxed. This is a very regressive tax scheme for people with lower incomes, paying 6.2% (currently). For the person making $100,000, a little more than one-third is not taxed, making his effective rate about four percent. Congress, in its myopic view of the future, did not watch population demographics while expanding the benefits. One addition I have previously mentioned, they added to the program: Social Security Disability benefits offered to immigrants who never contributed to the program. They treated payroll taxes as a bottomless pit. Now we are approaching a point that 1.8 workers will support one retiree. Congress cannot be blamed for the lengthening of life expectancy but should have taken note of it as they expanded Social Security benefits. When Social Security was started, retirement age was set at sixty-five; life expectancy was also sixty-five. Now life expectancy is eighty-three, and Social Security is obligated to pay on the average for eighteen years of retirement, and that length of retirement will continue to increase as life expectancy lengthens.

By the year 2002, Social Security will have an unfunded liability of three trillion dollars. Eventually, after the years 2012-15 (by current estimates), the unfunded liability will gradually rise to seven trillion dollars. Wait, you say, there is a trust fund. Yes, and no. What Social Security does each year is pay current obligations out of current collections. The money left over each year from the funds collected for that year buys treasury bonds, strictly according to law, thereby creating the "trust fund." Congress and the President claim that the budget is balanced as of 1997 by borrowing and spending the money represented by the trust fund bonds, wiping out the yearly deficit. The money is gone for the present. The bonds don't create income, except they are supposed to return something over three percent per year, depending on the interest rate for that year. What the bonds represent, in reality, to no ones' surprise when the issue is studied, are simply I.O.U.s on our treasury. They represent a future obligation, an unfunded liability. Since our government is not a profit-making entity (there are a few areas of income: national park concession fees, logging fees, off-shore and continental oil royalties, etc.), its income is primarily the tax receipts extracted from us year by year. There is no money behind those trust funds, and only by collecting taxes to pay off those bonds can they be made good. Currently, as of 1998, $100 billion a year are being put into those trust fund bonds, and all that is really happening is a future funding obligation is created, to be solved by future Congresses collecting more taxes from future generations. That protects current congressmen too cowardly to attack the problem. Senator Tom Daschle, who is a Democrat from South Dakota, in a 1996 interview with Robert Novak, responding to Novak's pointed questions admitted: "No, there is no such fund, per se." The Congress hypocritically calls the budget balanced, and watches an unfunded obligation grow. They ask for newly appointed commissions outside Congress to make recommendations, while the solution resides in the Rule of 72.

Since we are discussing trillions of dollars, something I can't imagine, lets look at this as though we are discussing a family of five. Mother and father are working to support the family and on the side create a college fund for the three kids.

Unfortunately, each year when vacation time comes for every-one, the only money available sits in the college fund, where it is trying to earn some interest. Either they take out a bank loan to take the vacation, or they raid the fund. Each year they raid the fund rather than pay a bunch of interest on a bank loan or on a credit card that is maxed out, and write them-selves an I.O.U. Their budget is balanced each year, everyone is happy with the vacations, but when the first kid turns eigh-teen and is ready for college, what do they do? They'll have to borrow the money each year, and pay interest on it, a reverse and negative effect of the Rule of 72. Everyone who has had a house mortgage knows how much larger the total sum of interest paid over the years is compared to the principal. If the family had not taken the vacations, the Rule of 72 would have helped grow that college fund. The family gave into instant gratification, just as Congress does. Have you noticed, unless the parents have some sort of pension plans at work, all they have to look forward to after the children are out of college is scrambling to save some retirement funds and hope Social Security will be there for them, as Congress keeps promising?

Why hasn't Congress come to grips with this? The rheto-ric and concern about what to do is finally being voiced by some in Congress. I think the foot-dragging is partially be-cause they cannot see past the next election, but mainly be-cause they do not want to give up control of any monetary program where they can make it appear that they are taking care of us and providing for us. "But wait," you should be thinking, "the fixes they have put in place so far are raises in payroll taxes; I don't like that." My response to you is to think about it; those taxes are somewhat hidden: everyone in this country is accustomed to "take-home pay," even though they know their total salary is a lot bigger. In the game Congress plays, the more that happens automatically before you see the paycheck, the less you are aware of how much is being ex-tracted. If you got all your salary, and then had to send in quarterly payments, you'd have a better idea of what is really being done to you. Don't think the fact that the employers having to pay half of the Social Security "contribution" is a good deal. The company simply raises the price of their product to cover the extra business expense and all of us end up paying that portion also.

All that is being suggested so far, until 1998, to fix Social Security is taking two percent of the 12.4% contribution and put it into individual investment accounts; raise the retirement age gradually to seventy, or even beyond that; set up a "safety net" supplementary fund, so no retiree has an income below the poverty line; and keep it all within the current Social Security system by setting up, over a three to five year period, a massive administrative program to handle 160 million private investment accounts. The philosophy in Washington continues to be one of not trusting the American citizens to be responsible for themselves, and not daring to take a giant step forward, to privatize the whole program and use already existing resources to administer the accounts. The longer we wait, the less the benefit from the Rule of 72. The sooner you invest at a compound interest rate, the higher the resulting sum at retirement: twelve hundred dollars invested per year by a twenty-five-year-old at eight percent (not an unreasonable scenario) will provide $351,428 40 years later for an age sixty-five retirement. Delay five years and collect $230,918, a loss of $120,510 or thirty-four percent! We need to pressure Congress to get a move on, or elect new folks who will.

Despite the fact that Social Security has been a government sponsored program for over sixty years, it does not mean that the government has to continue to run it. There can be some federally-mandated guidelines to a program being privatized, phased in so as to protect the already retired and the older working folks who deserve Social Security because it was promised to them. As a country we are all in this together, and we do not need one generation set against another. If Congress had started to work on this twenty years ago there would be a much smaller unfunded liability, but the problem can still be solved. It will just take longer than it should have. Courageous and far-sighted leaders in Washington are in short supply. With privatization the younger generations will end up much better off than under a government program with the help of the Rule of 72. As I write this, I am literally laughing inside at a vision of 535 Congress members looking quizzical and wringing their hands over the insoluble problem handed down to them from the time of the New Deal. How ludicrous. For how many years have we had company pension plans, IRAs, and 401(k)s permitted by Congressional laws? Much of our public is quite knowledgeable about the tricks of investing, and a fair portion of us have bought stocks and bonds for ourselves (forty-three percent). Perhaps in the 1930s and 1940s it was appropriate to set up a Social Security plan as it originally began. Now a fair portion of the public is sophisticated enough to recognize that conservative investing, not just income transferring, can bring very comfortable retirements.

There are several concerns voiced by Congress members and others, that may be a way of delaying a consideration of privatization, but also have validity. I think all can be solved, but here they are: 1) How do we handle the real issue of a sudden down turn in the market when someone is about to retire? Will they lose a sizable percentage of their retirement funds? 2) If the privatized funds are invested by a governmental group into some of our domestic companies, will the federal government become such a large stockholder it will have undue influence over the companies' policies and management? Further, a poll of citizens in 1998, showing how little we trust our government, found fifty-nine percent do not want to allow the government to make investment decisions (*Houston Chronicle*, 28 July 1998) 3). Is it safe to allow private citizens to run their own plans, with their own privatized accounts? 4) As we phase out giving money to older citizens who are on Social Security now and those who will have to receive it in the future because there is not enough time for them to build up satisfactory private accounts, how do we handle people who never earn enough to create a comfortable retirement account? In this group are included young widows, dependent children, disabled persons, and those who, for whatever reason, never earned enough to build up an account. 5) Will the administration of private funds cost too much? 6) Should we allow some people to exclude themselves from the program? There are answers for all of these objections and questions.

Investing money at an interest rate to produce income provides a much larger pool of funds for retirement than simply passing our tax money through a government agency to people who are retired, but investment at interest involves varying amounts of risk. In the bond market, the higher the rate for which you rent out your money, the higher the risk. The stock markets have their up and down periods, which happen on no particular schedule, since the markets are at the mercy of mass psychology as well as investing principles. Putting money into new small companies that are issuing stock is very chancy. Only two out of ten new companies hit a home run. My scenario keeps all of this risk in mind.

My plan can make us a very rich country, with more money in peoples' hands than can be imagined at this time. Answering question six, first, I think people should be able to exclude themselves, if they can prove their net worth in over a certain amount, say $500,000, or that they have a large enough private pension plan to provide a certain income, say $40,000 a year in current dollars. I realize, as a libertarian, that ideally we should let everyone opt out who wants to. However, on the psychological bell-shaped curve of personal fiscal responsibility, there will be people who burn up all their money, and in their later years will come with their hands out to be taken care of by the rest of us more responsible folks. It is better not to let that happen. The other five questions are taken care of by the plan I propose.

First separate Social Security spending from the federal budget. With budget and Social Security surpluses make those worthless bonds in the trust fund good by putting the money into proper investments. Appoint the top twelve to twenty-one investment companies and brokerage houses, as rated by private independent rating services, to handle the investments, and every two years drop the companies with the bottom one-third of fund growth, replacing them with new investment groups. This keeps the competition very sharp, and investment decisions out of the government's hands, reducing the possibility of government interference in private corporate decisions. I do not have the actuarial knowledge to pick exact ages in our working population, but our population needs to be divided into those who will receive Social Security as currently devised, and those who will be provided a national pension plan retirement. For example, I would start at age fifteen, dividing the population into ten year segments, ending with a group that is sixty-five years old and above. In my example, forty-five-year-olds and the three decades below would have their contributions go in large part to the pension plan, while for age forty-five and above some part of their contributions would go to pension plan and some to Social Security, with the employers' share also being contributed in some proportional way to phase out Social Security and bring in the pension plan.

Dividing the population by age into decades is very important to the safety of the retirement accounts. Following conservative investing principles, ages fifteen to thirty-five should go into mutual funds divided seventy-five percent stock—twenty-five percent bonds, and the percentages should gradually shift so that by age sixty-five, those people should be invested twenty-five percent in stock and seventy-five percent in bonds, protecting those about to retire from stock market downturns. Historical financial research for the period 1925 to 1996 has found that large-company stocks have had a compound annual return of 10.7%, small-company stocks, 12.6%, compared with 5.1% for long-term government bonds (statistics taken from Pamela Yip column, *Houston Chronicle*, 11 May 1998, quoting Ibbotson Associates of Chicago). Note that this seventy-one-year study covers the market crash of 1929 and the mini-crash of 1987. The stock market always recovers if given time. You just never know how much time. Bonds are not as volatile in price as stocks, since they are controlled by interest rate levels, making small changes again by simple arithmetic, prices to go up if rates go down and down if rates are up. These stock/bond mixes provide growth early in life when there is time to recover from downturns, and relative safety as retirement approaches.

There should, therefore, be mutual funds set up with differing proportions, and the retirement accounts should be readily portable to the appropriate fund according to age. These funds should be indexed to the stock market and set up by my proposed twelve to twenty-one investment companies, who are in competition with each other to keep the business. There should be a Federal Board of Investment Governors coming from national districts, just like the Federal Reserve Board to oversee the pension plan and make decisions about the private investment companies doing investment work. I would have the payroll withholdings go directly to the investment companies, with records of those transactions sent to the Federal Board. There is no need to have the money pass through Washington, where some will be wasted in bureaucratic salaries. Each American employee will have his own portable account carrying through from job to job, and automatically placed in the proper mutual fund for his age until retirement, and the income from that account in retirement will be taxed at whatever the income tax rates are at the time. At his death the account is passed in his estate to his family and other beneficiaries according to his will, since it is his private mutual fund account.

This solves the unfairness of the current system. Under the present system you only collect money till you die, no matter what you put into your account. There are no benefits if death precedes age sixty-two (early retirement) or sixty-five, the normal retirement. The system is especially unfair to the black population, and any other group that on the average doesn't live as long as whites. Yes, there are widows' benefits, but the system is still grossly unfair. Tongue-in-cheek, we should really be encouraging smoking, not trying to stop the roughly twenty-five percent of the adult population who are smokers. They die much younger than those of us who do not smoke, and the money they don't get supports the rest of us in delaying the failure of the Social Security System!

Answering opponents' objections under this plan, the risk of substantial loss of pension plan funds is greatly minimized. Indexed funds are now carefully set up to track the overall stock market averages and have been shown to achieve that result. Of course, a worker could stay employed after age sixty-five to make his account larger or to let it recover from a downturn. Life was never meant to be entirely fair, and we are in trouble now because Congress guaranteed us perfection in Social Security, a hopeless goal. A review of Dow Jones Industrial Averages (DJIA) since the Great Depression is reassuring.

The DJIA was fifty-nine on 1 January 1933, after flirting with the 400 range just before the crash in October 1929. By January 1937 it was 178. It then rose to 734 by January 1961, but moved sideways and was 734 in 1980. Yet in 1998 the DJIA was flirting with 9,000, almost eleven times higher than 1979. If Social Security had been set up as a pension plan with actuarial planning in the mid-1930s, let's say at a DJIA of 150, it would have been almost five times higher by 1961. The nineteen years of pause between 1961 and 1980 would still allow for a doubling of the Social Security funds by taking a 3.8% return in dividends and bond interest per the Rule of 72. Obviously, a very possible 4.5% return would have doubled the funds in sixteen years, etc.

Government influence in private business decisions is carefully buffered by using private investment companies in competition, making the investment decisions. And to reassure citizens' worries about trusting our government, the government takes no part in investment decisions. This plan does not allow private citizens to run their own accounts. Again, in an anti-libertarian decision, as I stated before, I do not think it wise to have self-control over the accounts. There is going to be a small segment of our population who will take wild investment guesses, and have their hands out to the rest of us at retirement age. Using private investment companies will not increase administrative costs prohibitively. They already have computer programs to handle millions of accounts. The administrative costs of IRAs are currently small. Social Security now has operating costs under one percent of annual contributions. There are many mutual funds that currently operate at costs of 0.5% to 1.5% of fund size. With the necessary reports to Social Security, perhaps another 0.25% cost might appear. As an example, management of my pension plan is currently running two percent of yearly income, with all reports to the IRS included.

What is left to consider are those unfortunate people who, for whatever reason, cannot be part of an earned pension plan. We must provide a safety net for them. I do not favor any form of inheritance tax: estate taxes bring in only one percent of current national yearly receipts, and that tax is damaging

aging the ability of families to pass on small businesses and farmland. Besides, why should we be taxing after-tax dollars carefully accumulated by fiscally responsible people? We should reward, not punish good deeds. However, in this instance a government-sponsored pension plan provided a retirement for mom and dad and an inheritance for their children. Why not have a small inheritance tax on these funds to supply the money needed to protect the unfortunate? The safety net program can be administered by the truncated Social Security Agency, left after the current program is phased out. That seems to make it fair to everyone.

There are pilot programs out there to prove that this can work beautifully. Chile has been conducting a privatized plan for seventeen years. It demonstrates a hidden benefit for our capitalistic society: the new investment money will further energize our economy, creating many new jobs and massive growth of our gross national product. Mr. Jose Pinera, a Chilean, President of the International Center for Pension Reform, and co-chairman of the Cato Institute's Project on Social Security Privatization, 10 April 1998, in the *Wall Street Journal,* described the Chilean result: "Since Chile embarked on this course, a flood of investment has benefited both individuals and the economy as a whole. As unemployment has fallen to its lowest levels in history, productivity has increased sharply, the savings rate has soared to around 25% of gross domestic product and economic growth has more than doubled to a 7% average during the last 13 years. If we keep up the present rhythm for another seven years, the size of the economy will have quadrupled in only 20 years." Note the Rule of 72, again. Seven percent compounded growth for twenty years quadruples the base amount. Naturally, our economy, being so much bigger at the start will not show that magnitude of growth. Seven other South American countries, Canada, Australia and Great Britain, all impressed by Chile's experience, are now privatized. Great Britain has gradually privatized over a two decade period. The system works well now, but by allowing each individual to make investment decisions during the transition, many people suffered heavy losses in investments (about eighteen billion dollars) because of high-pressure sales techniques by investment firms (*New York Times* article by Stevenson, *Houston Chronicle*, 19 July 1998, *WSJ*, 10 August 1998). My plan avoids that sort of problem.

E.J. Myers, author of *Let's Get Rid of Social Security* (1996), gives examples of a privatized federal and several local governmental plans in Texas that are very successful. In 1984 Congress set up the C Fund, a thrift savings plan for government employees only. It is administered entirely by Wells Fargo Funds, a private organization, not by the government. An employee who puts $3,500 a year in the plan will have $1.2 million in his retirement account in thirty years! We won't find an example like that anywhere in Social Security. Myers also describes local county plans in Texas that are equally as successful. Galveston County, investing with First Financial Capital Corporation of Houston, provides a twenty year retirement monthly benefit three to four times larger than Social Security would provide, and includes in the benefits disability insurance and a life insurance plan set at 300% of the employees' annual salary. Brazoria and Matagorda Counties also use First Financial with similar results, and the Houston Fire Department, privatized since 1937, provides retirement benefits over three times the amount that Social Security offers. Five states have started their own plans: California, Nevada, Maine, Ohio and Colorado. It is all simple arithmetic—the magic of compound interest and the Rule of 72.

If we could trust the Washington politicians to not spend money under their control (something that has never happened, and probably never will under our current election system), the Rule of 72 can be used in another way to solve our country's national debt and Social Security problem. In 1998, it has been predicted by the Congressional Budget Office that if the economy continued its current growth pattern, there will be a national budget surplus (with Social Security as part of the budget) of $1.55 trillion over the following decade. Social Security revenues will be $1.52 trillion (*Houston Chronicle*, Barlow, 28 July 1998). Investing that money at six percent in investments will result in a fund of over seven trillion dollars by 2032, the year Social Security is projected to crash. At four percent, about four trillion dollars will be available in 2032.

Unfortunately, Congress has always had a voracious appetite for unused funds. This amount of money lying around in a Washington fund will be very tempting unless a way is found to keep it safe from Congress. It is a way out of the Congress-induced Social Security mess as long as we can find a way to keep Congress from finding "emergencies" to fund. I would not save Social Security by this method but it shows that the Rule of 72 can bail us out.

Getting the folks in Washington to change their mind-sets about Social Security is going to be difficult. An opinion article by Albert B. Crenshaw of the *Washington Post*, printed in the *Houston Chronicle*, 8 June 1998, reviewed a "national summit" conference, held the first week in June 1998 in Washington. The facts presented to the conference are as frightening as ever regarding the way Americans save and are trying to prepare for retirement: "The personal saving rate is at a 59-year low; 80% of current retirees get the bulk of their income from Social Security; only a quarter of current workers are very confident they will have enough income in retirement; just under a third are not confident they will have enough, while 44% figure they will be okay if nothing goes wrong." The opinion article decries the shift from defined-benefit pension plans, caused by Congress-imposed tough restrictions, to re-placement by 401(k)s and other defined-contribution plans, which cost employers less:

> The rhetoric (supporting these plans) is full of buzzwords like "personal responsibility," "control," and an "end to paternalism" that make it sound as if workers are being handed something really desirable. And some are. Those who take advantage of the savings opportunities, the tax breaks, and the soaring stock market can, over time, put together a very large sum. Indeed, 401(k)s and IRAs with balances of six and even seven digits are already appearing. A young family making $28,000 a year is going to find it hard to put much into a 401(k) or max-out the $4,000 they can put into an IRA each year. The most important consequence of the current philosophy of self-empowerment, though, is likely to be the creation, in retirement, of an even wider gulf between haves

and have-nots than already exists in the working world.
Conversion of some or all of Social Security to investment accounts would exacerbate it further.

I interpret this to mean that a person should not try to be
too successful, or too fiscally responsible for himself. He might
have too much money compared to someone who was not as
responsible. Did you know that Marx and Lenin are alive and
well in Washington? Ask Ralph Nadar. He thinks Bill Gates
of Microsoft has too much money, and calls it "a problem of
distributive justice" (*Houston Chronicle,* 28 July 1998). If people
cannot take responsibility for their own retirement, Washington is required to rush in and bail them out. There is nothing
wrong with the following idea: Don't start a family if you can't
make it on $28,000! Is it an "entitlement" that you are allowed
to start a family when you are not financially able to do so?
This makes the rest of us responsible to bail out the idiots who
get themselves in trouble. In 1927 my father proposed to my
mother. He was twenty-three years old and had been working
six years. He said to Mother, "I have saved $6,000." She asked,
"Why are you telling me this?" "I want to marry you!" Do you
have any idea what $6,000 in 1920s dollars is worth expressed
in 1990s dollars? $56,000! Unfortunately there are few enough
Americans who take fiscal responsibility for themselves. They
have been taught that they are allowed immediate gratification, and look to Congress to be bailed out. This is the climate
in the country and especially in Washington. Unless this kind
of thinking is radically changed we are really headed for trouble.
Congress has set up Social Security as a gigantic giveaway, and
the public has been seduced into abdicating personal responsibility and accepting governmental responsibility for personal
retirement plans, making us pawns of Congress to get them
reelected. When Social Security was started, the country was
in terrible economic trouble. People needed help. Now the
country is awash in money and financial success, and we have
people who will drown in retirement, because of Washington's
seductive propaganda of the last forty years. My solution for
Social Security will work, but it won't change the awful philosophy out there. That will take moral and ethical reeduca-
tion.

There is another statistical method that citizens can use to judge what Washington is attempting to promise us as the result of a new program they are about to institute. It is a study of trendlines. There is an excellent discussion of this in Charles Murray's book *What It Means to Be a Libertarian* (1997). A trendline is a graph following the occurrence year-by-year of a phenomenon to be studied and perhaps altered. Murray shows a graph of automobile deaths per 100 million miles traveled starting in 1925. The trendline drops rapidly, and with the imposition of a fifty-five mile per hour speed limit in 1974, the downward slope is unchanged. The speed limit reduction had no effect on the increasing safety of auto travel, although the government tried to claim it did. Another trendline of great interest is the poverty level. Did the Great Society War on poverty make a difference when started in 1963? The answer is: no it didn't. The trend was sharply downward starting in the 1940s after World War II ended, and continued dropping at the same rate until about 1970 when it leveled off. Trendlines are a dynamic way of looking at the possible value of government interventions (Eberstadt, *WSJ*, 22 April 1996 and Thernstrom & Thernstrom, *WSJ*, 3 September 1997).

Another trendline, which is fascinating to me, is the rate of federal tax receipts as a percentage of gross domestic product (the size of our national economy). Over the thirty-plus years from 1960 until the early 1990s, the GDP grew from two trillion dollars to five trillion dollars. During this period we have had top income tax rates as high as ninety-one percent and as low as twenty-eight percent, yet the trendline of tax receipts as a percentage of GDP is virtually flat, varying from eighteen percent to twenty-one percent, and averaging 19.5% (*WSJ*, 25 March 1993 and 7 December 1994). These facts attest to the need for doing "dynamic scoring" in estimating tax receipts when tax rates are changed. Taxpayers respond to rates with their own individual decisions as to how to accept income, and thereby be liable for tax (see discussion Chapter Eight). The other effect of this trendline is to partially refute the claims of low-tax "supply-siders," who point to the Reagan tax cut of the early 1980s as the cause of a rapidly expanding economy with the tax receipts almost doubling during his eight-year term. If that is the case, then how to explain the extremely rapid growth of the economy following the Bush and Clinton tax increases in the early 1990s, the latter said to be the largest peacetime tax increase ever, resulting in the so-called balanced budget by 1998? The answer is the national economy is a slightly controlled 800-pound gorilla, influenced by many factors, one of which is tax rates, but primarily affected by the American population making many individual decisions to increase their own personal wealth. The principle is that trendlines are extremely valuable statistical guides and are worth studying closely to understand proposals at hand.

————————————

The bell-shaped curve has been mentioned on a number of occasions. As a measure of natural characteristics it is usually symmetrical, especially when measuring normal values of various chemicals in the body. In fact, a bell-shaped curve appears when measuring almost all of the biologic characteristics that make up human beings. It is symmetrical in measuring human mental characteristics like I.Q., and I believe that measuring personality characteristics, it will be generally symmetrical, but I should point out for completeness that these curves in certain circumstances can be skewed. But let's look at how a typical bell curve is used in studying thyroid conditions in patients, as a way of further explaining simple statistics.

Figure one shows a typical bell curve for the measurement of thyroid hormone blood levels, referred to as T4, shorthand for the fact that the hormone produced by the thyroid gland has four iodine atoms on it. The range of normal is from 4.5 to 13.5, cutting off "tails" of 2.5% of the population at either end of the curve. The curve is produced by studying people who appear to be normal. Therefore, normal people may well be out in those tails, but people who have too much or too little thyroid may be mixed in also. However, the statisticians assure us that with ninety-five percent certainty everyone else under the curve is "normal." Note it is not 100%. It is possible to be abnormal and be within "normal limits" of 4.5 to 13.5.

The problem is illustrated by figure two. Imagine a patient whose body was happily functioning at a T4 of 10.5. What

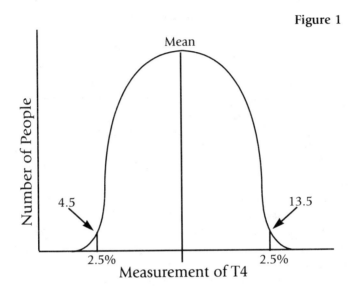

Figure 1

Number of People

Mean

4.5

13.5

2.5%

2.5%

Measurement of T4

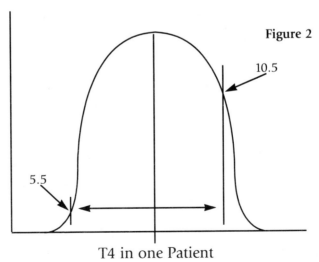

Figure 2

10.5

5.5

T4 in one Patient

thyroid hormone does in the body is run our rate of metabolism, the rate at which we are able to burn oxygen. It has to
do with how peppy we are, how much "energy" we have. It has
other bodily effects if too high or too low, but we don't need
to consider those changes to make the point at hand. My
theoretical patient at some point suffers from some damage to
the thyroid gland, and now it produces only a blood level of
5.5. The patient visits his doctor and complains of sluggish-
ness. If only the T4 test is used, the problem will not be
uncovered. Five and five-tenths is "normal" according to the
curve. Thank goodness for the way the body is set up. The
pituitary gland (the so-called "master" gland) sitting up under
the brain, reads the T4 blood levels and sends out its own
hormone to stimulate the thyroid gland if need be. That hormone logically is called Thyroid Stimulating Hormone, TSH
for short. The normal range for that substance is zero to four.
The doctor tests his sluggish patient for TSH and gets a result
of five. The pituitary is telling the thyroid to make more hormone and it cannot. The answer is to give the patient thyroid
pills to make up the deficiency. This story is simple, and if it
were more complicated there are several other interlocking
processes involving the thyroid and its control in the body that
can be tested to sort it all out.

I'm not trying to teach medicine but I am using it to show
how statistics may not be what they seem, and how underlying
factors may need to be understood in order to accept the statistical conclusions presented. How accurately the measurements underlying the statistics were obtained may be extremely
important. The entire method of obtaining the underlying
numbers must be understood to be sure of the conclusions.
The bell curve is a major underlying concept in the mathemat-
ics of statistical analysis. As mentioned, the little "tails" on
either end of the curve contain those findings that are considered to be beyond normal. The whole bell curve gives us the
full range of variation, and there is a math formula which gives
the "standard deviation," the statistician's measure of variation
from the average value. When a newspaper story covers a poll
and says its accuracy is three percent, the article is really giving
the standard deviation of the poll.

This brings me to polling data. Now that you have seen the bell-shaped curve at work, try to imagine 200 million people under that curve, who are American adults and could be polled for adult opinions. Advocacy groups, governmental agencies, think tanks, and news organizations have in the past two decades discovered polls as a tool for public relations, news making, and lobbying. Television news broadcasts, which are consistently losing their market share of viewers, have turned the nightly broadcasts into soap-opera-like feature magazines, with segments that say, "let us help you, let us protect you, let us instruct you, and let us tell you what other people are thinking." Polls are presented like peer pressure; if all those people in the poll feel that way, you should also. The polls claim they are accurate within three to five percent, while talking with 1,000 people on the phone. Stop a moment and think. What does that three percent implied accuracy statement mean to you? That the poll is ninety-seven percent a correct reflection of public opinion? My answer is, perhaps. What it really represents is a statistical probability, claiming that it is an accurate estimate of public opinion, as extracted by the contents of the wording of that poll, and, further, that the poll's accuracy is within plus or minus three percent of the real result, if the entire population were questioned. Plus or minus three percent really adds up to a spread of six percent. The three percent accuracy number is therefore only a mathematical prediction, based on statistical formulas and is no real guarantee as to the true accuracy of the poll which actually depends on who is willing to be questioned, how the questions are worded, and the order in which they are presented, as I will explain.

To the credit of American citizens, according to John H. Fund, a *Wall Street Journal* editorial board member, 13 August 1996, people are getting harder to poll: "Half or more of the people they try to contact can't be surveyed," not calling back on answering machine messages, or refusing to answer questions. "Pollsters must decide who they're likely to have undersampled and weigh their results accordingly." Take a moment and think about what that means. At least half the people who should be sampled at random are not! The sample includes only those people who are at home when the phone rings and who are willing to answer the questions. The telephone sample is skewed to begin with and in no way will match secret ballot voting, where no one is privy to your decisions. No pollster's finagle factor can unscramble this problem.

Simple arithmetic tells us that each person of the 1,000 people surveyed represents 200,000 opinions. An error of three percent of 200 million citizens is an error of six million persons, and five percent is ten million. That is the size, and larger than the size, of several of the smaller ethnic sub-groups in our diverse population. The Jewish population is about six million, for example. During the 1996 presidential election, only the Zogby poll ended up hitting the final result of an eight percent difference between Clinton and Dole (http://www.zogby.com). Zogby explained that this was accomplished by meticulously matching the polling sample with as exact demographic percentages of Republicans, Democrats, and unaffiliated probable voters as they could determine. It would appear the other national polls were not as careful. The sampling technique is very tricky, and since the pollsters simply declare their range of error without describing how they obtained the sample, the polls cannot be trusted.

Further, there is something in politics called the "push" poll. In this type of poll the questioner on the phone talks about two opposing candidates, and presents some very adverse material about one of them. Then the voting questions are posed. When this happened to me concerning a local Texas election, my answer was very careful. I would not vote for the adversely-described candidate, if the allegations were to be *proven* true to me. I have no idea how I was counted, if I was. The real purpose of the poll was to convince me to vote for the other guy. It is reported that Governor Laughton Chiles won his last election against Jeb Bush in Florida by use of these push polls.

The technique of push polls points out the fact that how questions are posed, in what order they are presented, and what influencing considerations precede the questions will control the answers. The more emotionally charged the issue, the worse the problem. Affirmative action is such an issue. The intent of the concept is well accepted as an important step forward to making equal opportunity available to minorities who have not had equal access to schools, jobs and as companies bidding on governmental projects. If people are asked if they favor affirmative action, of course they do. But if they are asked about the use of quotas, which implies that some people are being purposely included to make the quota requirement at the exclusion of other qualified people, then generally the poll will reject the concept. Quotas, used as an easy-to-follow numerical result by governments, are unfair in the minds of many Americans who are accustomed to "fair competition" in our capitalistic society, based on individual merit. So, governmental people often change the words from "quotas" to "goals," "preferences" and "set-asides," while really continuing quotas and still being able to count numbers.

In 1997 in Houston, Texas, a petition, carefully worded to bring out the concept of individual merit, not preferences, received enough signatures to force a vote on the methods of the affirmative action program of the city. Mayor Bob Lanier, a champion of affirmative action, immediately changed the question asked of the voters, essentially stating that following the dictates of the petition would end affirmative action for the city, and the ensuing vote preserved his program, although polls worded like the petition were strongly in favor of the petition.

Here are the two statements. The petition read: "The city of Houston shall not discriminate against, or grant preferential treatment to, any individual or group on the basis of race, sex, color, ethnicity or national origin in the operation of public employment and public contracting." Mayor Lanier and City Council changed the wording to: "Shall the charter of the City of Houston be amended to end the use of affirmative action for women and minorities in the operation of the city of Houston employment and contracting, including ending the current program and similar programs in the future." There is no way those two statements mean the same thing, and in a law suit brought by the petitioners, the judge sided with them by overturning the election after ruling that the language of

the petition and the ballot language were significantly different. The petition addressed the methodology of affirmative
action, not ending affirmative action itself. The only method
governmental bodies want to use is quotas and set-asides. Language must have clear meaning in petitions and in voting. The
passage of Proposition 209 in California ended affirmative
action in that state, and the Houston petition used language
very close to that of Proposition 209.

The underlying problem is that it is very unclear in the
minds of the American public whether the term affirmative
action means equal opportunity or preferences—and with good
reason. At the time the original Civil Rights Act was passed
in Washington in 1964, Senator Hubert H. Humphrey declared that he would "eat the law, if anyone could find quotas
in it." Despite the fact that they were expressly forbidden, the
first compliance officer of the Equal Opportunities Employment Commission (EEOC) used quotas and "praised the
agency for working 'in defiance of the laws governing its operation' " (Johnson, *History of the American People*, 1997). Our
courts have allowed quotas to creep in under the theory of
"legal realism," which argues that sociologic imperatives should
be allowed priority over the original intent of constitutions and
statutes, allowing legal decisions to advance social policy and
improve society (Johnson, *History of American People*). In other
words, the courts started legislating. No wonder the public is
confused. When I entered Bates College in Maine in 1946, I
learned that the college, way ahead of the affirmative action
concept, had inclusion quotas, mimicking the population distribution of New England. Those of us who were Jewish were
told that Bates had included 3.6% of us, against an actual 3.4%
Jewish population in New England. I resented the approach at
that time, and I still do. I wanted to be at their college based
on my own abilities and what I had to offer. Dr. Thomas
Sowell, a black conservative I have quoted before, states "One
of the many unfortunate consequences of affirmative action
has been that many minorities and females have no definitive
way to know, or to what extent, they got where they are by
their own efforts . . . group quotas stigmatize even legitimate
achievements" (*Forbes*, 10 April 1995).

It appears that at times poll results are deliberately falsified prior to elections and also after. Following the favorable vote in California, 2 June 1998, on Proposition 227 to abolish bilingual education, false polling results were reported by Charlie Ericksen, publisher of Hispanic Link News Service (*Houston Chronicle,* 11 June 1998). Prior to the vote several mainstream media surveys claimed that Hispanics favored Proposition 227 by as much as three to one. On the other hand, Hispanic media organizations found just the opposite, a sixty to eighty percent approval of bilingual education. On election day, the *LA Times*/CNN exit poll confirmed the Hispanic media finding, a sixty-three to thirty-seven percent vote against the proposition. Even after this exit poll was on the record, Ericksen found the *Chicago Tribune,* the *Washington Post,* the *Associated Press,* the *Christian Science Monitor,* and the *Dallas Morning News* all reported on 3-4 June 1998 a strong Hispanic vote for 227. Just because it is in print, don't believe it. Can our newspapers be trusted to give us unbiased news? When they accept any of this junk presented to them as gospel, they cannot be trusted. Honest journalistic research has become rare.

Fred Barnes, executive editor of the *Standard,* in a *Wall Street Journal* article in 1996, described "how to rig a poll," simply by using and misusing words. The following two questions were asked of the same 1031 people: "I would be disappointed if Congress cut its funding for public television." Fifty-four percent said not okay. Next question: "Cuts in funding for public television are justified . . . to reduce federal spending." Fifty-two percent said that would be okay. That is the same question, with different considerations added, and totally different results. Barnes presented a series of examples, and even pointed out a poll that asked forty-nine questions. They published the result of two questions that supported the public relations viewpoint they wished to present, and suppressed the results in questions that presented results that were negative to their viewpoint. Barnes concluded that we should "be skeptical of polls commissioned by advocacy groups." I could not agree more. Most people have not studied issues deeply, and respond emotionally and from sound-bite impressions they have developed. They answer the questioners according to the way the

questions are presented, and also as to how the responder
thinks the answer will please the questioner, especially if moral
or ethical slants are present in the question. Most polls are not
worth much with questions asked over the telephone and the
interaction that occurs with the questioning person.

Using and misusing words, the phrase just mentioned in
the last paragraph brings up another point. English is probably
the most precise language on Earth. We have a word or phrase
for almost every nuance of feeling or meaning. But still we
misunderstand each other more often than not. Most of that
misunderstanding is unwanted and unintentional, but it is
sometimes very deliberate. Did you ever wonder why lawyers
use such arcane words and phrases, or why doctor language
uses such big obscure terms? It is all invented vocabulary to
have very precise meanings that cannot be misinterpreted. It
works in medicine, but lawyers still argue over contracts. I
observed in my medical chapter that obtaining a very complete
history from the patient is eighty percent of the battle in achieving a proper diagnosis. The process is a battle of words and
feelings between the doctor and his patient. The final impression the doctor has of the problem is three times removed
from reality! The first remove is the patient trying to put his
feelings and symptoms into words. The second remove is the
doctor trying to hear what the patient is telling him, asking
questions of the patient to clarify his understanding of the
problem, and knowing that the patient is struggling with an
interpretation problem internally. The third remove is the doctor
comparing this information with his experience with other
patients who have told a similar story, and the doctor using his
own health problems to see if that will help his understanding.
The final result in the doctor's brain is an approximation, most
often a very close one.

The Haley Barbour court case comes from an ambiguous
sentence in his ad. I don't know whether it was deliberate or
not, but I suspect it was just bad planning in the rush to get
the ad out in print. In doing any statistical or scientific study,
there is no room for ambiguity, if the results are to be accurate.
The study must be carefully defined to understand the measurements being obtained, and the conclusions derived. To

illustrate, I am going to use "Planters Mixed Nuts," a three pound eight ounce can I buy at Sam's Club, and love to nibble from, a small handful at a time. The advertising hook below the title is: "Less than 50% peanuts." Let's stop. Did you read that and think you understood it? If you did, think again; analyze. How do you know what less than fifty percent peanuts means? I don't. All I know is when I open the can, it looks like a lovely mixture. I take out indiscriminate handfuls, and when I hit bottom, just peanuts are left, two or three handfuls. Now let's be scientific. The sentence can mean: 1) peanuts are numerically less than fifty percent; 2) peanuts are less than fifty percent by volume; 3) peanuts are less than fifty percent by weight. The scientist can find out easily. Divide out all the peanuts, and weigh, measure volume or count. The answer may be one, two or all three of the possibilities.

The pollster cannot do this; he cannot separate out people physically. He can only make theoretical assumptions in his sampling technique. The nuts represent various opinions, and also various cultural and political segments of our population. The poll taker must try to question a representative sample, which assumes that the nuts are smoothly and evenly mixed throughout the can (read "our country" or "his sample"). Is there any wonder that I think polls created to make news, or to push a position, or to bathe an advocacy group in self-praise are all junk news, not worth your time in watching or reading, unless you are willing to try and analyze what is presented, and only if enough information is given to allow analysis?

One of the worst developments that has happened recently in this country is that our Washington political leaders are governing by polls and by "focus groups." The latter are ordinary citizens brought together to act like a jury and pass judgment on policy proposals thrown at them. The polls are conducted by organizations hired by political parties to sound out opinions in the country. The people polled or in focus groups, are not experts and the results obtained have to be greatly influenced by emotion and by the wording of the questions. The politicians are governing by what is "safe" to propose to protect their own skins (read "reelectability"), not by determining the right principles, after careful research and expert testimony with which to lead the country properly. There are times when politicians must stop and educate the public as to what is most desirable, despite the appearance on a superficial first glance that the course is wrong, inappropriate, or too difficult.

Benjamin Franklin, in September 1787, at the end of the Constitutional Convention, was asked what was produced. He responded, "A republic, if you can keep it." George Will points out (25 May 1998 article, *Houston Chronicle*) that the "premise of republicanism comes from James Madison. 'In a republic,' Madison said, 'the people are the source of power but not the exercisers of it.' The principle of representation is the rivet securing the republican form of government. That principle is: The people do not decide issues, they decide who will decide—representatives in an assembly that can be a deliberative body." That is not truly happening now. The current approach by politicians, using polls to decide what is safe to propose, destroys the premise of republicanism. They do not lead, they test us and follow our opinions. If, in 1776, our brilliant patriotic leaders had guided themselves by a poll of the country, we would not exist today. At the start of the Revolutionary War, one-third of the population of the colonies wanted independence, one-third were loyal to England, and the other third would go either way. Luckily our founders weren't the gutless professional politicians we have today. They pushed forward, despite the fact their lives were at risk, while today the Washington politicians are afraid to follow necessary principles for fear of losing the next election.

Another example from this nation's founding years shows how narrow and shortsighted public opinion can be and why it should not be a guide for our congressmen. The framers of the Constitution knew that the four most powerful states— New York, Pennsylvania, Massachusetts, and Virginia—were vital to the success of the new federal government. They cleverly set a rule that the new Constitution would be adopted after nine states ratified, threatening the other four with the possibility of going it alone. New York was the most resistant, two of its three Constitutional Convention representatives having gone home in protest. Fifty-six percent of New Yorkers voted against ratification, and the New York ratifying convention was against the new Constitution by two to one, fearing they had more to lose than gain by joining the new nation. This explains why Alexander Hamilton, the remaining member of the New York delegation, arranged for the publication of the *Federalist Papers* in New York City. Thank goodness, the framer's plan worked! New York felt forced to join after the ninth state, New Hampshire, ratified. Immediate concerns cloud issues and confuse ordinary citizens. Our founders were miraculously farsighted and prescient. We need congressmen who are willing to study our current problems and apply a similar wisdom (Bantam Classic, *Federal Papers,* 1982, from the introduction by Garry Wills).

Chapter Seven

Bean Counters, Apathy,
and the Political Pendulum

Whatever else is said about the American citizenry, we try way too hard to find the perfect solution to our problems. Once we think we have found an answer by ourselves, or are convinced of an answer by others, it becomes the only answer, and all opposition is to be blasted aside. It is akin to sports competition. There can only be one winner. Finding a common ground among thinking people, recognizing an Aristotelian "golden mean," is to be avoided because the other side has had some of its points recognized, and there isn't an out-and-out winner. Occam's Razor, which I have described in the Introduction and in Chapter Two on medicine, is totally disregarded although it is entirely necessary, if we are to consider a nation under good will for all, as did the founding fathers. Competition in many aspects of life is not only desirable, but necessary to find or create the most efficient ways of producing results. Our capitalistic society demands competition to achieve the most productive business climate. That type of competition will usually end up with one winner. Competition among thoughtful people between ideas is also absolutely desirable, but should end up with everyone recognizing a win-win situation, a zero-sum game, in which everyone gains something.

Instead, we employ very aggressive and bellicose language to enhance our ideas and positions, overstating our opposition to the other side. As Neal R. Peirce, a syndicated columnist, points out we use "war (like) language: It's an explosive situation, torpedo that idea, stick to your guns; sports comments: no holds barred, beat him to the punch, play hardball, if you're not a winner, you're a loser; and (even) cannibalistic language:

go for the jugular, dog eat dog, bash their brains out, it sticks in my craw" (*Houston Chronicle*, 4 July 1998). We argue in slang hyperbole. Winston Churchill said of us: "Americans will always cooperate after they have eliminated other options" (Peirce).

Instead of cooperating from the beginning, we compete to win and manage to shove the political pendulum from far right to far left and back again, a 180-degree swing. A pendulum, by its very nature, wants to come to rest at the center of its arc. It takes tremendous energy to continuously swing it through 180 degrees allowing it to spend little time at the center. I'm not suggesting that every battle of ideas should split the issue exactly down the middle. Some problems will benefit from a slight tilt leftward and some just the opposite, but pushing to the extremes will always result in overreaction or overprotection. The best single example is the Prohibition Amendment and its disastrous consequences. Legislating morals is always on dangerous ground. Prostitution (in most states) and drugs are illegal, but we haven't stopped either as of yet, and frankly, never will. Abortion is currently legal, but the battle to make it illegal continues unabated. The Judeo-Christian bible is declared by some to be the final arbiter of all morals, but that leaves out the Muslim and Asian interpretation of morals.

We need to join a national debate with factors and beliefs from the right and the left. In debating tournaments the opposing debate teams have to be able to argue the question from either side, and often are able to win from either side because they have access to facts, statements, and unambiguous studies to support either side. Winning then involves how convincingly the arguments are presented to the judges. Often one approach may appeal more emotionally, but it may not win due to the presentation of facts and reasoned arguments. Nationally we have a distinct problem with an evenhanded presentation of "facts" and studies, and reasoned arguments. Slightly over eighty percent of reporters state they are liberal and left-leaning. Eighty-nine percent admit they voted for President Clinton (*Washington Star*). In liberal arts college and university faculties, liberals are about ninety percent. As

Gelernter has pointed out in *Drawing Life*, the intellectual elite (the faculties) tend to try to control the evolving national philosophic debate, and the press has been their handmaiden.

Allan Bloom made this quite clear in his brilliant bestseller *The Closing of the American Mind* (1988), the first major book to call attention to the loss of teaching and of direction in American universities, starting in the 1960s, and the sources of that loss. His appalling description of the dismantling of the core curricula by the colleges and universities in a cowardly fashion acceding to radical student groups in the 1960s, is a striking indictment of his fellow faculty associates. These professors were portrayed as teaching the values of the "Great Books," the philosophies of the white European males and the antecedent Greeks—Socrates, Aristotle and Plato—with no inherent moral commitment to those teachings. Their superficiality was demonstrated by how quickly they were willing to abandon all of this material when confronted by students who considered these teachings elitist, sexist and racist, and even "anticommunist." Bloom observed: "The university, of all institutions, is most dependent on the deepest beliefs of those who participate in its peculiar life. Our present educational problems are the result of a deeper lack of belief in the university's vocation. One cannot say that we must defend academic freedom when there are grave doubts about the principles underlying academic freedom." Bloom feels the radical students of the 1960s "discerned that their teachers did not really believe that freedom of thought was necessarily a good and useful thing, that they suspected all of this was ideology protecting the injustices of our 'system,' and that they could be pressured into benevolence toward violent attempts to change the ideology."

In the 1960s, that is exactly what happened. Bloom depicts a provost at Cornell as a mixture of "cowardice and moralism not uncommon at the time." In conciliating the black students, "the provost thought he was engaged in great moral work, righting the historic injustice done to blacks" (in the instance described, but this could be, and was applied to women and minorities as well). He also writes: "He could justify to himself the humiliation he was undergoing as a necessary sacrifice. He was both more frightened of the violence-threatening extremists and also more admiring of them . . . The American Association of University Professors Cornell chapter applauded the black activists who infringed the rights of the professors, and the national organization did nothing to protect academic freedom." The capitulation to students' demands is further captured in Bloom's assessment of "David Easton's disgraceful presidential address to the American Political Science Association in 1966. Behavioralism (i.e., the social science founded on the fact-value distinction, devoted to the study of facts and contemptuous of philosophy) had not, he admitted, been sufficiently sensitive to moral issues. Now he promised a post-behavioralism in which the great achievements of social science would be put in the service of the right values. The piper would henceforth play the tune called by the students." A perfect description of the inmates running the asylum!

Although Bloom describes a turning back to some core curriculum in the 1980s, the attitudes of the faculty do not appear to have changed, still fighting with the moral intensity, anger, and indignation of the 1960s all of the inequities that were truly present in the past, but with "solutions" that defy reason, because they are corrections that carry the pendulum back too far, thereby creating other inequities. Fortuitously, in the past year a series of letters to the Bates College Alumni magazine have been vigorously debating political correctness and multiculturalism, because of changes at Bates College that mimic the country at large, and these letters provide amazing examples of Bloom's descriptions and thoughts. These letters act as a distinct microcosm of the current issue, and I will now present them as distinct examples of the debate. I mean no disrespect to my alma mater; *U.S. News* has rated Bates in the top twenty small liberal arts colleges for many years, and I treasure the education I was given. I regret the changes.

In Chapter Three on "Victimology" I quoted my classmate, Charles W. Radcliffe, 1950 (Winter, 1998) as stating that "Political and social radicals of the 1960s have captured academia and turned all intellectual inquiry into issues of race, gender, class, in which there are groups of victims and victimizers, chief among the latter being white males and Western civilization itself." Earlier in his letter he quoted from a book review by Jonathan Yardley in the *Washington Post* (27 September 1997) supporting his contention. The book *Literature Lost, Social Agendas and the Corruption of the Humanities,* by John M. Ellis, offers an "acute analysis of 'a startling decline in the intellectual quality of work in the humanities and a descent to intellectual triviality and irreverence that amounts to a betrayal of the university as an institution.' " Yardley's conclusion: "This, as Ellis correctly argues, should be of utmost concern for every informed citizen of any political or ideological persuasion." Shades of Allan Bloom, a decade earlier! Radcliffe also noted in strong language: "Not since scholasticism throttled academic freedom in the Middle Ages have the basic premises of liberal education been under such attack as they are today by the zealots of 'political correctness' and multiculturalism."

Radcliffe drew an angry response in the next issue (Spring 1998) from William Tucker (1967), a professor of psychology at Rutgers University, which illustrates the thinking the academics developed in the 1960s in response to the "new morality" they allowed to be forced on themselves by the radical students: "Reality has eluded (Radcliffe), apparently unaware that he graduated from Bates in the midst of the American inquisition, a time when hundreds of teachers and professors were summarily dismissed for having the wrong thoughts and the House Un-American Activities Committee ordered colleges and universities to submit to the government lists of their textbooks and course readings." This concept is directly refuted by Bloom: "Another aspect of the mythology is that McCarthyism had an extremely negative impact on the universities. Actually the McCarthy period was the last time the university had any sense of community, defined by a common enemy. McCarthy, those like him, and those who followed them, were clearly nonacademic and anti-academic . . . In major universities they had no effect whatsoever on curriculum or appointments." Whom should we believe between these opposing views? It is simple. Bloom was a professor observing these events and fighting against changes in the core curricula,

and Tucker was a student at the time, absorbing the radical
student viewpoint. Tucker represents the radical students, and
demonstrates professors in academia today, markedly influenced by the 1960s, still impressing current students in the
1990s. McCarthyism was wrong, and so were the members of
the House Un-American Affairs Committee, very wrong; the
academic overreactions were also very wrong.

The next comment from Tucker, showing how captured
he is by the ideology of the radical 60s, is a complete reflection
and extension of the David Easton 1966 speech Bloom so
deplored, which stated that the social sciences had not been
sufficiently sensitive to moral issues and would be put in the
service of the right values: "After the social sciences spent
decades providing enthusiastic support for a host of repugnant
policies—Jim Crow laws, an attempt to overturn the *Brown*
decision, restrictive immigration to prevent the influx of infe-
riors from Southern and Eastern Europe, and involuntary ster-
ilization of 'defectives' like epileptics, 'cripples, tramps, and
paupers'—Mr. Radcliffe is now shocked to discover that these
disciplines are being politicized." Ignore this unrealistic hyperbole. Politicization attacks the root and meaning of the word
"university," which implies universal study and thought. University thought should provide intellectual insights with a broad
brush, analyses of ranges of possibilities to be considered in
approaching solutions. Should students be presented with the
declaration that only the political left has the true vision? You
might not recognize from the left's altering of history that
there were underlying expectations of equality in the Declaration of Independence and the Constitution. Slavery had to be
permitted to exist for a time until a stable country could be
formed. There is a need for compromise, and accomplishing
one major step at a time. Our founders knew this, but as
Bloom notes in the 60s, "the Founding was understood to be
racist."

In fairness to Tucker he does state "it is, of course, unde-
niable that inexcusable excesses have been committed in the
name of political correctness," but he ends his letter by noting
that "lurking beneath the surface of many of the attacks on
political correctness is the suspicion of, and hostility toward,

the life of the mind that Richard Hofstadter warned of long ago in *Anti-Intellectualism in American Life.* "If you don't like my intellectual arguments, you are being anti-intellectual, is a poor excuse as a method of debating ideas and is just a form of name-calling." Bloom has already identified the changes and the products of the 1960s radicalism as anti-intellectual, and he isn't name-calling, but making what appears to be a valid judgment. Of course the arguments of the politically correct multicultural proponents are intellectual attempts to convince the public, but so are the observations of their opponents. Both arguments need to be expressed and evaluated.

'Political correctness' is guilty of thought suppression in colleges and universities. Bloom clearly makes that point: "Indignation or rage was (in the 60s) the vivid passion characterizing those in the grip of the new moral experience. Indignation may be a most noble passion and necessary for fighting wars and righting wrongs. But of all experiences of the soul, it is the most inimical to reason and hence to the university. Anger, to sustain itself, requires the unshakable conviction that one is right." This anger and the sense that only one side is right is reported by Bates Alumnus, Leon Nicholas, 1993 (Spring 1998 issue). He had his Bush posters torn down within a few minutes of tacking them up during the 1992 election. He tried to put them up several times before simply giving up. He was distressed to learn that Gay-Lesbian-Bisexual Alliance posters had similarly been torn down in 1997 at Bates. When it is taught that *certain* ideas of our past culture can be trashed, it is logical for the student to assume that any ideas he doesn't like can be destroyed, thereby ending any hope of honest debate and realistic conclusions. This sort of thought control would not have been permitted on the Bates Campus in the 1940s and 50s. I was one of very few students in 1948 who rooted for Truman to win over Dewey. We had some fierce discussions, but everyone listened politely, and no one tried to trash my ideas out of hand. I must assume that the current climate of political correctness creates this atmosphere of idea-repression on the Bates campus.

What it is like to be a conservative faculty member, or worse, an avowed Republican, in the university setting, is clearly drawn by anonymous callers to talk radio, which I have heard, but not recorded, and by the following article: "Republican Professors? Sure, There's One," by Vincent Carroll, editorial page editor of the *Rocky Mountain News* (*WSJ*, 14 May 1998). He makes the blanket statement that "not only do most American colleges boast faculties markedly to the left of center, many have established policies that ensure a further leftward drift." Newspaper research found that registered Democrats outnumbered Republicans on the University of Colorado at Boulder, thirty-three to one, 184 out of 190. The university chancellor, Richard Byyny, is quoted as desiring a faculty diversity based on "gender, ethnicity, ability (sic) and sexual orientation." Mr. Carroll wonders "about the self-correcting ability of an academic culture so in-bred that it reflects only half of the political spectrum. What arguments will be overlooked? What lines of inquiry ignored?"

This article brought an immediate response from Laura A. Freeberg, Ph.D., an Associate Professor of Psychology, in a letter to the *WSJ* (20 May 1998). When her hidden role as a Republican was revealed, she was removed as department head. Luckily she had achieved tenure, but she has been refused promotion to full professor, and has had to file a law suit in federal court to force the issue. Official faculty meetings include Democratic fund-raising requests and "petitions are circulated, putting non-tenured faculty in a very difficult position." She advises the college student Republican group and says, "Student fliers are destroyed within 15 minutes of their posting . . . and faculty attend our meetings to 'stare down' the students who dare to participate." I find this absolutely frightening. The letter speaks for itself. The article also attracted another brief letter (*WSJ* 20 May 1998) from Robert L. Paquette, who is a faculty member in the Department of History, Hamilton College, N.Y. He is able to be openly conservative, was able to review his status with his college president, who agreed with him that he was the only conservative on a faculty of more than 150 members. He commented sharply that tenure-track is extremely politicized, although denied by current faculty, with the purpose of strongly favoring leftist philosophy.

Dr. Thomas Sowell has flatly stated that academia is in the hands of the left. His description of how left-leaning faculty is maintained indicates the letters I have quoted are right on the mark:

> Alumni around the country have become alarmed by the prostitution of college education to ideological indoctrination, and by the totalitarian mind-set behind "speech codes" and the kangaroo courts to which they have led. . . . Being right doesn't count. Saying what others accept is what counts. . . . Views to the contrary are not only screened out but shouted down, whether originating on campus or in lectures by outside speakers. Blatantly political questions get asked in academic interviews, and those whose answers are out of step find themselves out of luck. This is not academic freedom. This is a breech of faith (*Forbes,* 20 November 1995).

Whenever alumni complain, it is considered as interference with academic freedom. Sowell offers a solution: Quit giving to your alma mater: "The academic world is not a system that corrects itself. So long as donors continue to conform to academia's desire that they write checks and keep quiet, the dry rot will just spread further and penetrate deeper."

Alumni donations don't have the power another pervasive influence has, which is the federal government: "Colleges and universities became so accustomed to huge infusions of money from the federal government in the 1950s and 1960s that they were in no position to refuse the government-mandated rules and regulations about hiring, firing, affirmative action and sexual harassment that came in the 1970s and 1980s" (*WSJ,* 22 March 1999, review of *In Plato's Cave,* Alvin Kernan, by Merle Rubin). The money we send in taxes to Washington comes back in grants with strings attached, if not hawsers which drag the ships of freedom-of-thought only into liberal ports. This is another example of how insidiously Washington's control appears in our lives. Even with conservative administrations of Nixon and Reagan in the 70s and 80s, those regulations appeared. The bureaucracy is very difficult to control from the top down when that bureaucracy is so large and cumbersome, and is primarily responsible for writing regulations and administering laws, and especially when congressional oversight is so minimal.

My discomfort at discovering the problems of my alma mater, Bates, is not eased by finding that "they are all doing it." Not all. There are some religion-based institutions and some others that are avowedly conservative. One example is Hillsdale College (Hillsdale, Michigan), which declares that it has proudly earned a reputation as the "most politically incorrect college in America," and refuses all federal funds. They espouse our country's founding principles, believing "that core values like honesty, integrity, self-discipline, and abstinence (are) essential to the preservation of (a) free society and to the development of personal virtue." They decry the "new mantra: if it feels good, do it," and remind us that Benjamin Franklin warned "only a virtuous people are capable of freedom." To repeat myself, all ranges of thought must be presented on all campuses. The thinking student should not be forced to choose his institution of higher-learning based on his preconceived political leanings. He needs to challenge his beliefs to see if they will stand up to scrutiny and the arguments of others. He needs to be exposed to all thinking and be taught how to analyze, and learn to make intelligent choices from a broadly-based educational background. More frightening is the potential that the colleges will not change and will continue to turn out one point of view, one politicized form of intolerance. A letter in the *Bates Magazine* (Spring 1998) from Parker G. Marden (1961), president of Manchester College (Indiana), attempting to defuse the furor, offers the opinion that "at some point persons who are well educated start to think for themselves . . . if they have been exposed to the dialogue over differences, if they have had the opportunity to see values set in opposition with each other, if they have actually lived and worked with folks who are different, then they will develop ideas and conclusions of their own." But there is a distinct problem with that statement: under the current climate in the colleges, the students will be able to do this only after leaving college! College is where you should be taught to weigh ideas and form logical conclusions.

Marden is not sure that the "evils" of the time are as excessive as some think, but offers this solace: "At our colleges and universities, the excesses will disappear, the good stuff will survive . . . They will be different and better than they are today. It is an easy prediction. There will also be fresh 'excesses'—another very safe prediction." Sowell, who has studied the problem closely, doesn't think that academia is self-correcting. Even if it were, are we supposed to allow the colleges to swing from one extreme to another? What's wrong with trying to offer all sides of everything, a cafeteria of all ideations? Can we, in this country, ever control the pendulum? Marden, as a current faculty member, is simply using another preferred technique of the 60s, conflict-resolution—"Let's not fight about it; it is not as bad as you think. It will eventually go away." Bloom explains conflict-resolution as "bargaining, harmony. If it is only a difference of values, then conciliation is possible. We must respect values, but they must not get in the way of peace." Marden clearly reflects the changes of the 60s—you should not be "judgmental," there are no absolute values. Since the standard for values today is so relative, why worry about the current national collegiate faculties? Their values are as good as yours!

I don't think we should wait for change. We need informed alumni and citizens demanding a change now. I find the current "evils" in university teaching absolutely frightening. Political correctness is at times out-and-out reverse racism and sexism. A $450 million bequest to Yale University to set up a western civilization course in 1995 had to be withdrawn because of objections that it was, by definition, racist. African history courses have tried to state that Hannibal was black as was Cleopatra! Other more extreme examples include the head of the Afro-American Studies Department at City College (New York), who offered his student the following "facts": whites were biologically inferior to blacks, Jews financed the slave trade, and the ultimate culmination of the white value system was Nazi Germany (Johnson, *History of American People*). The head of the Women's Studies Department at Brandeis University began her course "with the basic feminist principle that in a racist, classicist and sexist society we have swallowed oppressive ways of being, whether intentionally or not. Specifically, this means that it is not open to debate whether a white student is a racist or a male student is racist. He/she simply is. Rather, the focus is on the social forces that keep these distortions in place" (Johnson).

At times there is omission of facts and entire subjects from university courses for fear they might offend a particular racial group. A Harvard professor went so far as to state "that a teacher should never 'introduce any sort of thing that might hurt a group' because 'the pain that racial insensitivity can create is more important than a professor's academic freedom' " (Johnson). Of course, we should not deliberately insult any group. Does this mean that we cannot analyze the mistakes we see in history when the mistake is by a specific group of people, for fear of offending current descendants of that group? No discussion of the Holocaust, it might offend the current German population? No discussion of slavery, it might offend the descendants of the Confederacy? No discussion of the Inquisition for fear we will upset Catholics? Utter nonsense. We are taught by the mistakes of history. The human race has advanced slowly from the Stone Age, and will continue to advance slowly. We must be patient with the slow advance; much as we would like to see it speed up, humans seem to tolerate gradual change best. Political correctness literally stops that progression by side-tracking everything in a one-sided polemical approach. That is beginning to engender a fierce opposition which will, in time, battle itself back into the debate. Once there can be a debate, advances in civilized attitudes will occur. Advances involve a generous dose of compromise.

For the time being, this country is producing college graduates (currently at a rate of twenty-three percent of the college-age population) who have been exposed to this far-left indoctrination. Exactly how many of the students succumb to this philosophy is not known, but the colleges and universities are turning out our current supply of teachers and journalists. These groups of professionals will be influencing public opinion by direct access to opinion-making mechanisms, schools, newspapers, TV, and magazines. I have described the leftist collegiate establishment. Earlier in this chapter I mentioned the political lean to the left of the journalists. Studies by Stanley Rothman, a political scientist, were published in the 1980s and clearly demonstrated media bias: from 1964 to 1976 journalists voted more than eighty percent for democratic presidential candidates. He and his co-authors found through very objective polling "that the U.S. major media are staffed by a surprisingly homogenous group: upper-middle-class northeastern urbanites who are disproportionately liberal. And they were able to show through content analysis that this viewpoint subtly shapes news coverage" (Peter Brimelow, *Forbes,* 17 July 1995). For Clinton (in 1996), their vote was eighty-nine percent as I previously noted.

Just how influential the profession of journalism is at the present time is open to debate. Newspaper readership is down, with many papers over the country looking more and more like they have fit in some truncated news reports to fill space between the advertisements. TV local news reports have lost so much viewership they have resorted to telephone sweepstakes ("if you are the tenth caller you win $5,000!") and to police-blotter sensationalism, with the most outrageous local crime of the day as the lead story to snare viewers by entertaining them. Shades of the Roman Coliseum and offering the public the spectacle of watching gladiators fight to the death either with each other or with animals! After the sensational news we are offered "help" spots, usually telling us the obvious, at a level of "wear sunscreen in the sun." National TV news has also stooped to these helpful features as viewership drops. Another sign of making news "entertaining" is the use of fifteen-second sight-and-sound bites—don't go into too much depth for fear of boring the viewer. Since the TV networks want high numbers of viewers, they have made the news programs appeal to the same intellectual level as the "sitcom" viewers. The briefness of the sound bite allows the commentator one brief comment, which may have some slant to it, and there is "no time" to slip in an opposing view for balance.

The TV networks have also thrown at us sensational "investigative" hour-long news magazine programs. At first I was seduced into watching, because of the paucity of this type of news elsewhere. I turned sour when some of these programs got into medical subjects in which I had a thorough knowledge of the factors involved on both sides of a controversy. I found them sensational, and slanted by leaving out material that was readily available and overemphasizing other material to enhance the sensationalism. This lack of honesty in subjects, where I had enough knowledge to understand the deceptions, soured me and I haven't watched since. How can these programs be trusted? Is television news real news, or is it entertainment, not to be believed? It is all part and parcel of enticing viewers as done in the local news broadcasts. More recently, the internet has blossomed with websites that offer all types of news information and investigations that can be downloaded, printed-out, and studied at leisure. Parts of this book were from sources obtained that way.

Replacing the papers and TV for news in depth is talk radio, where Rush Limbaugh, the most listened to, claims to reach twenty million different people each week. There are a number of these talk programs, and the successful ones have primarily presented a conservative viewpoint, while the liberal shows have struggled. Does this mean there is a large undercurrent of dissatisfaction in the population with the news they are presented, or are the great majority satisfied and therefore don't feel they have to turn to liberal talk radio to get the "truth," while the "dissatisfied" minority do tune in to the conservative shows? The 1994 and 1996 congressional elections suggest the country is tilted toward conservatism, and talk radio is filling a gap not presented by the journalistic profession.

There is another way of analyzing what has happened to the content and style of news offered to the public. In this capitalistic system, business leaders must find the most efficient way to make money to stay ahead of the competition. The newspapers and broadcast networks do demographic studies, and are responding to the interests and desires of the reading and viewing public, and giving the public what they appear to want. Viewed this way, it raises the probability that there is a large segment of our population that is dissatisfied with the way our government is being run, and doesn't want to hear much about it, since they feel they are not currently heard by the politicians to exert any control over Washington. They go to talk radio, news websites, magazines and news letters. At the other extreme is a satisfied group that doesn't care to follow events because in their view everything is going okay for them and are disinclined to read or watch much news. That leaves a group in the middle, who follow the news, some wanting more and some satisfied with the current content.

That there is a large disaffected group is born out by election results since the 1960s. In 1960, sixty-three percent of voting-age Americans turned out to vote in the presidential election. That dropped to just over fifty percent in 1988, bounced back to fifty-five percent in 1992, but was just under fifty percent in 1996. Viewed another way, both times Bill Clinton was elected it was by twenty-three percent of all people who had the right to vote! A study of primary voting, comparing 1998 with the past found that only 16.9% of all voting-age citizens voted in the democratic and republican primaries, down from 19.9% in 1996, and well below the 32.2% participation in 1970, which was the highest ever (*Houston Chronicle*, editorial, 6 July 1998). Based on these findings, the prediction is that turnout for future national elections will continue to drop. Look at this quote from an intelligently written letter to the editor of the *Houston Chronicle*: "Elections are not about who is the best candidate for the job, but about who has the most money to buy the election. Once in office the only thing on the agenda is to repay the campaign contributors in the form of voting for special-interest groups and lobbyists and, of course, getting reelected. If we non-voters thought for a second our vote would make a difference, we'd be first in line on Election Day. This is not to say I don't respect people's right to vote, but rather I respect their intelligent decision not to." This is not apathy, this is anger and antagonism. Undoubtedly there is the apathetic group that never takes an interest in national politics, but there is also the angry, disaffected group.

One of the most interesting twists is the discovery that as income rises, voting increases. At an income of $48,000 about sixty percent of people vote, and this has held from 1966 to 1994. But poor Americans are voting less. If income is under

$9,600, voting dropped from forty-two percent to twenty-two percent in the same time period. Slightly higher incomes have slightly higher voting rates. This offers some insight into the composition of the non-voting population (Committee for the Study of the American Electorate, *WSJ,* June 98), and makes one wonder if the paying for votes through "entitlements" as politicians have been doing will continue into the future.

What the diminishing number of voters ended up electing to run Washington is a divided government. In the forty-six years since 1952, the republicans have held the presidency twenty-eight years. At the same time, the democrats had complete control of the Congress thirty-four years. A *WSJ*/NBC News survey (*WSJ,* 13 December 1996) found that the voters are rather pleased with this arrangement, by a three to two margin. The citizens surveyed offered the opinion that this arrangement stopped extreme changes, and they did not want to set up a stalemate, but hoped for compromise agreements: "The public doesn't want bigger government, but it wants government to work." What I read into this is that the general citizen does not trust Washington to run the country in a coordinated way under one party control. There seems to be a weariness with all the partisan bickering, and the frantic winner-take-all attitude. Increasingly, at the state level, voter propositions and initiatives are doing an end-run around the state legislators, putting into play policies at which the legislatures have balked.

Since the Great Society of Lyndon Johnson, starting just after the passage of the Civil Rights Act of 1964, along with the drop in voter turn-out, trust in Washington has plummeted. Charles Murray has explored the American voters' mindset, based on information he has reviewed in a forthcoming book (*WSJ,* 23 December 1997). With his historian's perspective, he points out three tacit compacts, or expectations, between the public and the federal government:

1) The founding fathers designed a federal government that was not intended to be too intrusive or controlling of the individual. They were very afraid of a central authority impeding or trying to exert too much influence or power over individual citizen's activities, purposely designing the three equal

branches, and in the legislative arena two deliberative bodies of equal power. They also attempted to keep the federal government and the states co-equals in the Ninth and Tenth Amendments by setting them up in balance: The Ninth recognizes the practical impossibility of listing all areas where the federal government might enter with a role to play, while the Tenth reserves to the states powers not delegated to the central government, establishing constitutional limits on government at each level (from a book review of *Grassroots Tyranny*, Clint Bolick, Cato Institute in the *WSJ* by David Osterfeld, 1992). In the 1960s, the federal government became more and more intrusive. Murray observes: "Today, there is no social or economic problem of which a president can say, 'That's not the government's responsibility.' And so, naturally the government is blamed when problems are not solved. This irritates everyone. People who opposed the government's intervention in the first place are irritated, but so are the people whom the intervention was intended to help, because whatever the government does is never enough." This violates the psychological principle that pride in ourselves comes from solving our own problems whenever possible, and the government limiting its role to those problems that require national action.

The scope of the Ninth Amendment has been enormously enlarged at the expense of the states' powers in the Tenth Amendment, starting with the New Deal during the Great Depression of the 1930s, with the major imbalance appearing with the major changes of the 1960s. During the 1996 presidential election, Senator Bob Dole carried around a card with the Tenth Amendment in his pocket, and he would pull it out to remind everyone how much it has been eroded. I wish he also had the Ninth and had talked about balancing them, because balance and the use of compromise is what the founders wanted—to keep government at all levels from interfering too much with individuals.

2) The second compact or expectation was that Americans, with their religious and moral precepts, would argue out the conflicting ideas of moral disputes, and when there was a clear consensus, then the federal government would act. Murray gives three examples—slavery, suffrage for women, and prohi-

bition—each of which was settled by an amendment to the Constitution, the latter requiring two amendments, to undo the initial mistake, trying to control individual habits, making them victimless crimes. Starting in the 1960s, the federal government and Congress jumped into the moral debate. The Civil Rights Act of 1964 was, in my view, absolutely essential to make the country fully recognize the guarantees of civil rights already clearly stated in the Constitution. From it we have gotten the political term "affirmative action," which has such different meanings to different people and has unfairly resulted in government-sanctioned inclusion quotas. Murray observes that the federal government "has by law and jurisprudence" gotten itself involved in the moral debates over abortion, gay rights, prayer in schools, and I would add other disputed areas that have an ethical tone, sexual harassment, environmental overprotection and endangered species controls taken to the irrational extreme of denying private owners their right of use of their property. Additionally, the "war on drugs" is repeating the same mistake as prohibition, criminalizing an activity of individual choice, driving up the cost of a drug habit, and as a by-product, creating real crime to supply the money needed. All the issues come from both right and left, and need a great deal more seasoned debate before the country comes to a consensus and the federal government then assumes an active role. The federal government, for the moment, should encourage and facilitate debate in a neutral manner.

3) The third compact or expectation described by Murray involves an attitude: "The national government made it easy for us to pride ourselves on being good citizens. If the ordinary Joe did nothing more than make an honest living and take care of his family, he was as good an American as the highest in the land . . . Through the 1950s remarkably few federal laws (or regulations) affected individuals or businesses." However, with the onslaught of governmental activism in the 1960s there "has been [a] geometric expansion of law created. Today there are more thousands of ways in which Americans can break federal law than anyone can count; not just as misdemeanors, but as felonies. The result is that millions of good Americans must

reasonably fear their national government. Nor is the government reluctant to enforce this sprawling edifice of law. (There has resulted) a widespread harrying, pestering, hectoring, obstructing and fining that afflict citizens who were not only unaware of breaking the law, but in fact have done nothing wrong in any substantive or ethical sense." Laws must make sense to citizens if they are to be respected. People must see the "good" in a law. It must be seen to contribute to the proper functioning of society. Murray concludes: "Because so many regulations are so unconnected to anything resembling right or wrong, people who want to be law-abiding find themselves picking and choosing the laws that they deem worthy of respect."

Murray's view that a more activist federal government is seen by many of our citizens as interfering and oppressive, rather than helpful to society, appears to be borne out by the polling data studied since the 1950s. I have criticized current polls as a "snapshot" in time conducted to create news or even a point of view (Chapter Six), but polls studied over a forty-year period can be used to form trends and patterns, as the errors in questions asked and the possibility of induced answers are diluted out by comparing polls from several organizations with answers from many thousands of different respondents. The following questions were used: 1) Do public officials ignore what ordinary people think? In 1952, thirty-five percent said "yes" in the 1990s, sixty percent agree with the statement. 2) How many politicians are crooked? "Quite a few" or "all" was agreed to by about twenty-five percent in the early 1950s, and in the 1990s, fifty-three percent have that opinion. 3) Is the government run for the benefit of a few big interests instead of the benefit of all the people? In 1964 it was twenty-nine percent yes, and by 1997 had risen to seventy-four percent. 4) The most startling finding are the responses to this clear-cut question: "How much do you think you can trust the government in Washington to do what is right?" Americans answering "just about always" or "most of the time" averaged seventy-five percent during the Eisenhower and Kennedy years, then the percentage started plunging in the Johnson years, reaching twenty-five percent in 1980, climbed back to an average forty percent during the Reagan administration, then dropped again in 1992 and have averaged under twenty-five percent since. This decline began and has continued with the marked increase in the activism of the government in the 1960s.

This decline in "trust" parallels almost exactly with the reported decline in Americans' opinion of Congress. Polls asking how people would rate the job Congress is doing found fifty-six percent felt it was fair to good in 1948, rising to eight-eight percent in 1958 (Gallop polls cited in *Congress, The Press, and the Public*, Mann & Ornstein, AEI/Brookings, 1994). There was a sixty percent rating at the time of the Civil Rights Act passage in 1964. Roper polls peaked at seventy percent in 1965, and all polls, in composite, then dropped dramatically and have averaged around thirty percent starting in 1971 until the early 1990s. There was a brief rise during the Gulf War against Iraq, and an immediate drop to less than twenty per-cent in reaction to the House banking scandal in 1992. During 1997 the Gallop poll approval rating varied around thirty-five percent, but strikingly rose to fifty-seven percent in February 1998, when Clinton became mired in his sex scandals and the Republican Congress sat back and did nothing, only to fall back to forty-four percent by May 1998, when Congress and Clinton became more active. These polls clearly support Murray's contention of loss of trust in our government since the 1960s. Obviously, the peaks and valleys of approval are event-driven, but what is very clear in 1998 is that the public is happier with Congress and the presidency when they are doing nothing to change the nation. This fits exactly with the desire of Americans to keep a divided government, mentioned before, which tends to slow Washington from moving too fast in any direction.

Mann & Ornstein's book attempts to blame the hard-to-understand arcane functioning of Congress, and the criticism of Congress by newspaper and TV journalists for the public's low opinion of Congress. David S. Broder (*Houston Chronicle*, 8 July 1998) described a conference held in June 1998 between congressional campaign consultants and journalists. He con-cluded the cynicism of both consultants and journalists, in creating and covering election campaigns, are turning off voters and creating a "dismally low trust in our system of choosing our leaders." I disagree with him and Mann & Ornstein. As James K. Glassman, a Washington columnist says, "Officials on the tight little island inside the Beltway aren't in touch with what other Americans think and desire" (*Houston Chronicle*, August 1997). The picture Congress presents of itself in general is of a pompous, overly-privileged group, and those outside the "Beltway" know it. Further, the governing laws and regulations passed by Congress since 1965 are perceived by the public as oppressive and unnecessary.

Congress treats itself much differently than the rest of us. They have voted for themselves a pension plan that is worth two to three times the best corporate plans in the country. They do not pay social security taxes. They can retire with full pension benefits at age sixty-two, after serving in Congress only five years, at age sixty after only ten years, and at age fifty after serving twenty years! (Cal Thomas, *L.A. Times Syndicate, Houston Post*, August 1994) They have enjoyed cheap car washes, subsidized haircuts, free prescription drugs, special parking privileges, a private gym with masseuse, and subsidized dining rooms ranging from cafeterias to opulent dining rooms. The list is longer, but the point is made (Mann & Ornstein). They would still have a House Bank that allowed kiting of checks and free loans; they couldn't continue when it became public in a General Accounting Office Report in 1991, but while secret, it was okay. At the same time, they keep promising a fix for Social Security, and can't find the courage to do it. They then claim the budget is balanced as of 1997 by throwing in the Social Security surplus which is needed for the future. They continue an overly complex IRS code, which allows them to sneak in tax preferences for their supporters in return for campaign contributions. Their attitude is easily discerned as: "Let future Congresses worry about it. We will promise a lot, but make no possibly controversial moves now so we can be reelected. To stay in office, we will continue the confusing rules about soft-money contributions so as to fight off challengers."

Until republicans took control in 1994, Congress exempted itself from the fair employment, equal opportunity, and freedom of information regulations all businesses had to follow. The lack of ethics in the House banking scandal is topped by indictments in the 1990s of Senator Dan Durenberger of Minnesota, for allegedly billing the Treasury for the lease of a condo he actually owned. Representative Nicholas Mavroules of Massachusetts was jailed for misusing his office for personal gain. Most infamously, Representative Dan Rostenkowski of Illinois, after over forty years in Congress, was indicted and convicted of embezzling government funds, and spent eighteen months in jail, only to come out and start enjoying that huge congressional pension (Mann & Ornstein). Another ethical lapse is "hear no evil, see no evil" by congressmen of other congressmen: in Texas, in 1997 Representative Henry B. Gonzalez (of San Antonio)—eighty-two-years-old and sick— decided to sit out the last eighteen months of his final term (nineteen of them) at a salary of $136,000 at home! His excuse was that he wanted to save the cost of a special election! Finally the pressure of newspaper articles, and the fact his son was campaigning to succeed him, forced him to return to Washington for the last fifteen days of the 105th Congress (*Houston Chronicle,* 5 July 1998-24 September 1998). Isn't his pension enough, and shouldn't the House have demanded his resignation? No courage.

Gonzalez would have probably remained just as popular in his district whether he resigned or not. The public's disaffection with an amorphous body of Congress is not paralleled in their feelings about their own personal congressman. Approval ratings for home district congressmen run twenty-five to forty percent higher than ratings for the institution (Mann & Ornstein). There is good reason for this. Remember that huge pile of money that goes to Washington every year. The local congressman arranges to bring some back to the district. He is known to his voters as a person who has their interests at heart, and more often than not, when he runs a reelection campaign, he runs it against Congress, agreeing with their complaints against the institution. Most voters seem to miss the point that unless their representative has seniority and a leadership role, he has little chance of making changes.

There is an historical perspective regarding our nation's poor opinion of congress, if one tries to make the assumption that service in congress should create a good breeding ground for the presidency. It doesn't. In the twentieth century only Warren Harding and Jack Kennedy went directly from the Senate to the presidency—that is just two out of twenty-five elections! The most common background is a governorship. Granted, Harry Truman, Lyndon Johnson, and Gerald Ford all had congressional service, but each got to the presidency by being a vice-president, after being in congress. Without question, the nation's tendency is to elevate someone outside Washington to be president. Even Nixon, who served in congress and was vice-president for eight years under Eisenhower, was an outsider for eight years before his election. Dissatisfaction with congress may be much older than Mann and Ornstein realize, and may occur in ways they did not address.

Remember the letter-to-the-editor I quoted from the purposeful non-voter? I think that letter is right on. Yes, there is apathy. However, the dissatisfaction levels with congress rise as people are more educated. I would equate apathy with less education and an increased feeling of helplessness and hopelessness. The more educated have tended to vote more, and if now they are becoming more dissatisfied, may have chosen not to vote as a protest, given the choices they find in the voting booth. The very best citizens don't want to run, and the would-be challengers do have a problem with money because of the way the campaign contribution laws are written.

The progressive disapproval and dissatisfaction with congress from the 1970s until the 1990s is shown in polls concerning various groups and institutions in the country measuring "confidence," and other polls asking for opinions of "honesty and ethical standards." It is no surprise to find that the progressive disapproval pattern includes journalism. Gallop poll rankings of different professions questioning levels of honesty and ethical standards (as high or very high) found the congress at the lower end of the rankings with only 16.5% in 1976, and sixteen percent in 1993 of respondents agreeing. Congress had higher rankings in the 1950s, but the questions asked in those polls do not allow direct numerical comparison. Journalists

had a much higher ranking at thirty-three percent in 1976, but
dropped to twenty-six percent in 1993/4. The polls regarding
a "great deal of confidence" (averaging two sources) showed
congress dropping from thirty-three percent in 1973 to 12.5%
in 1993/4, while newspapers fell from thirty-one percent to
twenty percent and television approval declined from nineteen
percent to twelve percent (Mann & Ornstein). The public is
turned-off by congress, by our government, and by the journalists who report issues and who have been openly critical of
the way congress and the government has handled its responsibilities. With regard to the journalists, I don't think this is an
example of "shooting the messenger," but a perception of the
general ethical and moral decline in the country, especially as
exemplified by the class of politicians that has developed in
Washington since 1960 and in which the journalists have taken
part.

Sixty-one percent of us thought "the state of morals in
America today is 'pretty bad and getting worse'" in a poll
reported in 1996 (*WSJ*/NBC News, *WSJ*, 13 December 1996),
compared with only forty-one percent in 1964. The distrust in
government and journalism is "tarring with the same brush."
I think the overall ethical/moral decline and the attitude that
there are no absolute values, with the admonition not to make
judgments about people ("don't be judgmental") are the causes
for this attitude. People feel adrift and powerless if there are no
accepted moral and ethical values to the way society is functioning and the way the leaders of government are acting.
Government officials act as if they don't care what people
think of them in terms of morals, as long as the officials can
buy votes with entitlements and special favors: "Look at what
I can do for you, not at the way I act as a person."

Mark Helprin captures the problem exactly in his brilliant
essay, "Statesmanship and Its Betrayal" (*WSJ*, 2 July 1998):
"(We have) a political class that in the main has abandoned
the essential qualities of statesmanship, with the excuse that
these are inappropriate to our age. In the main, they are in it
for themselves. Were they not, they would have a higher rate
of attrition, falling with the colors of what they believe, rather
than landing always on their feet—adroitly, but in dishonor. In

light of their vows and responsibilities, this constitutes not merely a failure but a betrayal." He describes these Washington politicians in a withering but honest way:

> They who, in robbing Peter to pay Paul, present themselves as payers and forget they are also robbers. They who, with studied compassion, minister to some of us at the expense of others. They who make goodness and charity a public profession, depending for their election upon a well-mannered embrace of these things and the power to move them not from within themselves or by their own sacrifices but by compulsion from others. They who, knowing very little or next to nothing, take pride in eagerly telling everyone else what to do. They who believe absolutely in their recitation of pieties not because they believe in the pieties but because they believe in themselves.

There is no question that statesmanship in the 1990s is not present in Washington, only political games and subterfuge: We are told the budget is balanced, but it isn't; we are told that some groups are more deserving than others to make up for inequities of generations past, when to have one cohesive population all groups should live in good will together and be allowed to share equally; we are told they have our best interests at heart, when all they want to do is buy our votes for their perpetual reelection. As Helprin observes, the statesman stands honestly for his own vision of what is best for the country, despite the pain and injury that policy might cause. He accepts the challenges, knowing "there would be little enjoyment of the job." The statesman knows that for every good deed "there is a counterbalance. Benefits are given only after taxes are taken . . . A statesman knows a continuous stress of soul." This is why our great presidents have appeared to age so much while in office. He says: "Statesmanship is not the appetite for power but—because things matter—a holy calling of self-abnegation and self-sacrifice . . . Statesmanship remains the manifestation, in political terms, of beauty, and balance, and truth. It is the courage to tell the truth, and thus discern what is ahead. It is the mastery of the symmetry of forces, illuminated by the genius of speaking to the heart of things."

No wonder the apathy. Our population is not stupid. They see the type of congress we have, and understand full well the shortcomings, the lack of truthfulness, the confusing claims and the unkept promises. Everything is kept deliberately fuzzy. That way if an idea doesn't fly too well and votes might be lost, the fuzziness allows for a re-interpretation that might go over better. This kind of unwillingness to take a firm stand on important issues and principles turns up in the laws produced. In the bills, ideas, and even the meanings of single words are not well-defined and so, it is left up to the courts to try and fathom congress' meaning as best they can. It appears "that the essential problem is that congress has been deliberately vague and knew full well that they would want the courts to step in and solve the issue. The pattern is that congress doesn't want to face up to its responsibilities and then blames the court afterward for its decisions. Congress, through deliberate ambiguity, present(s) the court with choices and the court (is) doing exactly what it should be doing—trying to make sense of them" (quote of Robert A. Katzmann, judicial scholar from Fred Barbash, Deputy Ed., *Washington Post*, in *Houston Chronicle*, 19 July 1998). It is easy to imagine congress saying to itself: "Blame the courts for the interpretation; tell the public the judiciary should stop legislating, and we can get reelected without taking the blame." What makes the large omnibus bills that are passed today even worse is not only their size of over 1,000 pages, but according to an article by Representative Don Manzullo (Republican, Illinois), most of the members of our "Cliff Notes" congress read only brief summaries, and have no idea of what is really stuffed into a bill (*WSJ*, 1995).

This brings me to the heart of the matter. The "affirmative action" aspect of the Civil Rights Act of 1994 and the multicultural diversity-praising philosophic theories touted by the Intellectual Elite of the leftist collegiate faculties work hand-in-glove, as if the political parties and the faculties actually planned a campaign to control governing the country by a divide-and-conquer technique. First, split us up into multiple ethnic and special interest groups. Then, knowing that under forty percent of eligible citizens will vote in a non-presidential election and just under fifty percent in a presidential year, the political parties can consult their focus-group polls, and check their computer databases to target partisan groups most likely to vote. Next, they can decide what they need to promise the groups they anticipate getting to the polls, and with what kind of voting turnout. Finally, they put together a campaign with enough issues and promises to buy the votes, cobble together a coalition and steal an election. This is actually the approach in the 1998 congressional election taken by both parties, realizing they have to by-pass the majority of apathetic Americans. In California (always a leader), detailed voter histories are kept, along with neighborhood census data, targeting registered voters to contact (*WSJ*, by John Harwood, 13 July 1998). The collegiate faculties and political parties did not actually plan what has happened, and we cannot blame the political parties for taking advantage of public apathy any way they can.

There is no evidence of statesmanship in this electioneering technique. When we should be offered elections based on principles, instead we are given vote-gathering promises, which are the result of a computer-driven manipulation of artificially derived sub-groups of our population, and hardly anyone is noticing that it is happening. Paradoxically, in part this is because the Civil Rights Movement of 1964 has been so widely accepted, and has proved to "have a positive impact on today's values" according to eighty-four percent of our population, responding to a *Wall Street Journal*/NBC News poll, 13 December 1996 (*WSJ* of that date). It is clear that the vast majority of people are pleased with the civil rights progress since 1964, allowing, understandably, that blacks want more and faster progress. Societal changes take time. Ingrained attitudes die hard. I remember discussing race relations in the south with an Army Colonel I had hospitalized in 1959. He told me that his daughter felt like I did, that segregation had to be ended, and he knew she was right, but with the teachings he had received since childhood, he could not bring himself to help in the fight. As the song in "South Pacific" tells us: "You have to be carefully taught." Removing racism eventually comes down to what is taught by parents to their children. Of course children are born without prejudice.

Because the "good" inherent in the Civil Rights Initiatives has been so broadly and reasonably accepted by almost all of us, methods of achieving the goals have been allowed to slip into place, that by and of themselves, damage the unity of our society and end up negating a large portion of the good that has been achieved. The pressures applied to our population by the government's methods of using quotas to enforce civil rights laws and regulations is already setting one group against another by counting percentages and numbers, rather than using individual merit in a fair society. This leads to group competition because it implies an inherent and unreasonable expectation that a group's percentage share of the population should be reflected in like kind in every aspect of societal activities. When those percentages don't work out, because in reality that is an impossible result to achieve, intergroup antagonisms will appear and lead to increased racism. Two kinds of inequities appear with the use of quotas: first, the exclusion of the qualified, in order to fit in others less-qualified; and, second, the failure to meet a quota, because the group inherently does not yet have enough individuals capable of, or interested in, an activity, and may never have them. Blacks and Hispanics are roughly equal in numbers in our country. How many Hispanics are in the National Basketball Association? We cannot overcome biologic differences, and therefore cannot make everything equal. We cannot make IQs equal. We can have an equality of opportunity, but unfortunately there will never be an equality of outcomes—some of us can achieve more than others. It is allowing each of us to achieve something we can achieve, to be all we can be that is important, not artificially creating equal percentages of everything.

An example of the first inequity, qualified college candidates being shunned aside to allow minority quotas to be filled, is the Bakke case back in the 1970s, which ended up in a Supreme Court decision: that he had been treated unfairly in his application for medical school admission in California simply because he was white, and the white numbers had been filled. This did not end affirmative action programs at the collegiate level in California, but the Hopwood case in Texas in the 1990s ended the program at the Texas State schools.

Four white students sued the University of Texas Law School on the same grounds, but with a twist: UT Law School had two totally separate admission procedures for white and minority applicants. The federal appellate court handed down such a strong decision that the Attorney General of Texas ordered all Texas State schools to shut down their programs. A clear victory for the equal protection clause of the Fourteenth Amendment to the Constitution: it is unconstitutional for any state to "deny to any person within its jurisdiction the equal protection of its laws." What is the consequence of forcing schools to accept students under a quota-driven government mandate which demands the quotas or lose educational grants? "Minority students admitted with lower qualifications fail to graduate more often than students admitted under normal standards, whether those students are black or white. Those who do graduate tend to come in at the bottom of their class" says Dr. Thomas Sowell (*Forbes*, 10 October 1994). Those minority students, who matriculate at second or third collegiate level, graduate with much less difficulty and with a better feeling about themselves than those using the quotas to open the higher universities, then stumble and fail or who barely graduate and feel their degree is tainted because of the artificial boost they know they received.

John McWhorter, a linguistics professor at University of California at Berkeley, who is black, makes several important observations. He agrees with Sowell (who is also black) in many ways and yet he doesn't. His contention is that many of the black kids don't do well in college because it is an "echo of a well-known tendency of black children of all classes to associate school with 'whiteness.'" There is nothing wrong with "whiteness," unless whites are considered the enemy. These kids are as racist as racist whites or worse; they have been taught within their own community that it is "us versus them." "If it is something that white folks want us to do, then it is not for us," and all they are really being asked is to do, and helped to do, is get an education and succeed. Their minds are being poisoned, for they are being told they are racially separate from our general society, and therefore should be treated differently, and they are taught to expect to be treated differently. As

McWhorter observes, they are told they are victims, and despite the "massive progress on all levels since the 1960s, many influential blacks insist upon reading all remnants of racism as evidence that no substantial change has occurred." He finds that black children who are entering California campuses without preferences, under the non-quota reality of Proposition 209, are considered by the liberal faculty as "not being committed to the black presence on campus. In other words, victimology and separatism have gotten us to the point that the black child who fulfills the goals of affirmative action and no longer needs it is a sell-out." Liberal faculties, through their love of multiculturalism and diversity, facilitate continuing racial antagonisms and rivalries. Should blacks come onto a predominately white campus with a chip on their shoulder, or should they arrive prepared to join actively in one student body, where natural diversity helps teach each group about the others?

Where McWhorter does agree with Sowell is that the affirmative action programs have benefited primarily middle-class black children: the statistics document that only twenty-five percent of black children applying to Berkeley have parental incomes under $30,000 a year (*WSJ,* 16 July 1998). The proponents of the programs have tried to maintain that it is the disadvantaged who have been benefited. Both agree that the California collegiate faculties mourn the loss of the affirmative action system by quota, as it was practiced in that state, and, without "the merest acknowledgment of class, merit or fairness . . . speculate on how to reinstate racial preferences in other guises" (McWhorter). Both agree that black students have lower test scores on average in college. Sowell thinks that too many black students still have poor high school academic training despite integration of school districts, and only a finite number have the capacity to handle the top-flight challenge of schools like Berkeley. They will prosper scholastically and psychologically at a slightly lower level school. They were pulled into Berkeley-like schools by the suction of the quotas, setting them up for failure or graduation with a comparatively poor record. McWhorter feels that the black students could improve, if only the faculties would cease ignoring the issue of lower grades, as they strive for their major goal of diversity. That is "In essence (they are) implying middling performance is inherent to the race. This assumption prevents black students from pursuing top grades and acing placement tests."

The inequity of the quota system in education sets race against race, removes the fairness of competition between individuals based on merit, and damages our collegiate educational system by keeping out the more qualified, in order to fill racial quotas, resulting in more failing students. Diversity simply for the sake of diversity, without the equality of outcome created by competition, is extremely damaging. All this comes at a time in history when our country needs as many highly-trained professionals as we can produce to maintain our superior position. We are filling the need now partially through immigration, which I favor (see Chapter Four), but since many foreign-born experts come here for lower salaries, this is another way that resentments are set up between groups of people.

Bean-counting in education has failed, and has perversely affected race relations. Congress and other governmental units have created a cookie-cutter mentality by chopping up our population into as many as eighteen racial/ethnic groups (the Seattle Public Schools survey; Michael Medved, *WSJ*, October 1997) and implying that each group will be guaranteed equal outcomes in every sphere of human endeavor. That is, if your group is eight percent of the general population, then eight percent of each type of job or profession will be represented by your group members, and they will always win eight percent of the bids available for contract work, and so forth. Preposterous and impossible. This is the second inequity I mentioned earlier. Different groups, for historical and cultural reasons, have different interests and desires. There is no reason to expect that the individual representatives of any group will try to enter any field or arena in exact percentages. Turned around, should the country demand that each racial/ethnic group supply exactly the percentages of its members for every area of endeavor? Ridiculous and ludicrous.

With all the political foolishness that has gone on, it is no surprise that this cookie-cutter mentality really exists. President Clinton, as a racial initiative, began a series of racial forums in 1998, and his first one ran into immediate trouble because it did not include a Native American. In April 1998, in Houston, there was more trouble. The local Hispanics threatened to boycott that forum because they were under-represented on the "cookie-cutter" basis; after some political concessions in a private meeting with Clinton, they did attend. A month later, the *Houston Chronicle* wisely set out to explore Hispanic political thinking in view of what happened, and assigned the project to Lori Rodriguez, who produced a thorough, excellent article (of course, only an Hispanic reporter could be trusted to unearth honest feelings in interviews, in this climate of interracial/ethnic battling that has developed—rubbish!).

As background, the city of Houston has had an exemplary history in race relations. In the 1960s, the city desegregated public and some private facilities very quietly. The white leaders consulted privately with the black leaders. There were no disturbances between races, and the changes were accomplished very quickly. At this time the Hispanic population was quite small. Houston's ethnic racial mix in 1998 is a forerunner of what the country will look like in fifty years: forty-one percent white, or "Anglo," as it is referred to here (a contraction of Anglo-Saxon, which certainly does not fit all whites; as a Jew I am not an Anglo); thirty percent Hispanic; twenty-five percent black; and four percent Asian. Some of the more affluent blacks have moved to the suburbs, and the Hispanic population has grown rapidly. As another important aside, nationally "Hispanic" covers a multitude of ethnic/racial possibilities: it is primarily a linguistic classification covering blacks, whites and native Indians; it is also a cultural classification covering South America, Central America, Puerto Rico, and immigrants from Spain! Under this stupidity of classification, the Civil War naval hero Admiral David Glasgow Farragut, would today be called Hispanic. His father was an immigrant from Spain (Medved, *WSJ*, October 1997). In Houston, "Hispanic" primarily means "Chicano" or Mexican.

Lori Rodriguez (*Houston Chronicle*, 31 May 1998) found that Hispanic political leadership in Houston wanted their fair share of political jobs at all levels and in all branches of government, and expected that share immediately. A population that has migrated to Houston in the past two decades, mainly from Mexico, has already learned the American ideal of instant gratification. Their main rivals are, of course, blacks who have been around much longer. They are better organized and much more well-established. Think about it: if two candidates for an appointive position each have equal credentials, but one of them is much better known personally to the selection board, who know his work ethic and morals are excellent, it is obvious who will be selected. Human nature is such that networking and a seasoning of relationships must develop first, and then a newly-arrived population group can work into the total structure of a society. This is clearly borne out in the city of Houston work force: the forty-one percent Anglo population is exactly matched in the work force; the twenty-five percent blacks have 36.3% of the city jobs; the thirty percent Hispanic group has 18.4% of city work; and the 4.1% Asian group has 4.3%.

The Hispanic leaders recognize the natural rivalry with blacks, and understand "that what one group gets often comes at the expense of another." A black politician understood the dangers of such a rivalry: "Neither of our constituencies are in such positions of economic empowerment that we can justify or risk alienating the other. That is failed politics." The Hispanics have a distinct political problem—their folks don't vote. In a typical city election, blacks turn out thirty percent of the vote, Hispanics only ten percent. An Hispanic leader understands: "With blacks, you've got to be an equal partner. They are not going to give you half the pie as long as they are delivering whatever share of the vote they're delivering and you're not delivering your share." This is another aspect of the time it takes to work into a society. You have to teach your group to be good citizens, take an interest in how government is working, and get out the vote. Non-voting Hispanics are not apathetic like so many established Americans, they are not educated politically.

So we see a black/Hispanic rivalry that they must work to overcome, while they seek to achieve their preconceived percentage share of everything. Viewing this, how do we become one American population with many cultural and ethnic contributions to a society that works together, ignoring percentage divisions and awards, allowing the best individual for the position or job to do the work, particularly as we go from predominately white to multiracial? My own American College of Physicians (I am a Fellow), in a 1998 member survey, has fallen prey to this mess, much to my disgust. They offer nine ethnic/racial classifications for the question, "With what racial/ethnic group do you primarily identify," but do allow "other," and "I do not care to provide the information at this time." I decided not to answer the whole survey: I don't know why they think they need that sort of information. Dinesh D'Souza says: "Civil rights activists condemn proposals to eliminate racial classifications. They seem unconscious of the irony that they are perpetuating the racial lexicon of their oppressors and rejecting the color-blind principle for which generations of black leaders from Frederick Douglas to Martin Luther King, Jr. have labored. Consistent with King's vision, the government should stop color-coding its citizens. A new generation of Americans should be able to think of themselves as Americans, and not have to go through life checking racial boxes that force them into artificial categories" (*Forbes,* 2 December 1996). When Tiger Woods won the Masters Golf Tournament, the blacks tried to claim him, but he wouldn't allow it, stating that he was a multiracial American (he is white, black and Asian). That is the kind of attitude we need.

The dangers of interracial rivalry, as America moves forward, are illustrated by the ruckus Councilwoman Martha Wong, an Asian-American, created in June 1998 in Houston. The city should be studied by the rest of the country to try to avoid the same mistakes. She jumped right into a cookie-cutting diversity fracas by writing to Houston Mayor Lee Brown, a black, "There is obvious overrepresentation of African-American employees and a shockingly low representation of Asian-Americans and Hispanic employees" in the Health and Human Services Department. The Department has 52.7% black employees, against the city population of twenty-five percent; Hispanics had 24.3% of the jobs versus a city population share of thirty percent; the Asians had 5.9% of the

Department jobs, with a population share of 4.1%; there were 1.4% native Indians, against an unknown population (imagine this statistic is not being kept!); and the whites had 15.8% of the jobs, with a city population of forty-one percent. Wong then voiced concerns about the "work ethic" of the department's employees, saying a friend told her the employees were lax (*Houston Chronicle,* 24 June 1998).

As you can imagine, the city's black leaders responded angrily. In their letter they told her: "You owe an apology to the people of Houston, who are diligently trying to overcome two centuries of neglect of women and minorities." One black leader stated the obvious: "We can't let this type of divisive statement stand. We have some hard fights ahead of us, and all members of the minority community should be pulling together." Within a week Wong wrote a letter to black community leaders apologizing for her remarks, and saying that she would like to study a "history of hiring practices that will explain this imbalance" (*Houston Chronicle,* 2 July 1998). The answer is obviously the explanation I gave before. The blacks got there first and secured government jobs of a type they couldn't get in the private sector. In the past two decades the Hispanics and Asians arrived, and they are playing catch-up. But note, no one complained about the white under-representation in the Health Department. No one cared, not the whites; and the minorities certainly didn't care, as for them the whites were obviously a non-issue. Remember, overall white employment by the city matched the population percentage. As one might predict, the letters-to-the-editor of the *Houston Chronicle* did reflect biased confusion. A writer with an Hispanic name declared that the blacks were racist to attack Wong, and essentially demanded that blacks should be removed from their "excess" jobs to make room for a proper percentage of Hispanics. The situation was seen only through the lens of his own racial loyalty.

Is this any way to have a population come together as one nation? Of course not. But it's happening because of government bean counting and insisting that we should be divided up into our little segments. Think about the Balkans: seven hundred years of race, religious, and ethnic wars; Serbs against

Croats, Christians against Muslims. The world has their troops there to try and keep the peace, but fighting and civil wars continue wherever the troops are not present. We are Balkanizing our own country. Why can't we look at history and learn? There are ways out of this morass: to overcome apathy among citizens, changes must be made giving the population a strong sense that they have control over Congress and Washington. This involves removing Social Security from Congress' control, developing a very simple income tax/flat tax scheme, and changing the campaign contribution rules and perhaps even the way congress is elected (covered in Chapter Eight, as I consider the major steps in correcting the country's problems).

Multiculturalism as a political force must be stopped. Alumni must influence the trustees of their institution by any means that are effective, by reasoned argument and/or by withholding donations, to create a faculty balance between multicultural diversity-loving professors, who denigrate the white European males of the Enlightenment, the source of the major principles of this great country, and teachers who take the opposite view. I am not asking to replace politically correct, multicultural far-left faculty. First achieve a balance and let the students hear the debate and reach their own conclusions. Politically correct may be a form of thought control, but it should not be eradicated by its own methods. Congress should be pressured to reassert that portion of the 1964 Civil Rights Act which did not permit the use of quotas in bean counting, and the courts should continue to be petitioned to recognize the primacy of the Fourteenth Amendment and its equal protection clause, removing the quota system by the legal system.

There is another way to view the dangers of multiculturalism. It is, in fact, a form of stereotyping, by pointing out group separateness and implying differences. Some stereotyping is hard to avoid, because it is valid: blacks make great basketball players, and are superstars in other sports also. Many Jews and Asians are very studious, and high achievers. But look at the next thought: Muslims hate western culture and are terrorists. Not true. A few have been, but obviously most are not—"No one likes being prejudged; we all want others to view us as individuals" on our own merits (James Taranto, *WSJ*, 12 August 1998). Malicious stereotyping brings ugly consequences, but some "stereotypes will always be with us, (because they are based on) actual experience." There is no harm in observing that different cultures create slightly different humans who bring differing interests and skills to our combined population. We need those skills and differences; "Organizations that set out to refute stereotypes typically say they speak on behalf of some minority group or other. But by claiming to represent a 'black view,' or an 'Asian view,' they themselves are stereotyping. Multiculturalism, with its emphasis on group identity (is nothing) more than an exercise in stereotyping. If advocates really wanted to weaken the force of stereotypes, they would embrace a strong *American* identity. For what unites Americans is the ideal of individualism—an aspiration to transcend stereotypes," says Taranto.

If we do not stop multiculturalism, we may go the way of Canada, which began a governmental campaign to promote it starting in 1971, and even going to the extent of a constitutional change requiring "the preservation and enhancement of the multicultural heritage of Canadians." It has been a disaster, with Quebec threatening to break away as a major result. Jan Brown of the Canadian Reform Party feels that "every dollar spent on multiculturalism is a dollar spent on the breakup of the Confederation." The chairman of their Commission on Canada's Future, a federally appointed body, declared that "state-funded multiculturalism was an anthology of terrors: (Causing) balkanization, ghetto mentalities, (the) destabilization of Quebec, reverse intolerance by immigrants for Canadian culture and institutions, and the devaluation of the very idea of a common nationality" (Mark I. Schwartz, a Canadian author, *WSJ*, 5 April 1996). Doesn't that all sound like what is beginning to happen here?

This is an intellectual war and must be fought on many fronts. The battlecry should be: "Jelly beans, unite!"

Chapter Eight

Dictator for a Day

All of us daydream. Having spent twelve years thinking about the contents of this book, I have come up with some solutions for the problems I see in the country. I also daydream that if I were dictator for one day, by edict, I could put my solutions in place, and improve the country. Not General Pinochet style, with an alleged 20,000 people killed in Chile, but by benign rule. Of course in our republic, I know these ideas must be debated, and then over a period of time once generally acceptable changes are agreed to, the compromises are put in place to correct the errors of current practice. Still, it is fun to daydream. Like everyone else, I like instant gratification, although that is rarely possible. I feel so thankful that my grandparents and their parents had the courage to come here, and let me grow up and become an active adult citizen of the most wonderful democracy on earth. Feeling so strongly that I should make some contribution to the national debate, I ask you to indulge me and study my daydream. All of these changes are possible to achieve and are reasonable. These alterations in our methods recognize that human beings are not perfect, and that less than idealistic solutions must be used to overcome the fallibility of people in general.

In Chapter Five, "It's Not Nice to Fool Mother Nature," I tried to demonstrate that one of our human shortcomings is to look out for ourselves first. True altruists, like Mother Teresa, thinking only of others and doing only for others first, are extraordinarily rare. Our extremely short span of civilization has developed the teachings of altruism, but not its universal acceptance. Wariness was built into us in the Stone Age period, for most of us less than 3,000 years ago in time, a fraction of the three-plus billion years of our human evolution. We have developed an enormous code of laws and ethics in a short time, and we do respect them in general, but it is my view that the idealistic hope of a practiced universal altruism and self-sacrifice in all of us is a couple millennia into the future, if we manage not to have global atomic warfare in the meantime.

Along with the three branches of government given us by our founders, now we have a fourth unelected branch of government, the bureaucratic agencies, which control our lives more than they should, and carefully take care of themselves, as shown in Chapter Five. They, our employees, control us, the employers! And worse, our congress exerts poor control over the bureaucracy for us. How many times has the congress had to change to Internal Revenue Service rules of conduct? Further, we feel we have poor control over congress and poor responsiveness from them as to our requests and wishes, unless we have contributed enough money to their campaign. The members of congress, like the bureaucrats, have built walls of self-protection around themselves to assure they can stay in office perpetually. No wonder there is citizen apathy, an apathy we can currently afford, because of the system the founders started. Although partially limping along, it is still such a miraculous invention that we continue to live in a rich and powerful nation.

The answer to the apathy is to find ways to re-exert control over congress, and thereby demand that they rein in the bureaucracy. The first step is to remove from congress the control over money that directly affects each of us. Start with Social Security. They keep offering possible solutions for the Social Security incipient bankruptcy, a mess they caused. It is akin to leading a horse with a carrot by saying, "reelect us and we will solve it even though it is such a difficult task." The privatization of Social Security, as demonstrated in Chapter Six, accomplishes exactly that. Difficult task? Horse feathers! Great Britain, Chile and others have already solved it. What is so difficult here is overcoming congressional cowardice: re-election comes first, and they cannot afford to offend anyone!

The second, and somewhat more important step, is to simplify the income tax code, taking away the quid-pro-quo giving of tax write-off favors for campaign contributions. This is somewhat putting the cart before the horse, in that the very expensive election campaigns drive the IRS code changes, but as dictator, I plan to simplify the code and reform campaign finance simultaneously, which congress could do all in the same session. We have been presented with a flat tax plan and a national sales tax plan. Both have good and bad points. The flat tax, by offering a large deductible ($35,000) before a tax kicks in, protects lower income people from a very regressive burden. It cannot get to the laundered and hidden income in drugs and other crime estimated to be $250 billion a year. Only a sales tax can do that when the crooks spend their money. A flat tax also cannot catch barter, which is also estimated to be quite large; but again, the money saved in barter will be taxed when spent. A sales tax on everything can unfortunately be very regressive for low income folks, unless some basic items are excluded, but has the advantage of being able to use a sales tax system at the state level already in place, and also has the advantage of taxing consumption, and therefore resembles a progressive income tax. In this case, it is the individual who makes the consumption choices and thereby creates his own increasing taxes as he consumes more.

There are those who would "tear the IRS out by the roots," to quote Representative Bill Archer, who favors the sales tax, and opposing him are those who favor retaining the IRS with a flat tax. IRS opponents worry that if the IRS is retained, a low flat tax could later be raised. However, either tax could always be raised in the future, so that argument doesn't hold water. Since both plans have advantages and disadvantages, I would have both. The IRS shouldn't disappear. Some agency has to collect the sales tax if the income tax is gone, and it might as well be a remnant of the IRS. Further, raising the tax rates can be made difficult: Requiring a two-thirds or three-quarters congressional approval to increase taxes, except in the case of a congressionally-declared war. To solve the problem of protecting the lower income families from paying sales taxes on baseline necessities of living, a list of those basics, made tax-free, could be developed and identified for non-taxable status by the product identification codes now in use. These products would include staple foods, basic work clothing, and transportation, the latter by excluding from tax the first $10,000 spent for a car or truck. Inexpensive rental property would not be taxed.

I am not competent to pick percentages for these two taxes. And I can tell you that the Treasury and the Congressional Budget Office are not good at predicting tax revenues when there are changes made. They tend to make arithmetic predictions, not psychological ones. For example, they assume blandly if a fifty billion dollars yearly revenue comes from a twenty percent capital gain tax, a twenty-five percent tax will bring $62.5 billion, but that is not what happens. At twenty-five percent, many investors will hold on and not sell, and Washington may see less than fifty billion dollars in revenue. Conversely, drop the capital gain tax rate to fifteen percent, and the revenue may be predicted by the arithmetic method to drop to $37.5 billion, but in actuality often it will rise to sixty to seventy billion dollars as people sell to take advantage of the lower rate. By studying the past revenue responses to tax shifts, one can use "dynamic scoring" to make predictions; that is, take taxpayer psychology into account. In view of these problems, if both tax systems are started, they may well need adjustment to meet the government's needs. The major result, however, is to remove from congress the ability to grant tax favors to contributors, a distinct and decisive advance in regaining citizen control of congress.

Before leaving this subject of simplified taxes, I would like to point out that they will save many billions of dollars now spent on CPAs and tax lawyers; businesses will be simplified by not having to use tax-driven strategies. Monumental record keeping will be a thing of the past, another cost and time saver. It is estimated the savings would equal twenty-five percent of all the money the IRS collects in taxes! (Jim Barlow column, *Houston Chronicle,* 16 April 1998) The IRS is expected to collect $1.7 trillion in 1998. A twenty-five percent saving is $425 billion! In exchange there will be *no* deductions—no charitable deductions and no mortgage deductions—much to the horror of the real estate industry and the charities. Both will survive. We are a charitable nation, and only twenty-eight percent of us use the mortgage interest deduction now.

House prices will drop, if at all, only by the percent used for the income tax deduction, and then will go back to rising again with inflation. Estate taxes should be ended, as they now contribute only one percent of national revenues, and make it very difficult to pass on to family small businesses and farms. Capital gains should be included in taxable income at the same flat rate, since it will be much lower than the current rates. I see no harm in including Social Security income in a person's general income, if there is a $35,000 deduction to start with. Especially if privatized, it belongs to the person's net worth and should be treated like any other pension income. Municipal bonds can be maintained tax free to continue to help the issuing governmental units find money for improvements. This is a system that has really helped support the physical infrastructure of the country. Since the country does without tax income from these bonds now comfortably, a tax on the bond income need not be started.

A final worry which needs to find an answer is the tendency of congress to complicate the tax code, of which they have a frightening history. The flat tax needs to be inviolate in form, with no deductions or additions allowed. Only the rate should be allowed to change, by super-majority vote as I have suggested. This may require an amendment to the Constitution to guarantee that nothing can be added to a flat tax code. The same amendment could require a balanced budget, excepting, of course, times of war. A required balanced budget would act as a further control over congress, stopping them from using our money to buy their reelection, but not completely. There will always be a tendency to dip into the pork barrel and bring home some juicy little project to the district or state to help with the next election.

Our population has developed a pattern of apathy and cynicism about politics, which is now an ingrained habit. There is also a lassitude, born of a degree of contentment with the growing wealth and power of the country since World War II. Are things really so bad, if we are so comfortable? As was shown in Chapter Seven, in politics a bean-counting analysis is performed on all the big and little segments of our population. Which segments will vote for us if we offer which in-

ducements? What kind of turn-out can we expect from this or
that group? Does the candidate have "name-recognition?"
Name-recognition really bugs me. It requires all the intelligence of a flea circus. What is that worth in terms of knowing
the candidate's positions and principles? Now the campaign
manager enters all the factors into the program and the computer tells him how to set up a winning campaign. Winning
at all costs, and it is the country that bears the costs of fragmented sound-bite campaigns, with all the nasty invective that
the candidates throw against each other. Nothing about this is
statesmanlike, with the one possible exception of the 1994
campaign, when republicans won back the house by national-
izing their campaign using the Contract With America, offering a vision of their philosophy for the future. It worked, but
interestingly as the G.O.P. embarked on it in the House of
Representatives, the country at large became somewhat restive,
worried they might go too far too quickly. Did republicans
really intend all this change?

   The founding fathers never anticipated the appearance of
professional politicians, who would spend their lives living off
government salaries, and then retiring on overly-generous pensions. Spending time in the federal government was a noble
self-sacrifice for one's country, not a power-seeking, money-
making event. A political position can make one's fortune in
perfectly legal ways. Mayor Louis Welch served ten years in
Houston. When he retired I remember (it was published in
the local papers) that he had entered office with a net worth
of $50,000 and left office with $1,050,000. I don't know how
he did it, but more than likely, in a rapidly-expanding city, he
joined others investing in raw land, in areas destined for future
city progress. President Lyndon Johnson entered the Senate
with essentially no net worth, and it was widely reported when
he left office that he was worth about ten million dollars. He
could not have done that on his senatorial or presidential salaries. He undoubtedly invested in opportunities enhanced by
governmental activity. This is investing based on "insider information," legal for politicians, but absolutely forbidden when
that information relates to stocks and bonds. The Securities
Exchange Commission takes a very dim view of trading on

"insider information," and they can administer severe penalties for it. Why not apply the same moral principles and forbid this activity for politicians?

Removing the seductive qualities of salvaging Social Security and creating IRS favors from the control of congress, attempting to limit spending through a balanced budget amendment, and trying to remove the "profit motive" from political office only solve part of the problem. As long as such a large segment of our citizens are apathetic and cynical, we can be manipulated by these artificially conducted "elections." There is another step, and that is by setting up term limits and campaign spending controls all in one large plan. In proposing this, I recognize that it is not an idealistic, philosophically-pleasing prospect. Given the self-preserving, self-interested, self-aggrandizing nature of humans in general, it is a reasonable method to limit the ability to spend a lifetime in politics. The term limits approach is not perfect, but I feel it offers the best method available to rein in our current crop of politicians. I developed these ideas about term limits in the mid-1980s. Imagine my surprise to hear Governor John Connally give a speech at a Methodist Hospital Medical Staff meeting in 1989 supporting the very idea. A national leader and I were on the same wavelength. I will present my plan first, and then discuss problems attendant to it.

The Constitution is not absolutely clear as to whether the control over state elections for congressional representation resides with the states or with the federal government. Several states set term limits for their congressmen. It was challenged in court and in 1995, by a five to four vote, the Supreme Court declared that state-imposed term limits on federal officials was not constitutional. Such a close vote suggests that a slightly more conservative composition of the Supreme Court could reverse that decision. The nation should not be subjected to that type of instability. Term limits should be set in place by constitutional amendment. In 1976, a Supreme Court decision (*Buckley v. Valeo*) equated campaign contributions with free speech, thereby protecting the contributions under the First Amendment: they cannot be limited. The term limits amendment will need to include a clause controlling contributions.

This is my proposal for the amendment: A person should be limited to twelve years in congress, either in one House, or as a total of service in both. The length of service must be keyed to a multiple of the Senate term of six years. Six seems quite short to me, considering the complexities of current government, and eighteen years tends to bring us back to the problems we have now. Twelve years is the best compromise. A span of twelve years should permit learning the intricacies of how Washington works and how to control the bureaucracy. House terms should be expanded to four years (instead of the current two), with half the House elected every two years, along with one-third of the Senate (the current arrangement for the Senate). With term limits shortening stays for politicians in Washington, this election pattern allows for more continuity in congress. My reason for increasing the House terms to four years is that the current House of Representatives is like living in a revolving door—with two-year terms, the first year is spent in legislating and the second year in getting ready to try to be reelected. The longer House term provides for more stability and hopefully more statesman-like activity. The four-year House term and one six-year Senate term results, if combined, in only ten years of service in the legislative branch. Under the term limit plan, there might be some individuals who resign after two years of a second House term to run for one Senate term, and serve all twelve years, but it is a politically risky approach, and not likely a course taken by most individuals.

I would limit a politician to no more than a twelve-year exertion of influence in congress by forbidding retiring congressmen to stay on as congressional aides, or as lobbyists to congress. Lobbyists are a form of representation without election. With congressmen staying for shorter periods, there will be less networking in congress by lobbyists, if the lobbyists have to come from outside Washington and cannot come from within congress. Let congressmen stay their twelve years and get out—a truncated term as the founders anticipated. However, I see no reason why they cannot serve in the judicial branch, or in the executive branch, after or before serving the twelve congressional years. With their expertise in Washington government, they should be able to make valuable contributions to the other two branches of government.

I would also reduce the current rather regal congressional perquisites. Their pension plans and the annual contributions must match exactly what the general population is allowed, and no more. Franking (free postage) must be limited to direct replies to direct inquiries; no general mail-outs to the district, which is a subsidized form of campaigning. Their medical care plan must match medical plans available to our citizens, and so forth. My point is that they are our employees and should be treated the same as we are treated as employees in American business. I would also have congressional salaries paid by the individual states, each to their own representatives and senators. This idea is nothing new. This proposal was debated before the Constitutional Convention: when a decision was finally made to federalize the salaries (by an eight to three vote of the states), it was on the basis that the states might not be willing to pay enough to attract the best people. Instituting state control of salaries might result in different salaries in different states. So be it. In American business, only if you own the company do you get to set your salary. Congress does not own the country. This might help exert more local control over our representation in Washington, if the folks in the House and Senate have to look to the state legislators for their income. It may return more governmental control to the states, or at least give the states more leverage in instructing their congressmen on how to vote in the state's interest. Currently, federal governmental power is much greater than states' power. The founders anticipated a more balanced arrangement. Local control and solution of problems with the more intimate knowledge possessed locally results in better and less-costly solutions than ones imposed from Washington (see Chapter One: My Story of Fixing the Bayou).

The next step is to control campaign contributions. The problem is to work around the 1976 Supreme Court decision that the contributions are protected under the free speech rights of the First Amendment, and therefore cannot be limited. I have a plan that I think will pass constitutional muster. For each representative, permit him to collect money for his personal campaign only within his own district from his own private constituents and from local businesses and unions. No money may come into the district from national headquarters of businesses or unions. The political parties may collect large sums of money on a national level, but may not supply that money directly to candidates. They may use the money to present general campaign material illustrating their political philosophy, their program proposals, and of course, a request to vote for candidates from their party, but they may not campaign for specific candidates by name. The same rules would apply at the state level for senatorial candidates.

This approach will make it easier for challengers to try for election because both sides will have a fair chance at collecting roughly equal war chests. I believe this solves the First Amendment problem, because it does not limit contributions in amount, but limits them to geographic area, where specific voters for specific candidates live. The rights of the legitimate voters are not abridged. Why should money from New England interfere in a race in Texas, just to state the proposition in a different way? The national parties retain their right to collect as much money as they wish to present their views and philosophy to the country. Knowing just how sleazy the handling of "soft money" by the politicians has been in the past and seeing how unwilling the congress generally has been to provide campaign contribution reform, very strict audit trails will have to be put in place to insure compliance with my plan; the plan should be reinforced with severe felony punishments, including immediate removal of the representative or senator from office if campaign contributions were improperly handled.

There is one other change I would institute. Currently, when a congressman leaves office, if there is any money left in the campaign coffers he can keep it as income. I would require that the money be put in the national presidential campaign fund. I have not suggested changing the funding and conduct of the presidential campaigns. Being national campaigns in which the presidential candidate heads his party and represents it, the First Amendment controls appear to dictate not trying to change anything, nor do I think that anything need be changed.

If citizens regain control over congress, in part by making their employment less imperial and approximately equivalent to executive positions in the private sector, and by limiting their terms, we will have a better chance of regaining control over the bureaucracies. This will first require the country to rethink the functions of a federal government. Currently we are micromanaged by congress and the bureaucratic agencies, while the original intent of the founders was to have a representative body to set national policy for the states to follow. Instead, the federal government over-controls the states by collecting taxes and then sending a portion of the money back to the states as grants accompanied by a mass of restrictive regulations regarding the program involved. At times there are regulations set at the federal level for state-run programs, which cost the states money for which there are no funds, the so-called "unfunded mandates." This is all backwards. The founders intended that the federal government would set policy and allow the states, as local laboratories, to try different methods to handle the new policy. Government oversight should be just that: assuring that policy, when agreed to in congress (the national forum), is carried out, not that each nuance of the policy be controlled by Washington bureaucracy, accompanied by mountains of paperwork. The Federal Welfare Program has been sent back to the states, each of which manages it differently, and the welfare rolls dropped significantly. Devolution of power to the states works.

One of the objections to term limits is the loss of knowledge in handling the intricacies of Washington. This might tend to shift power to congressional staffs, lobbyists, and bureaucratic "experts." Not true. It's been said that "Every Capitol Hill observer knows that it's the most senior members (of congress) who are most dependent on staff and lobbyists, not the hot-shot young freshmen" (*WSJ* Editorial, 11 October 1990). The new members don't owe favors to anyone, and enter congress full of idealism and fervor. Older members tend to overspecialize in one area (*WSJ*, Albert R. Hunt, 2 July 1998), and are experts in "the arts of packaging, log-rolling, creative accounting and other forms of deception. (They) are experts only in the law and in political machinations" (Thomas Sowell, *Forbes*, 23 September 1996).

As I have shown in Chapter Five as a prime example, congress has been led into a mess in the water diversion projects in the western states by trusting "expert" bureaucratic studies. We cannot expect members of congress to be experts in everything, or anything. I think we can expect the bureaucrats to continue to mislead them, driven by bureaucratic self-interest. Congress must be policy makers and consensus makers, and rely upon true experts in setting up new policies and laws. Lobbyists and bureaucrats have hidden agendas. The experts must come from outside government, and must represent both sides of the political spectrum. Consultants from the private sector and from "think tanks" are necessary. Congress is responsible for oversight of the huge bureaucracy that has been created. It literally is too large for them to do that, and therefore I assume they are accepting reports without on-site verification. The bureaucracy can be controlled, first by using outside experts to analyze and research reports supplied by the bureaucracy, and secondly by deciding which bureaucratic agencies should survive. Of the departments in the President's cabinet, only State, Defense, Justice, and Treasury are vital. All the others are dispensable to varying degrees, since they were grossly enlarged or created by the Roosevelt New Deal or Johnson's Great Society.

A congress rejuvenated and vibrant with idealistic newcomers, not wed to trying to stay there forever, and not beholden to a bureaucratic constituency, will have the courage to rethink policy for the country, devolve power back to the states to experiment and run programs (with just enough government oversight, not control, to see that national policy is met). Also, they will have the courage to set up "sunset" committees to decide which cabinet departments and which agencies are to be terminated. The "sunset" committees also will use outside consultants and think tanks, again covering a broad political spectrum. I cannot repeat often enough that we need decisions by consensus, not pendulum swinging from extreme to extreme. Thus, bureaucracy can be controlled and partially eliminated. Devolving programs back to the states will help in oversight of the bureaucrats by dividing the job between the congress and the fifty state legislatures. However, the self-important attitude of bureaucrats cannot be underestimated. In Houston, a city councilman, who serves under a six-year term limit, was told by a city employee, "I have been here fifteen years, I will be here fifteen more. I know the exact moment you are leaving office, and I will outlast you" (*Houston Chronicle*, 28 June 1998). Who is more important, the government official representing voters, or the bureaucrat? Who is running the store? I cannot imagine that conversation occurring in private business. This is why congress must reassert firm control over a smaller bureaucracy, using outside consultants and experts. Civil Service rules do not allow instant dismissal of a government employee with that attitude, but I would think a government employee with that attitude would damage his career with a comment like that on his record.

There is another way congress can gain control over the bureaucracy. Currently they write laws as general policy statements and then expect the agencies to write regulations to refine what congress promulgated into law. This process is called "delegation," but for over 100 years after the Constitution was ratified, the supreme court would not allow congress to delegate its legislative powers. Then early in the twentieth century, the concept developed that non-political "experts" could do a better job at writing laws. In FDR's administration, Roosevelt asked congress to allow him to appoint experts and also delegate their legislative power, so his administration could experiment with solving the Great Depression. Both congress and the supreme court were frightened about the future of the country and Roosevelt threatened the court with his court-packing plan (increasing the court to fifteen), and delegation was approved, according to David Schoenbrod, a professor at New York Law School, (*WSJ*, 6 December 1998). Professor Schoenbrod offers the opinion that technical experts are not insulated from politics, but "by the 1970s, experience had shown that most agency heads are not experts but lawyers or other generalists up to their necks in politics."

Congress likes delegation. It offers a wonderful way for them to dodge the bullet and avoid criticism, and the current group is certainly expert at that: "When constituents complain about regulations being too weak or too strong, legislators blame the agency. Our elected lawmakers cast themselves as heroes and their creations—the regulatory agencies—as scapegoats. Delegation is ersatz democracy." There is a large group of constitutional lawyers in the bipartisan Constitutional Caucus, liberals and conservatives, who feel the constitutionality of delegation should be reconsidered. One clear reason to support delegation is that congress appears to lack the time necessary to write complete laws. My term limits suggestion of increasing House terms to four years helps solve the time issue. Running for office every four years instead of every other year frees up another whole year for legislating in the House. Short of declaring delegation unconstitutional, there is another suggested method of congressional control over regulations: set up a statute mandating that congress review and vote on all regulations, reserving for legislative rewrite any regulations that do not pass the review. This would save judicial time. Now, law suits are brought into federal court to judge whether an agency's regulations fit the intent of congress, as pointed out in Chapter Seven, a system congress likes, because they can then blame the courts for interpretations the public doesn't like.

You will quickly realize what this has done to the federal courts. Letting the bureaucracy interpret the intent of laws, aggressively and inventively write regulations, while always hoping to enlarge their own roles has increased the number of court battles. In 1998, almost 54,000 cases reached the federal circuit appeals courts, sharply up from 33,360 in 1985. The load has become so great that these courts have added staff lawyer positions to screen the cases, and in reality actually decide cases by giving the judges brief summaries and suggested decisions. Now less than half the cases are argued before the judges and only one-quarter of the decisions are published in full. Many decisions are now one word: "affirmed" or "denied." To compound this highly controversial problem, only eleven judges have been added to the circuit courts since 1985 (167 from 156) and the judges have resisted adding more! A law suit attacking this system is currently before the Eleventh Circuit Court (William Glaberson, *New York Times/Houston Chronicle*, 14 March 1999). This is another perversion of our governmental system, stemming from congress avoiding its responsibilities while attempting to micro-manage our lives. Note the constant pattern of congress preferring systems that buffer them from criticism. We must insist that congress does a more complete legislating job, living up to the responsibilities for which we elected them, writing the regulations themselves, or at least reviewing and approving regulations written under delegation, and directly accept responsibility for the results. Under the pressure of having to do much more work in legislating, congress will be much less inclined to proliferate agencies, and more willing to devolve power back to the states. Further, by taking direct responsibility for the laws, the legislation produced should become simpler and less onerous. Currently the bureaucracy, as the fourth branch of government, is running our country, but is not elected. Oversight by congress is myopic if not minuscule. Bureaucratic creation of regulations, which become the law of the land; by trying for perfection become more and more restrictive, and more criminalizing of individual behaviors, simply put, is wrong and must end. A.V. Dicey is quoted as saying: "The true importance of laws lies far less in their direct result than in the effect upon the sentiment or convictions of the public" (Legal philosopher, A.V. Dicey, quoted by James Bovard, *WSJ*, 16 May 1997). Roman Arnoldy adds that "As more and more things a person might do become unlawful, the more our whole society tends to become criminalized, and the more it loses respect for the law. In other words, the less logical our laws, the less respect they command" (Roman F. Arnoldy, *Houston Chronicle*, 3 August 1998). There is no logical rebuttal for these quotes. As dictator, I would remove delegation by fiat.

The other advantage to downsizing the bureaucracy and decentralizing programs back to the states is the potential enormous savings. Tremendous amounts of money are wasted in Washington. Centralized government is extremely inefficient, as reported in J. Peter Grace's book, *Burning Money, the Waste of your Tax Dollars* (1984), a popularized version of his report to President Reagan, after being appointed in 1982 as chairman of a presidential commission to study government waste. One example of the waste he found: only 30 cents of each anti-poverty dollar actually reduced poverty, "The other 70 cents (went) to the non-poor and for administration of the programs (72 of them!)." The private watch-dog group, Citizens Against Government Waste, came out of the commission, and each year still reports annual Washington waste approaching $200 billion. Read the book. Its findings are frightening. There are so many programs, so many overlapping authorities, so many overlapping requirements, and overlapping benefits resulting in over-administration and in uncontrolled overpayments. Do you remember the $700 toilet seats for the Armed Services? Grace describes a seven dollar hammer the Defense Department bought for $436. Think of the obvious: there are generous costs in having federal tax receipts go to Washington, and then make the round trip back to the states as part of mandated grants. Downsize the bureaucracy, decentralize it to the states, send less money to Washington, and raise state taxes, where under local control, there should be less waste and more judicious spending.

Another objection to term limits is that voters are limited in their choices at the ballot box. That is true, in the sense that existing congressmen are forced off the ballot by term limits. There are two parts to the answer for this point. First, I said in the beginning of the chapter that humans are fallible, they have faults, and to overcome those human failings, at times a less than idealistic solution must be sought. In Chapter Seven I made the point that voters tend to have a good opinion of their own congressman, but not congress in general. Second, "term limits are not, and have never been, about voters ousting their own senior representatives. They are about ousting the senior representatives of other districts. Ousting one's own senior representative is simply the price one must pay to achieve this result." Currently the congressional seniority system and "pork barrel politics create perverse incentives for each district to vote for senior incumbents." Senior members "deliver the bacon" much more assuredly with the clout they enjoy. This helps explain why we like our congressman, but not congress. Voter self-interest brings federal projects to their local district. Yet in polls the nation is strongly in favor of term limits by two to one or more. The limited choice objection implies that term limits are antidemocratic. That is not true. The current seniority system is not democratic. All congressional members should have equal power to represent their citizens. Currently, they do not and this partially disenfranchises their voters, another example in which the Equal Protection Clause of the Fourteenth Amendment is ignored at the federal level. Einer Elhauge writes that "Term limits are a rather logical corrective to a seniority system that itself has no basis in democratic theory" (Einer Elhauge, visiting professor of law, University of Chicago, *WSJ*, 14 March 1995).

This discussion by Professor Elhauge clearly implies that in a term-limited congress, seniority should and should not exist in our current system The seniority system provides unequal representation, which is not democratic. Committee chairmanships should be changeable at the start of each two-year congressional term. We should see a much more courageous and active congress, much more responsive to the electorate with all of these changes in place, and especially a congress with the interest and courage to take on real control and true oversight of the bureaucracy.

Perhaps we will see a less pejorative group, with less hyperbole, and hopefully with more truth. Perhaps the English language can be brought back to proper meanings. "Partisanship" has become a code word. If a politician is partisan he is not working with the other side to develop the best bill, and is not cooperating. Since when does a debating society have two sides that cooperate with each other? A debate to create a law is a battle of ideas, reasoning and words to reach a compromise somewhere near the center of an issue, giving each side some winning and some losing points. Only in a debate contest is there a winner and a loser. "Extremism" is another such word. "Extreme" now means dangerous, totally unreasonable. I think term limits are a relatively extreme solution, in view of the principles with which this country was started, but I obviously think this is a logical extreme to overcome the foibles of human beings. Perhaps the truth will come out, especially about the so-called "balanced budget" which arrived in 1998. Based on 1998 income and expense, the budget is in balance, but based on future unfunded obligations, as of 1998 it is totally out of balance. Also, the truth about that infamous obfuscation of the 1996 campaign which assigned the word "cuts" to what was actually a reduction in previously-planned yearly increases in the Medicare program, and therefore just a smaller increase. Must our political campaigns continue to be based primarily on mud-slinging and deliberately confusing fifteen-second sound bites? No, if we can reform congress and overcome voter apathy. If apathetic voters remain so turned-off that all they will spend time listening to and watching are the sound bites, then the current pathetic political campaigns will continue. Only thirty-five to forty percent will vote and the others will remain in an uninformed and confused political fog, manipulated by the politicians election managers. What a horrible outlook for the country.

What has gotten us into this state of affairs? Guaranteed perfection. All those promises from disingenuous Washington politicians—they promise anything to get reelected. Create a ponderous bureaucracy to do the job. Create a "Nanny State" to hand out "entitlements" to special interests and to newly-minted "victims." Glorify multiculturalism and diversity as excuses for giving special awards to segments of current generations for the obvious mistakes of past generations. At first the citizens of this country got sucked in and believed all of this tripe. However, the results and promises are not there. It is all a mirage. Centralized government is ponderous, inefficient, enormously expensive when compared to the results, and very slow-moving. Do you want efficient, inexpensive, fast-moving results? Look to the competitive, profit-motive private sector. Who is at fault? The past and present congresses. No wonder Mark Helprin (Chapter Seven) cries out for a revival of statesmanship in Washington.

Worse, this nannyism from Washington is eroding the individual drive and self-confidence of our citizens and also eroding our guaranteed freedoms, the true entitlements of our citizenship. Those rights are: "life, liberty and the pursuit of happiness." The logical extension, "if individual rights are to be respected, the (citizen) should be able to do anything he wants, so long as it doesn't infringe the rights of somebody else. He decides himself what is best for himself without governmental interference" (Arnoldy, *Houston Chronicle*, 3 August, 1998). Think about it. A person should not break the speed limit or yell "fire!" in a theater. Both actions endanger others—but gambling, smoking, prostitution, and drug usage are victimless crimes, for the individual is only making himself the victim. If the government prosecutes a drug user, he is now a criminal because of his own moral indiscretion. What good does that accomplish? Arnoldy writes: "Our government is seeking a thousand ways to "help" the citizen while abandoning him when he needs help (by criminalizing him) and then presuming to legislate what is best for him—what to eat, what to wear, what to do, while we tell the world we have the greatest freedom on Earth."

Look at the cult of victimology in the so called anti-smoking crusade of 1998 by the federal government. As a physician I counselled my patients against smoking. I could fill several pages with a complete discussion of all the possible side effects of smoking. Did I remonstrate my smoking patients? No, I treated them as adults. They heard the reasoned facts, and then they were on their own to make their own choices. Not so with our government. First they assert an unproven issue as though it were true: second-hand smoke causes cancer. Worldwide studies do not support this conclusion. Shades of the approach to global warming, then the nanny state takes over: "People start smoking because they, poor things, are putty in the hands of advertisers; smokers cannot stop because nicotine is too addictive. The last rationale is inconvenienced by the fact that there are almost as many American ex-smokers as smokers" (George F. Will, *Chronicle*, 31 July 1998). Then the attack that drove Joe Camel off the billboards: ninety percent of six-year-olds recognize him, based on interviews with twenty-three Atlanta preschoolers (Will). A sample that small is scientific garbage, and certainly doesn't prove that the twenty-one who recognized Joe will smoke later in life. The government seemed to assert: "Wicked corporations preying upon helpless individuals are responsible for individual behavior." (Will) Dennis Prager (quoted previously in Chapter Three) viewed the anti-smoking campaign as "the largest public relations campaign in history teaching Americans this: if you smoke, you are in no way responsible for what happens to you. You are entirely a victim." Our government is telling us it is okay not to assert any personal responsibility. We have become a country "that regularly teaches its citizens to blame others— government, ads, parents, schools, movies, genes, sugar, to- bacco, alcohol, sexism, racism—for their poor decisions and problems" (Prager in Will) .

If I were dictator, I would immediately end the nanny state's attempt to legislate morals and habits. I would legalize drugs, dispensing them at low cost in state clinics, and requir- ing counselling for the customers. Our dangerous crime wave, our walled and gated sub-divisions are a direct result of the high price of criminalized drugs. We seem to have learned nothing from our social experiment of prohibition. Criminaliz- ing drugs does create victims, those innocent citizens who are burglarized and robbed for the money to buy drugs. Taking the street value out of drugs will do more good for the country than trying to stop drugs from getting to users. Barry R. McCaffrey, director of the Office of National Drug Control Policy, as support of the war on drugs, lamely pointed to crimes with victims as an excuse for continuing the govern- ment policy: "While we agree that murder, pedophilia and child prostitution can never be eliminated entirely, no one is arguing that we legalize these activities" (*Houston Chronicle,* 2 August 1998). Entirely off the point! One person harms an- other. The drug user is his own victim, and he alone must accept responsibility. Further, if I were dictator I would legal- ize prostitution, primarily with the medical intent of control- ling venereal disease, especially AIDS. Oops, I should have said sexually transmitted diseases, which is more politically correct. Many prostitutes are junkies, supporting their habit with paid sex. What better way to gain control over one av- enue for AIDS?

Peter Grace's view of the nanny state is very cogent. He describes "the welfare-state mentality of those legions who see the government as the national nanny, there to supply baby with all his wants, cradle to grave. In contrast to the spirit of the risk-taking entrepreneurship, welfare-state aficionados crave security . . . a guaranteed job at a guaranteed pay. In the welfare state, risk taking and productivity become alien concepts . . . Policies that move us toward the welfare state are often justified on the basis of the common good, yet, in analyzing these policies, we find their basis in selfishness rather than selflessness . . . You find (this mentality) wherever entrenched protection and security is the watchword, where innovators are feared and hated." Remember, politicians are deathly afraid of dramatically changing Social Security, as an example. Grace points to France as a prime example of how severely debilitating the welfare protectionist mentality is on a nation: "The French welfare state has become a society of mistrust. Everyone fights over how to divide up the economic pie, with little thought to making a bigger pie . . . (There is) a never-ending series of conflicts over who gets to be protected the most."

Nannyism creates an environment for jealousy between haves and have-nots, and encourages the have-nots to look to the government for a handout to equalize their economic status in life. Ralph Nader has called for "distributive justice." He thinks Bill Gates of Microsoft is too wealthy (see Chapter Six). Free enterprise, the best economic system, is based on risk and reward. As this letter to the editor states: "The tendency today is to look at people who are financially successful as a result of their creativity, ingenuity, aggressive spirit and persistence, with accusing eyes for hoarding the nation's wealth. We imply they should be ashamed of their success. It is no wonder our kids don't have a work ethic. We criticize the people who work hard for their success. It seems to me the best way to distribute wealth is by doing it the right way—the old-fashioned way—work for it" (*Houston Chronicle*, 3 August 1998). The following is a valid government role in this area: setting economic policies that encourage entrepreneurs to begin new businesses and create jobs. This has always been the largest producer of new jobs. Government can also provide low-cost job training programs, with my preference, run at the state level.

The nanny state damages immigrants before they get here; for example, those from Communist Russia. Before Communist Russia ended, I cared for Russian refugee Jews who came to this country, full of optimism (as was my grandfather). They were very successful, but several had severe ulcers. Why, I asked, were they so stressed? Because, if we fail, what government program here will save us? The thought had never occurred to me, with my American background. They came here partially brainwashed by their communist upbringing, thrilled to be here, but worried that there were not enough "safety nets." Too much nannyism destroys the drives and ambitions people should have. Freedom to succeed is balanced by freedom to fail. What our government, at many levels, should offer is not to care for "victims" but offer inducements to take an initial risk, and encouragement to try again after a failure: Small Business Administration loans and tax-abatement programs are well-known examples.

The nanny state is a government trying to protect its citizens from everything, thereby attempting to increase the importance of government, and increasing the omnipotence of federal politicians who are constantly thinking of the next election. This is why it is so important to regain control over congress and make the congressman's position not one of privilege, but of service. Washington should not be a place of competition for power and money, but a place for the competition of ideas among statesman-like people, who respond to a calling to serve their country, much as people are called to the clergy. As Jack Kennedy said in his inaugural speech: "Ask not what your country can do for you, ask what you can do for your country." We need bright, selfless men and women to come to Washington and courageously create policies that truly advance what is good and right in our country, giving every person a chance to achieve all he is capable of achieving.

Finally, we all must come to appreciate that the social experiment called The United States is a first of its kind, in a much different way than even imagined by the founding fathers. We were, and are still, the first of a kind in our form of democratic republic, created in a momentous summer in Philadelphia by fifty-five amazing statesmen, who with a deep understanding of the political philosophy of the Age of Enlightenment, created the most unique political document on Earth, our Constitution. That document, if not twisted beyond recognition, if maintained in its original intent by strict constructionist interpretation, can serve this country with a life of its own, forever. What is different than the founders anticipated is that their willingness to anticipate immigration and our willingness to allow it has created a country that is attempting to amalgamate almost all of the races and cultures on Earth. "E Pluribus Unum," from many one, doesn't apply to just fifty united states. It applies to all the peoples on Earth who want to come here, partake of our freedoms and opportunities, and join our experiment in human behavior, truly making one nation out of all branches of mankind and an unending variety of cultures and philosophies of life. In doing that, we must overcome a holdover attitude from our Stone Age days: we are most comfortable with "our own kind," the folks from our own tribe. We must come to accept people who look different, who think differently, because the philosophic background of their culture provides a different outlook on how to live.

This does not mean that we have to give up our original inherited culture, based on European thought. That is the cultural heritage that allowed this great nation to begin. Yes, the heritage came with mistakes, recognized now because of two more centuries of developing political philosophic thought, building on past thinking. We must not lose our way; we must recognize mistakes of the past, but we must not try to atone for them now as though we somehow must share the guilt for those past omissions. We must see those mistakes as we learn from a true study of history, and not by revising history. We must not repeat those mistakes again and thereby bring fairness to everyone. We must not try to apologize for those mistakes—they were not our fault. These current generations are liable for the mistakes of the past only in the obligation to recognize them, and not allow them to happen again. All to the end that we can all learn that we are all the same, under the skin, one species, an E Pluribus Unum of hundreds of tribes.

For this country to survive in its best form, we need all parts of this disparate population to come together with one thought: we are all citizens of the greatest country on earth, we

have a deep avowed patriotism for her, we will defend her to
the death, and we will work on cooperating together, debating
our differences until we reach compromises that make all segments comfortable with the solutions proposed. The current
campaign for multiculturalism and diversity, instituted with a
shallowness of thought that is appalling, falls far short of my
vision for this country. The campaign insists that we atone for
the past by creating unfairness in the present. The way we
atone for the past is by creating fairness in the present. During
the 1998 trip President Clinton made to Africa, it was openly,
and I feel idiotically, debated whether he should apologize for
slavery. He didn't create slavery or condone it. My ancestors
came to this country after slavery here was over. They and I are
not to blame: I owe nothing to the descendants of slaves on
the grounds that they are the descendants of slaves. I owe
them a recognition of equality of opportunity and a concept of
fairness in all our dealings together.

This concept of fairness must dig under the surface to
create complete fairness. Overtly, we are a fair way down the
road to ending racism and discrimination. The laws and practices are in place but covertly we are not free of prejudice.
"Whenever I find myself in a group of white males only, the
conversation inevitably turns racist. Even though overt racism
has been mostly replaced by covert racism, the terrible and
totally un-Christian results are the same: Many of God's children are denied fair treatment": a confessional letter-to-the-
editor (*Houston Chronicle*, 5 August 1998). The inevitability
that whites will, in the near future, lose their majority status in
this country offers a practical reason for insisting upon an
eventual end to covert racism. That is the wrong philosophy.
Morally and ethically we all know covert racism is wrong, and
should end now. Overt and covert racism is not limited solely
to whites. There has been ample evidence of anti-white black
racism. There is no question that each racial group is more
comfortable within their group, and may tend to feel, "my
kind is better," again based on our recent Stone Age background psychology. Japan has a well-publicized problem with
this (Japanese-American letters to the editor, *WSJ*, 14 August
1998).

To bring ourselves to form a cohesive population, we must not follow policies that will increase group antagonisms. Name-calling, artificial competition, and antagonism between all the races represented in this country are only accentuated by the multiculturalism, diversity-worshipping affirmative action quotas and set-aside programs. They set group competing against group over preset percentage expectations, instead of allowing individuals to contest fairly with one another based on individual merit. Dividing us into eighteen ethnic/racial/geographic/ linguistic groups (Chapter Seven) chops us up into large and small competing segments, on top of competing segments that already exist. This country has had segments of differing interests since its beginning, and one of the wonders of our form of government has been the innate ability to compromise and reach solutions for the differences of thought. There have always been regional and sectional differences in lifestyles and philosophies. The attitudes in Boise are not those of Boston, nor are those of Albany, Georgia compared to Albany, N.Y., or Phoenix matched with Pittsburgh. Add to the mix economic diversification: economic strata of people, from very poor to very rich; different types of economic production in different regions, the factories of the mid-west "rust belt" compared to Silicon Valley in California, one producing physical products, the other intellectual properties.

Dividing us up into groups it is even more complicated than it seems at first: No one should really lump all "Anglos" or "white people" into one group. Blond, blue-eyed northern Europeans don't look the same as the more swarthy Mediterranean folks. Many eastern Europeans have a somewhat Slavic look. Further, all of them received a slightly different set of cultural precepts: Arab and Jews are white, they are the same sub-race, Semites, but culturally they are not the same. Now lets add all the different religions to the mix. Do you see what is happening mathematically? Eighteen artificial governmental groups multiplied times geographic sections, multiplied times economics, multiplied times all the different kinds of white folks, multiplied times all the different religions, and our population is chopped up into hundreds if not thousands of special-interest segments. The prime issue is to create one cooperative population out of this huge pile of different colored jelly beans, not piles of the same colored beans, all separated and counted.

To show how foolish this "diversity" policy can be is to review a Census Bureau report from 1998, estimating that "Hispanics" will overtake blacks as the largest minority group in seven years. The foolish part is their concern of how to define "Hispanic" in arriving at a total number for the group. It's been written that "The gap between the Hispanic and black populations can be viewed as somewhat narrower than the raw numbers suggest. As an ethnic rather than a racial group, Hispanic Americans are categorized not only as Latino but also as either black, white, Asian/Pacific Islander or American Indian. When the 925,000 Hispanic blacks—a group generally made up of some Puerto Ricans, Dominicans and Cubans—are subtracted from the total black population, the difference in size between the country's two largest minority groups shrinks even more" (Holmes, *New York Times, Houston Chronicle,* 7 August 1998). How stupid! This report makes it sound as if the two minorities are vying in some competitive way to be the biggest minority. If the Census Bureau dumps the black Hispanics into the Latino group, will the blacks complain, or bring a law suit in federal court? I'll bet most of their members don't care. What if some jelly beans are multicolored? Remember Tiger Woods. The blacks tried to claim him, but that young adult golfer makes more sense referring to himself simply as multiracial and American. After all, he is really white, Asian and black. Is one blood stronger than another? Must we continue to follow the "one drop" rule developed in the time of slavery, when one drop of African blood defined who was a slave?

Governmentally imposed artificial diversity is wrong, but turned around and viewed in just the opposite direction, exposure to multiple cultures and to diverse people is an extremely valuable experience, and very educational. Their views can be measured against our western teachings, and as in any good debate, new ways of looking at life will be created. No one pattern of thought is perfect, and no ideas should be discarded or ignored because of past mistakes in the development of that pattern. The more exposure we have to different people, the less different they will look and seem. It all takes time because of our innate tribalism. We are a very diverse population and will become even more so. We must not allow ourselves to live only in segments, but must teach ourselves to interact as one cooperative population.

In my daydream as dictator, I would end all of the governmental multicultural diversity programs. They are just a set of shallow political ploys, again sounding like another attempt to guarantee perfection, but really quite dangerous to the American experiment. We are obligated within the framework of our Constitution to continue to have a diverse and yet united population, and that takes continual discussion, work, and compromise. There is no question that Americans can be both diverse and united. There is the prime example of World War II. Volunteer Japanese-Americans and Negro-Americans (as they were called then) were on the front lines in some of the toughest fighting, despite the internment of Japanese out west and the continuing overt discrimination against blacks. These volunteer soldiers knew this country was worth their sacrifice, they were optimistic the racial mistakes would be overcome, and we are, slowly but surely, overcoming the racial mistakes.

Now, we need to overcome the current multicultural mistake. One hundred years ago the country debated whether the eastern and southern European immigrants could assimilate, because they were "different." They did. Recently we have begun debating assimilation all over again, because some of us feel it is best to preserve every newcomer's culture first and not worry about our cohesiveness as a nation (see Chapter Four). We can easily learn from our past. Peter Salinas said: "The history of the United States has demonstrated that it is the easiest thing in the world to reconcile ethnic diversity—including the maintenance of distinctive ethnic cultures—with an unshakable commitment to American unity. That is what assimilation, American style, is all about" (Paul Greenberg, quoting Peter Salinas, *Houston Chronicle*, 11 July 1998). Our American culture has always been willing to absorb the most interesting, the most useful and the most amusing parts of the quite different cultures that have been brought here. Greenberg writes: "The most vibrant of cultures tend to be the most open, welcome and willing to learn from others." We can respect the culture of others, we can debate with them differences in philosophy, we can enjoy other cultures, and yet join with them in one overall American culture, an amalgamation of the best from all of them. That is what we have been doing in the past, and very successfully, until the multicultural protectionists came along. We will do it again. Paul Greenberg put it very well: "We are *both* diverse and united, and whole-hearted in both those callings. And we *enjoy* our differences. Or at least we do when we are not being dam fools." The way we solidify our unity is by a recognition of shared absolute values, moral and ethical teachings we all can believe in, based on profound thought from the past and as a part of all cultures. It is patently obvious that a relative value system is destructive of a strong unified society of the type we have under our Constitution. The Federalist Papers make this point over and over.

At this point I must mention the one disappointment I have with my fantasy. There is no way a dictator or a nation can legislate or dictate the moral structure of its population. What I have been describing as solutions to our problems are mechanical and political tinkerings under the hood of the engine of our republic's vehicle—the Constitution and the structure of laws developed from it. The strength of that structure is completely dependent on acceptance of those laws by all of our society. The failed experiment of prohibition is clear proof of that principle. The bedrock foundation of that acceptance is moral absolutes and unchanging ethical standards within each of us. Moral relativism and situational ethics have pervaded a sizeable segment of our population since the 1960s, with an "if it feels good do it" approach to life, as our country slides toward paganism (Don Feder, *A Jewish Conservative Looks at Pagan America*, Lafayette, LA: Huntington House Publishers, 1993), while the courts and congress slide along, going with the flow.

Here is a recent example of congress helping with the moral slide by putting forth a superficial do-good approach without recognizing the underlying moral fault in their offering: In 1998, fifty million dollars was made available to the states to "create abstinence-education programs teaching the benefits of delaying sex until marriage" in the classrooms (Lewin, *New York Times* in *Houston Chronicle*, 4 April 1999). Sounds good, but my obvious objection is, why should we be sending money to Washington only to have it returned to us to teach children what their parents and religious affiliations should automatically be teaching but currently are not doing well? Washington sees the problem, and answers with the wrong solution. The *Times* article describes the "Law of Unintended Consequences" taking over with states not following the intent of the law, urging delay of sex without mentioning waiting until marriage. Advocates of comprehensive sex education in the schools complain that this new law "interferes with offering contraceptive information." There is a progressive moral decay in this country, aided and abetted by the recent spectacle of the impeachment of President Clinton, followed by an obvious sham trial in the Senate that did not convict him for his perjury. After all, said the country through the polls, lying about sex is okay. Everybody does it; most of our congressional leaders have affairs. So what? How can the kids learn right from wrong if the country at large seems to think this way? Throwing more and more money at the problem is not the answer. Changing the downward moral drift of the country is.

A series of recent books have decried this change. Rabbi Daniel Lapin just published *America's Real War; an Orthodox Rabbi insists that Judeo-Christian values are vital for our nation's survival.* He is absolutely on target. Judeo-Christian values underlie our Declaration of Independence, the Constitution, and the construct of laws that has followed. The moral relativists, with their faculty supporters in our universities, have the moral fiber of silly putty, their consciences taking any shape they want, and bouncing all over the place. The key word is conscience. It is formed in each of us by age twelve to fourteen, constructed by teachings from one's parents, close relatives, surrounding community, and the influence of one's religion. How do we change adults' morals? Not easily, but by continuing to attack the relativists not only in the written word, but also by the deeds and actions moral absolutists show in the way we live our lives and conduct ourselves. Also by fighting to elect moral absolutists to political office at all levels, by being active in politics—not apathetic. We are in a culture war in which absolute morals and ethics must win over the vast majority of the population or this nation will continue its obvious slide downhill.

There will always be a tension between individuals who naturally want as much freedom as possible and society, which requires some rigidity of structure (and laws) to provide the proper protections for individuals from each other, and to protect its citizens from the intrusions of other countries. Our population must learn to have the moral strength to understand this tension and to control their individual desires accordingly, or we will continue to lose the original strengths provided to us by our founding documents.

Yes, my daydream has a defect. I cannot legislate or dictate morals. Yet the fantasy I have written about is not ethereal. We face some very real challenges, and there are very real solutions out there. We need to find the courage to face the issues, wake up from our apathy (if that personally applies), and demand that statesman-like people carry this country forward from its miraculous beginning, to the future that is promised by that beginning. That future is certainly possible for us to obtain, if we are interested, knowledgeable, committed, and actively participate in the political and civic process. You owe it to this country to be that kind of citizen. Perhaps you will want to go to Washington as a patriotic "calling," like a founding father, not simply seeking fame, power and money, which is so often the case now. As I said in the beginning of the book, folks like that are out there. You might be one of them.

The Coming Collision
Global Law vs. U.S. Liberties
by James L. Hirsen, Ph.D.

Are Americans' rights being abolished by International Bureaucrats? Global activists have wholeheartedly embraced environmental extremism, international governance, radical feminism, and New Age mysticism with the intention of spreading their philosophies worldwide by using the powerful weight of international law. Noted international and constitutional attorney James L. Hirsen says that a small group of international bureaucrats are devising and implementing a system of world governance that is beginning to adversely and irrevocably affect the lives of everyday Americans.

Paperback ISBN 1-56384-157-6
Hardcover ISBN 1-56384-163-0

Cloning of the American Mind
Eradicating Morality Through Education
by B. K. Eakman

Two-thirds of Americans don't care about honor and integrity in the White House. Why? What does Clinton's hair-splitting definitions have to do with the education establishment? Have we become a nation that can no longer judge between right and wrong?

"Parents who do not realize what a propaganda apparatus the public schools have become should read Cloning of the American Mind *by B. K. Eakman."*

—Thomas Sowell, *New York Post*
September 4, 1998

ISBN 1-56384-147-9

What Would They Say?
The Founding Fathers on Current Issues
by Glen Gorton

Thomas Jefferson, John Hancock, George Washington —
If these men could once again walk through the halls
of Congress, surveying the present scene, what would
they say? We are being told by the Clinton administration that things like honor and integrity don't matter as long as the rate of inflation is kept down. Our
Founding Fathers disagree. They believed that high
moral character is an essential ingredient of leadership. Into the heated atmosphere of today's social and
political crossfire comes a refreshingly new point of
view from -- the Founding Fathers. This is not another analysis of the men and their times, but rather,
the penetrating and concise testimony of America's
greatest heroes. Herein lies the strength of this 240
page anthology: the Founding Fathers themselves.

What Would They Say? is divided into three parts:

• Part One has quotes under topics covering Character,
Patriotism, Federal Power, Crime, Taxes, Education, Gun
Control, Welfare, Term Limits, and Religion.

• Part Two gives the reader an animated and personal
glimpse into the life of each of the 28 men quoted.

• Part Three contains a copy of the *Declaration of Independence*, the *US Constitution*, and the *Bill of Rights*.

ISBN 1-56384-146-0